THE BLACKOUT MURDERS

An air raid warden wearing his civilian duty gas mask c1940

The Blackout
Murders

NEIL R. STOREY

PEN & SWORD
TRUE CRIME

First published in Great Britain in 2023
by Pen & Sword True Crime
An imprint of
Pen & Sword Books Limited
Yorkshire - Philadelphia

ISBN 978 1 39907 102 4

Printed and bound in the UK by CPI Group (UK) Ltd, Croydon, CRO 4YY

Pen & Sword Books Limited incorporates the imprints of Atlas,
Archaeology, Aviation, Discovery, Family History, Fiction, History, Maritime, Military,
Military Classics, Politics, Select, Transport, True Crime, Air World, Frontline Publishing,
Leo Cooper, Remember When, Seaforth Publishing,
The Praetorian Press, Wharncliffe Local History, Wharncliffe Transport,
Wharncliffe True Crime and White Owl.
For a complete list of Pen & Sword titles please contact
PEN & SWORD BOOKS LIMITED
47 Church Street, Barnsley, South Yorkshire S70 2AS, United Kingdom
E-mail: enquiries@pen-and-sword.co.uk
Website: www.pen-and-sword.co.uk

Or
PEN AND SWORD BOOKS
1950 Lawrence Rd, Havertown, PA 19083, USA
E-mail: Uspen-and-sword@casematepublishers.com
Website: www.penandswordbooks.com

*In memory of sadly missed crime historian and
friend Martin Fido (1939–2019)*

Martin Fido (left) and the author in the old Bow Street dock when
it was on display at the National Justice Museum

Contents

An evocative image of a London street during the blitz, 1940

Introduction

Want to get home alive?
Look out in the Black-out!
Ministry of Transport, 1940

Over the decades since the end of the Second World War, the experience of the British people on the home front during that conflict has become swathed in a comfortable popular history, clouded by nostalgia, where everybody pulled together, maintained stiff upper lips and chirpy cockneys sang *Roll Out the Barrel* as they sheltered in London Underground stations while Nazi bombs rained down night after night. There *was* a 'blitz spirit' where people really did help each other pull through and there were wartime home front organisations that went to extraordinary lengths to help people and relieve suffering; many folks simply would not have come through had it not been for those efforts. There were also remarkable and selfless acts of bravery by individuals and groups working in extraordinary situations fighting fires, conducting rescues and transporting casualties throughout the blitz on London and cities and towns across Britain.

In his wartime speeches, Prime Minister Winston Churchill spoke of defiance and the official message from the plucky British people to the world, propagated by the Ministry of Information, was 'We can take it.' The problem was not everybody could 'take it' and some people snapped. Nostalgia often conveniently forgets that wartime conditions with the streets shrouded in the inky darkness of the blackout provided superb cover for criminal activities. Strings of robberies were soon being carried out under the cloak of the enforced darkness while many of those who had been mulling over committing a crime saw it as their golden opportunity to finally 'have a go'.

It was not just the blackout which drove them to act either. The police preferred to recruit ex-servicemen with good character military records to become constables. The problem was that those leaving the forces were retained on the Army Reserve for a number of years after their discharge and were eligible for call up in the event of war. This meant thousands of trained officers were lost to police forces across the country in September 1939. Special constables (SC) and war reserve police constables (WRPCs) were recruited to fill the gaps but standards and efficiency suffered. In 1939 and early 1940, police were stretched to the limit dealing with refugees fleeing from the Nazi heel in Europe, the registration of 'enemy aliens', reports of 'fifth columnists' engaging in suspected sabotage and signalling to the enemy using lights at night, and air raid incidents, in addition to their day-to-day duties. Guy Liddell, the man who would head MI5 B Branch responsible for home security for most of the war, recorded in his diary: 'We are of course up against many difficulties, not least of which is trying to follow people in the black-out and the present means for investigation which are at our disposal seem to be very meagre.'[1] These deficiencies became widely known and many were drawn to crime at this time because they stood a very good chance of getting away with it.

As the war progressed and Britain was subjected to air raids and ordinary men and women were conscripted for military service there was another spirit that emerged, one of living for the day because 'tomorrow you might be dead'. Both men and women did rash things that they would probably never have done under any other circumstances. Wartime conditions presented a perfect storm for petty crimes and a crime wave ensued.

Despite there being stringent laws against looting, bombed houses provided tempting and easy pickings for those inclined to do so. Shortages saw a burgeoning 'black market' for anything that was in short supply, and there was a brisk trade in stolen and counterfeit ration coupons. By 1941, in the London area alone the Metropolitan Police had made over 5,000 more arrests and recorded 4,000 more indictable offences than it had in 1939. Criminals of the time even became acceptable, as we see in the loveable rogue 'spiv' characters epitomised by cheeky 'Joe' Walker on *Dad's Army*. Yet delve deeper and you will also find some of the most horrific crimes from muggings using extreme violence, assaults and rape by sexual predators, to psychopathic violence, murder and even serial killers on our streets during what were both metaphorically and literally Britain's darkest hours.

The notion of a blackout is a simple enough device used to foil attacks by enemy aircraft who otherwise would find the lights of large towns and cities a great navigational aid when they were

---

1. KV4/185 8 December 1939

BLACK-OUT
ZERO
HOUR
TO-NIGHT
UNTIL 4.21 A.M.
MOON 2.22 MOON 3.9
RISES A.M SETS P.M.

Blackout times were published in both national and local newspapers during the war years

seeking out the target for their bombs. If all lights were extinguished or screened effectively enough to black out the area it would greatly hamper any such attack. Britain had experienced 'blackouts' during the Zeppelin raids of the First World War but, at that time, people had not been accustomed to the amount of street lighting and certainly not the electrical signage of those who had grown up in the 1920s and '30s. The blackout for the new generation would come as quite a culture shock, to the degree that even one of the most impassive official historians of the Second World War would observe that the blackout 'transformed conditions of life more thoroughly than any other single feature of the war.'[2]

Helpful hints on how to make suitable blackout arrangements with curtains and wooden screens were explained in the booklet *The Protection of Your Home Against Air Raids* which had been delivered to every household, along with the first issue of civilian gas masks, at the time of the Munich Crisis in

2. Quoted in Calder, Angus, *The People's War: Britain 1939–45* (London 1969)

One of a number of guides produced to assist the public during the Second World War

September 1938. As the storm clouds of war gathered during the summer of 1939, public information posters, leaflets and films shown before the main features in cinemas urged people to make those blackout arrangements in their homes and reiterated how the blackout could be achieved to the required standard. Drapers and drapery departments in city stores advertised their stocks of blackout cloth in local newspapers with eye-catching adverts advising their customers to address their blackout sooner rather than later.

The first large-scale trial blackouts were held across the country during July 1939, and on the evening of 1 September 1939, two days before the declaration of war with Germany, Britain had its first official blackout. Despite there being an optional respite from the more stringent full blackout regulations to a 'dim out' being announced in 1944, most areas would continue a full blackout until the end of the war in Europe in May 1945.

No-one could be exempt from the blackout. Households would spend an average of five to ten minutes every evening ensuring their blackout arrangements were in place. Anyone failing to comply with the blackout regulations would be visited by a police officer and served with a notice to appear before their local magistrates where they would usually receive a fine of ten shillings – equivalent to about half a week's wages for a working man – for their first offence. Hefty fines and even prison sentences could be hammered down on persistent offenders.

All road transport, be they bicycles, motorcycles, cars, buses or lorries, had to dim and screen their lights in accordance with blackout regulations. To aid visibility, street kerbs and door frames had alternate sections painted white and lamp posts had white rings painted around them. Messages were also stencilled on streets requesting people to walk on the left side of the pavement. There was a host of other products to help you be seen in the blackout, from luminous button badges to be worn on the lapel to white coats, umbrellas, arm bands and gas mask bags.

Despite the best efforts to avoid them, the blackout caused accidents on an unprecedented scale both in domestic settings and particularly out on the streets and roads. Everyday objects changed pavements into assault courses and injuries and accidents were caused by things that would have been quite innocuous in the light. People crashed into each other, into doors, lamp posts, pillar boxes, walked off the edges of railway platforms and harbours or plunged into watery or dry docks.

Some of these accidents ended in tragedy. Among those to reach the newspapers were Margaret Davies of Worsley, Lancashire, who suffered fatal injuries after falling from a settee while taking down a blanket she used for the blackout. Beatrice Page, the wife of the rector of West Wickham, was electrocuted while arranging her blackout curtains, George Peck of the Southall Gas Light and

A Metropolitan Police constable hanging up an air raid warning sirens sounded notice, 1940

Coke Company stumbled over a low wall and was impaled on an angle iron at the works where he had been employed for more than twenty-six years, and coastguard William Pearce took a fatal dive when he went over the cliff while bicycling to his duty post at Margate.

The worst death toll of all occurred on Britain's roads where fatalities trebled in the first month of the war. In one particularly dreadful incident, solicitor's office clerk Mildred Matthews (39) was making her way to Charing Cross to catch a train home during the blackout on 14 December 1939 when she was knocked down by a vehicle in Trafalgar Square. The driver probably did not see what had happened and drove on, leaving her lying on the road. When the No 11 bus passed over her, her clothes got caught up in the drive shaft and she was dragged 5 miles to the Hammersmith bus depot, which was lit inside, and it was there her body was finally spotted under the chassis.[3] In January 1940, it was reported that blackout-related deaths exceeded

3. *Westminster & Pimlico News* 12 January 1940

British casualties on any battlefront. During the first fifteen months of the war 11,424 people were killed on our highways.[4]

Although matters did improve on the roads, many people did not like going out alone at night in the blackout and would avoid it if they could as they simply didn't feel safe. Think about it, would you? Those who did venture out were often going on duty for wartime organisations and night work. Others might go out to meet friends for a trip to the cinema, pub or a dance. Groups were fine but it was the solo journey to or from the duty post, workplace or friends where fear and dangers were most likely to be encountered. During blackout hours, especially when wartime posters began to pose the question 'Is Your Journey Really Neccessary?', most people did not venture far and tended to go where they felt confident. After all when the enemy bombers started coming over you would not want to be caught out in an air raid if you didn't know where the shelters were. Thank goodness for battery torches with screens and low-power bulbs that were permitted but had to be switched off if the air raid warning sounded. But then even these became scarce when batteries were in short supply.

In an attempt to reduce road accident fatalities the *Lookout in the Blackout!* safety campaign was launched early in 1940 and produced posters, magazine and newspaper adverts headed by terrifying statements such as 'Want to get home alive?', 'You'll never forgive yourself if you kill someone', and warned those walking out in the blackout: 'YOUR turn may come tonight. There's danger in the dark.' This book proves such warnings need not apply exclusively to accidents; death stalked in many guises in the blackout.

Such is the backdrop for the murders in this book. My interest in historic true crime was kindled by some of the books in my school library and second-hand bookshops in the early 1980s and I have collected and read crime books ever since. As a young historian researching the wartime history of my county in the 1990s I interviewed and corresponded with many men and women who had served in the emergency services and lived on the home front during the Second World War. The stories they shared with me were moving and powerful but I also learned from them that there was a far darker side to life in wartime Britain. Over the last twenty years my lectures, books and research have taken me all over the country and I have

---

4. *Daily News* 11 January 1940; *Daily Mirror* 19 December 1940

An air raid warden setting off on patrol in the blackout, 1940

discovered many more such stories. As case files are released into the public domain, and more newspapers become digitised and searchable online, I have been able to research those stories like never before. I am also fortunate to not only know many respected crime historians, medical and legal professionals and retired police officers but to have had the chance to discuss these cases at length with a number of them over the years.

In this volume you will read accounts of some of the most horrific murders that took place on the home front during the Second World War; indeed some of them rank among the most shocking crimes in modern British history. Others will be far less well known but their stories are no less powerful, poignant or tragic. Readers will gain insights into the darker home front narrative and with that learn of the men and women who strove to maintain law and order under the most challenging circumstances or developed, what were in their day, groundbreaking forensic methodologies and techniques to identify bodies, recognise if foul play had occurred and bring murderers to justice. I also bring to light murders, some of them infamous, some almost faded from memory and some that local people seem to want to forget that remain unsolved to this day. Above all, I hope this book will show those who were murdered are not forgotten.

Neil R. Storey
2022

FLOOD-LIGHTING OF EDINBURGH CASTLE FROM THE GRASSMARKET.

A floodlit Edinburgh Castle viewed from the Grassmarket before the blackouts started in 1939

Wait!

Count 15

slowly

before moving in the Blackout

Poster issued by the National 'Safety First' Association offering advice to help keep members of the public safe during the blackout

CHAPTER 1

Into the Darkness

When I leave the Club, I am startled to find a perfectly black city.
Nothing could be more dramatic or give one more of a shock than to
leave the familiar Beefsteak and to find outside not the glitter of all
the sky-signs, but a pall of black velvet.

Harold Nicolson, 1939

The First Blackout Murder (Edinburgh 1939)

For Britain, the Second World War began on 3 September 1939 and the first murder in a blackout was committed less than two weeks later. It would take quite some period of adjustment before the people of Britain became accustomed to the night-time blackouts. In Edinburgh, just like the rest of the nation, blackout blinds and thick curtains masked the windows of homes and businesses, street lamps and even the floodlights of Edinburgh Castle were switched off and the streets of 'Old Reekie' were plunged into darkness. Shopkeepers had already expressed their anxiety to local authorities that the darkened conditions would lead to smash-and-grab-raids and there had already been some instances of malicious mischief. The police stepped up their patrols, got more CID men on the streets and advised all their officers to be even more vigilant. That said, there were more dark places in cities than ever before and no matter how many police were out on the beat the darkness was against them.

Shortly before 2.00am on 15 September 1939, an Edinburgh City police constable was making his rounds on the leafy, tree-lined park land of the East Meadows when he spotted something that stood out, white against the gloom under a tree near the Archer's Ground at North Meadow Walk. Upon investigation, the white shape turned out to be the prostrate half-naked body of a dead woman. Some of her clothes had been removed and thrown back over her body, other garments and her few other personal effects were scattered over the ground nearby. When the policeman shone his torch onto her face he could see that she had been badly beaten but was not unrecognisable. She was known to the police – 52-year-old mother-of-three Isabella Ralph (aka Pope or Donnelly). Separated from her husband she was of no fixed abode but had lived in a number of lodging houses in Edinburgh over the years. At the time of her murder Isabella was living at 17 James Court, Lawnmarket.

Initial enquiries revealed Isabella had last been seen alive at about 9.00pm on the night of 14 September, when she had been spotted by officers outside a pub in the Cowgate. Police immediately launched an appeal for information. The story ran in many Scottish papers and was picked up by several national and regional newspapers, especially in the north of England. Somewhat ironically, a few of the first reports of what was rapidly dubbed 'The Blackout Murder' were printed above the blackout times published in the papers. A number of people responded to the police appeals; they had seen Isabella in the company of a dark-haired man in his mid-twenties 'of respectable appearance', 5ft 11ins tall, slim build, fresh complexion wearing a grey checked office suit and a dark cap.

This description was published in the newspapers, but the best lead came from a lorry driver who had picked up a man on the road between Preston and Glasgow. When they had stopped at a roadside cafe just north of Carlisle, his passenger had broken down and confessed that he had committed a serious assault on a woman in an Edinburgh park. The lorry driver immediately went for assistance but when he returned the man had gone.

Officers from Edinburgh CID travelled to the Borders and the north of England to interview other heavy transport lorry drivers regarding the 'mystery man' hitchhiker. Their enquiries were rewarded when they identified 24-year-old John Henry Connell as a strong suspect and arrested him in Dumfries where his family resided. According to his statement Connell had been working as a bricklayer at Rosyth until he took a bed in a lodging house in Grassmarket, Edinburgh on 14 September. He stated that he intended to spend the night in the city and went to a pub in the Grassmarket where he drank heavily. Around 9.00pm he had met Isabella in the public house; she had wanted to go on to another pub together and it was she who suggested they should go to the Meadows.

While on the way there Connell discovered £3 10s was missing from his pocket and when they got to the Meadows he accused Isabella of taking it. She denied it, he became angry and there was a struggle. Connell punched her in the face and about her head with his clenched fists. Isabella began to scream and that's when he said he took her by the throat to quieten her. He recovered the money but she started to scream again so Connell compressed

The pubs, shops and cheap lodging houses of the Grassmarket, Edinburgh

her throat and she collapsed. He claimed he thought she had just fainted. He then threw what clothes he had removed from her back onto her body and fled the scene. Connell blamed his outburst of rage and his murderous attack on Isabella on having been in an intoxicated state.

Initially arrested on a charge of murder, Connell was brought before Sheriff Principal Charles H. Brown on 26 October 1939. At the opening of the hearing Thomas Muir, the procurator fiscal, stated that the Crown had decided to proceed on a charge of culpable homicide – a lesser charge which did not carry a death sentence. The sheriff felt that, in light of the gravity of the case, it was his duty to send Connell to the High Court for sentencing.

Despite the Lord Justice Clerk pointing out that 'There must have been great violence, the woman's ribs were fractured', Connell's counsel replied, 'He did not think she was seriously injured.' In passing sentence, Lord Aitchison addressed Connell stating: 'I am satisfied that the result of your conduct was the very last thing you anticipated but you took this woman's life through violence which you inflicted upon her.' Connell was sentenced to three years penal servitude.

Wannabe Gangsters (Wood Green, London 1940)

The fears of many shop owners that the blackout could be used by criminals as an opportunity to try their hand at robberies, were realised in numerous cities, towns and villages around the country.

A typical British pub in wartime

The situation was exploited not only by skilled and hardened criminals but by groups of criminal 'chancers' and wannabe 'gangsters' who were attempting crimes cloaked under the enforced darkness, some of which had fatal consequences.

By the night of 17 October 1940, the Luftwaffe had inflicted over a month of consecutive night bombings on London, and newspapers were announcing figures of nearly 7,000 dead and more than 10,500 injured in the September raids. The city was in blackout and it was a quiet night at Alexandra Park Tavern which stood on the High Road, Wood Green, not far from the Empire Theatre. Mrs Gwendoline Louise Wehrman (43), known to most at that time as Miss Gwen Cox, was manager of the off-licence attached to the tavern and was working behind the counter.

At approximately 9.15pm a young man, later identified as Felix 'Johnny' Jenkins (19), went into the bar and purchased a packet of cigarettes, using the opportunity to scope out who was there.

Returning to the car that had brought him there (a car that Jenkins had borrowed from his employers without their permission), he reported back to the rest of his gang who had been waiting inside.[1] They were a rather motley crew of young men: Frank Greenaway (18) of Raynham Road and Colin Geoffrey Grey (18) of Northumberland Park – who, like their erstwhile leader Jenkins, hailed from Tottenham – and Edward 'Eddie' Alfred Hare (18) who came from Edmonton.[2]

They decided the off-licence was ripe for a hold-up. Leaving Frank Greenaway behind the wheel with the engine running for a quick getaway, the raiders pulled scarves up to mask the lower half of their faces and stepped out of the car. Jenkins strode in first followed by Grey and Hare, who blocked the doorway as Jenkins approached the counter and pointed a Luger automatic pistol at Gwen Cox. Mustering up his best gangster style Jenkins issued the demand, 'Put your hands up. It's your dough we want.'[3]

These youthful raiders were hamming B movie gangsters so badly Gwen had to ask, 'Is this a joke?' As she did so she deftly picked up a beer bottle aiming to send the young man off with a ding, but instead a shot rang out from the Luger. The bullet hit Gwen in the chest and she died in seconds. Annie Higgins, who had been at the counter talking to Gwen just before the raiders came in and witnessed the events as they unfolded, did not think Gwen had managed to strike Jenkins with the bottle before the shot was fired. The raiders fled empty handed; Jenkins and Grey piled into the getaway car and Hare stood on the running board clinging to the side as it sped away.[4]

The group were not done for the night and only a short while later they robbed an Edmonton electrical shop of over twenty radios. Detective Chief Inspector (DCI) Ted Greeno of Scotland Yard and Detective Inspector (DI) Coates of Y Division were soon on the case. Their enquiries with informers suggested the crime had been the work of a north London gang of teenagers. Following up these leads it soon became apparent the youths had ideas of being gangsters, but they were inept. One of them had a sideline of robbing people at gunpoint he had given lifts to, but he bragged about it later. He was tracked down and he soon led police to the rest of the gang. Johnny Jenkins lived on Hale Road, Tottenham.

---

1. *Evening Telegraph* 8 November 1940
2. *Belfast News-Letter* 23 October 1940
3. *Evening Telegraph* 8 November 1940
4. *Ibid*

When the police came knocking, his mother produced the murder weapon from the drawer of her manual sewing machine.

Every gang member would give their own statement of events of that fateful night. What they had probably not realised was that under the law of joint enterprise all the raiders, if found guilty of murder, could have been sentenced to hang. As DI Coates commented to the press, when these young men were charged with the crime of murder not one of them made any reply.

In his interview, Jenkins claimed Miss Cox *had* managed to strike his wrist with the bottle she had picked up when she challenged him. DCI Greeno examined the hand and wrist in question but could find no trace of injury or bruising.[5] However in court, Jenkins' defence team offered a scenario suggested by an expert witness that the gun *could* have been triggered by the impact of the bottle on his wrist. A plea bargain was made whereby the robbers would all plead guilty to manslaughter and in doing so avoid the gallows. When the judge handed down the sentences, Jenkins and Greenaway each received three years and Hare and Grey both got eighteen months.[6]

'Let Him Have It' (Durham 1940)

The phrase 'Let him have it' used to order an opening of fire, often from Tommy guns, was one of the stock phrases synonymous with American gangster films that were so popular among British audiences during the 1930s. It also became both notorious and controversial at the trial of Derek Bentley in 1952. The situation emerged when Christopher Craig (16) and Bentley (19), two very amateur criminals influenced by gangster films, had attempted to rob Barlow & Parker's warehouse in Croydon. The pair were on the roof when Detective Sergeant (DS) Fred Fairfax moved in to arrest them. Bentley was rapidly in police hands but Craig managed to slip away to elsewhere on the roof. Craig was then cornered by the detective and drew his revolver. Fairfax appealed to Craig to hand over the weapon but as he did so he claimed Bentley called out 'Let him have it, Chris!' Craig fired his weapon, hitting a detective in the shoulder, and as other police officers made their way onto the roof Police Constable (PC) Sidney Miles died instantly when he was shot in the head.

---

5. *Bradford Observer* 23 November 1940
6. *Belfast Telegraph* 10 January 1941

Much of the trial would hinge on whether Bentley had said 'Let him have it' with the intention of urging Craig to hand the weapon over, or to open fire, and it was hotly debated in the courtroom. Bentley and Craig would also counter claim that Bentley had never uttered the words in the first place. Both were found guilty of murder but Craig was under 18 and as a minor could not be sentenced to death. Under the law of joint enterprise, despite not actually firing the fatal shot himself, Derek Bentley went to the gallows. The case was the subject of the 1991 film *Let Him Have It* starring Christopher Eccleston. Derek Bentley's family fought for a pardon for decades afterwards and his conviction was finally overturned in 1998. What is not generally realised is that a case with many similarities, even the use, or not, of the phrase 'Let him have it' had occurred twelve years earlier in 1940.

In the early hours of Thursday, 29 February 1940, local miner Jesse Smith was cycling to work through the country village of Coxhoe in County Durham from his home at The Grove. At that

The Coxhoe Co-Op, Durham where burglars tried to escape capture by jumping through the shop window on the night of 29 February 1940

time of night the streets were always quiet and darker than ever because of the blackout, so when he spotted the flash of torchlight through the window of the Co-op it really did catch his attention. As he turned to look and see what was going on the light was rapidly extinguished, but not before he caught a glimpse of a man's face.

Something was amiss and Jesse sped off to the local police station to report what he had seen. PC William 'Billy' Shiell (28) was on duty and rushed to the shop to investigate picking up WRPC William Stafford halfway along the street. When they arrived at the Co-op PC Shiell knocked at the front door. When they were there another miner named William Wilson came over to see if he could help.

Shiell told Wilson and Stafford to go round to the back of the store and asked Smith to keep watch at the corner. Stafford soon discovered a bolt had been withdrawn on the gate at the back of the premises. Scuffling noises were heard at the rear of the shop and Stafford called out, 'They are here at the back.' Shiell and Smith ran to the back and no sooner had they had arrived they heard a crash of breaking glass at the front. Shiell ran around to the front and saw two men running across the road. PC Shiell blew his whistle, shouted at them to stop, kept his torch beam on them and pursued them around the corner into Patterson's Opening and onto waste ground near Long Row. In his own statement Shiell recalled: 'I chased them and cornered them behind Wesley Place. One of them pulled a revolver out and the other said, "Let him have it, he is all alone", and he shot me – just one shot in the stomach at the side.'[7]

As Stafford ran round the building he could see Shiell and the two suspects about 100 yards in front of him and joined the pursuit. He could see Shiell was keeping the suspects in the beam of his torch as he closed in on them, but then he heard a shot ring out and saw Shiell clutch his stomach and drop to the ground.

When Stafford and Wilson reached Shiell the suspects had fled and the brave constable was bleeding badly. They were not going to leave him lying in the dirt so the pair part lifted and part dragged him to the nearby home of furnace worker Robert Sinderson at 53 Long Row and laid him on the kitchen floor. It was there that Shiell managed to tell them what had happened and said to Wilson, 'Go and get the ambulance and call for the sergeant on your way up.' When Mr Sinderson asked PC Shiell if he could get him anything, he asked for a glass of water and a cigarette. When the ambulance arrived, PC Shiell was taken to

7. *Liverpool Evening Express* 6 May 1940

Durham County Hospital where he was given treatment for the wound.[8] PC Shiell's comrades in Durham Police volunteered to give him transfusions of blood arm to arm to help save his life but sadly the doctors could do little for him and informed detectives that he only had hours to live.

PC William Shiell, the much-loved husband of Frieda and father of little Barbara, died from his wound the following day. He had, however, been able to describe the events of that fateful night and provide descriptions of his assailants in a sworn deposition given from his hospital bed. PC Shiell was given a full honours funeral befitting a police officer killed in the line of duty. It was attended by the Mayor of Durham, magistrates and hundreds of representatives from police forces in Durham and Northumberland. Hundreds of local people lined the route of his cortege as it made its way from his home at 6 The Avenue in Coxhoe to St Andrew's Church, Spennymoor, where, only a few years earlier, he had been married. The pallbearers were six of PC Shiell's police colleagues from Coxhoe. [9]

The police investigation, led by Detective Superintendent (DS) Tom Holmes and Superintendent (Supt) J. R. Johnson, uncovered more clues – a bag of housebreaking implements that had been found in an outhouse at the rear of the Co-op and a ladder that had been stolen from another premises, which the thieves had used to climb onto the roof to get in through a skylight. There was also a vicious-looking dagger with a six-inch blade which, judging by its clean appearance, had not been lying in the lane for long. Witnesses came forward to say they had seen a car in a lane near the Co-op and when the area was examined by police, distinctive tyre tracks were found.[10] Subsequently, a burnt-out Vauxhall 10hp saloon, which had been stolen a few days earlier from the home of Doctor Traill, the medical officer of health for Chester-le-Street, was discovered on moors near Holmfirth in Yorkshire.[11]

A £100 reward was offered by Durham Police for any information that could lead to the apprehension of the perpetrators, but it would be the criminals that gave themselves away. The burnt-out car had pointed detectives towards Yorkshire, and the tyres from Dr Traill's stolen car and the tracks found in the lane at Coxhoe proved a good match. Additionally, goods known to have been taken in the burglary were sold in Leeds just days afterwards and detectives knew they were on the right trail.

---

8. *Newcastle Journal* 1 March 1940
9. *Ibid*
10. *Ibid*
11. *Yorkshire Post* 10 April 1940

Vincent Ostler (24), a motor mechanic well known in his local area as a seasonal ice cream salesman, and William Appleby (27), a joiner and undertaker, both from Hawksworth near Leeds, were soon identified as highly likely suspects from the assembled clues and were arrested. Of the pair Ostler, the son of a retired police sergeant of the West Riding Constabulary, put up the most resistance when police came to arrest him. He refused to answer the door, an entry had to be forced, a violent struggle ensued and Ostler had to be overpowered before officers could get handcuffs on him. He even continued to struggle after he had been cuffed. When Ostler's home and garage were searched, items identified as some of those from the Coxhoe Co-op were discovered.[12] The pair were suspected of having committed many offences in the north and Midlands over a two-year period, stealing goods from housebreaking and burglaries with an estimated value of more than £20,000.

Ostler and Appleby were remanded at Durham Police Court on the day of PC Shiell's funeral and appeared before Mr Justice Hilberry at Leeds Assizes in a trial that ran 6–10 May 1940. Ostler, who had a previous conviction for threatening a policeman with a firearm, offered a defence that he was simply not there and was in bed asleep in his own home at the time of the crime. Appleby confessed that he had been one of the robbers but claimed he had not known Ostler was armed and denied he had said 'Let him have it' when the pair had been cornered by PC Shiell. He insisted that he had said, 'Come on, let's give him a clout.'[13] Ultimately, what he did or didn't say was immaterial. As Derek Bentley would discover twelve years later, under the law of joint enterprise, despite not actually firing the fatal shot himself he still received the full force of the law as an accomplice.

Appleby and Ostler admitted to a string of robberies but denied being in Coxhoe on the night of the shooting. Nevertheless, they were found guilty of murder and although there was a recommendation for mercy from the jury in the case of Appleby, both shared the death sentence and were hanged at HM Prison Durham on 11 July 1940 by uncle and nephew Thomas and Albert Pierrepoint with Stanley Cross and Alec Riley as assistants. There was no posthumous gallantry award made in honour of PC Shiell, and his widow lived off a pension of ten shillings a week with two shillings and sixpence for little Barbara.

---

12. *Ibid*
13. *Bradford Observer* 9 May 1940

CHAPTER 2

Snapped?

Science has not yet taught us if madness is or is not the sublimity of the intelligence.

Edgar Allan Poe

The increasing intensity of air raids began to take its toll on the frayed nerves of the British people in 1940. Over the war years the combination of air raids, false alarms, blackouts, lack of sleep, shortages and rationing strained some families to the limit. Occasionally, morals fell by the wayside and for others life became cheap. There were outbursts of frustration and violence. For some it was too much, and they simply snapped.

'It was for the best' (Hackney, London 1940)

At the very start of the shows that may well have inspired our interest in the darker pathways of humanity, be it *Alfred Hitchcock Presents*, Rod Serling and *The Twilight Zone*, *Roald Dahl's Tales of the Unexpected* or my own personal favourite, Edward Woodward's introductions for the precious eleven episodes of *In Suspicious Circumstances*, the opening monologues would often ask the viewers to consider a poignant question such as what would you have done under the circumstances presented in the programme you were about to be shown.

In that same spirit I pose two questions to ponder when reading the stories in this chapter. Consider if it were you and your home city that were being subjected to bombing by enemy aircraft, not just for one night but night after night, and you don't have the benefit of hindsight to know when it will end. Nights when you would hear the warning sirens and make your way to your little corrugated iron Anderson shelter down the garden. There you would sit and wait until you heard the unmistakable drone of the engines of enemy bombers, the crump of distant bombs and then explosion after explosion as they get closer, and you are left in that horrible limbo of will you be next, or will it pass over and you get to live another day? Add into that mix the day-to-day issues of life and work, love and relationships, especially if something

Devastation at Harrington Square, London after an air raid, September 1940

drastically upsets that difficult balance – could you weather it all with stoicism? How much could you take before you snapped? And perhaps darker still, do you dare contemplate what you could be capable of *after* you snapped?

Before the days of a National Health Service, when there was far less public awareness and adoption of healthy eating habits, and more people smoked than not, many people in their sixties and seventies looked and felt old and were quite happy to see these as the twilight years of their lives. Even though there were old age pensions, many still had to work to make ends meet and often ended their years living hand to mouth just managing to 'get by'.

One such couple were Ida Ethel Rodway (61), who worked as a boot and shoe machinist for A & H Meltzers at their Pretoria Shoe Works in Tottenham, north London, and her husband Joseph (71) who was a retired horse-drawn delivery driver. They had been married for nearly forty years and relatives would recall that they always seemed happy and not a cross word passed between them. On 21 September 1940, the house where they were living in rented rooms at 11 Martello Street, Hackney, was bombed. Fortunately, the couple were already in the Anderson shelter in the garden when the bomb detonated and destroyed much of their home and possessions, although they still caught some of the force of the blast. Neither suffered any serious physical injuries but Joseph was taken to Hackney Hospital in a badly distressed state. He had to leave less than a week later when the hospital required his bed for other casualties.

Mrs Rodway had not been hospitalised but, as a family friend would comment, it was believed she had been receiving treatment for neurasthenia, a kinder and less stigmatised word for a condition commonly known as shell shock.

Life had not been kind to Joseph. He had been one of the last generation of men to work as drivers of horse-drawn transport

A young woman rescued from the debris of her home after an air raid, 1940

but times had moved on – steam and petrol vehicles were being used instead – and Joseph had not been in regular employment for ten years. He had also been losing his sight for years and became totally blind in April 1939; consequently he was pretty much entirely reliant on Ida. She had to take more and more time off work to look after him and lost her job as a result, so they were living on Joseph's meagre pension and dole money. After losing their home and nearly all their possessions, the couple had been reduced to sleeping on a floor at the home of Ida's sister, Florence Clapp, at 39 Kingshold Road, Hackney Wick. Joseph's mental health had also deteriorated and he was often confused and disorientated. Ida confided in her sister that she wished the bomb that destroyed their home had killed them both.

Shortly after her sister left for work at about 7.40am on 1 October 1940 Ida Rodway snapped. What happened next was written up in a statement she gave to police shortly after 11.00am the same morning:

> I thought to myself, 'What shall I do? Here am I stranded with nowhere to go. Whatever shall I do?' I know my sister would not keep me there forever. My husband was in bed on the floor. I had been up since about seven o'clock. I was dressed. I was

Londoners removing what possessions they could salvage after their home was destroyed in an air raid, 1940

going to take him in a cup of tea, but I never gave him the tea. I got hold of the chopper from under the dresser in the kitchen and the carving knife. I went into the bedroom and he was sitting up in bed. I hit him on the head with the chopper. The head of the chopper fell off. He said 'What are you doing this for?' I said 'I am led to desperation.' and took hold of the knife and finished him off. I was worried to death with no one to help me.[1]

In fact Ida Rodway had not only cleaved her husband's skull with a hatchet, she had also cut into his throat so vigorously she had nearly detached his head from his body. She then covered his head with two pillows, cleaned herself up and went to alert the authorities. She encountered their upstairs neighbour Lily Beauchamp on the street, to whom she said, quite calmly and in a matter-of-fact way: 'I have murdered my husband. I want to find a policeman. Will you get one of the wardens?'[2]

When questioned about why she had killed her husband Mrs Rodway took pains to point out they had not quarrelled, explaining that: 'He was my husband. I was worried about him. He was blind. We were bombed out of our home and I had nowhere to go and nobody to help me. I was worried to death. I don't know what made me do it.'[3] In much the same way that thousands of beloved pets had been destroyed in September 1939, when many feared severe food shortages and the air raid regulations did not permit dogs or cats to be taken into public air raid shelters, Mrs Rodway appeared, in later police interviews, absolutely convinced she had done the kindest thing for her husband under the circumstances and that it had 'been for the best'.[4] She had even taken the knife and chopper to a local knife grinder shortly before the day of the murder.

Arraigned at the Central Criminal Court on 14 November, Ida Rodway was brought before Mr Justice Wrottesley. A psychological assessment had been carried out by the medical officer of Holloway Prison who said Mrs Rodway had told him she 'intended to plead guilty, as that would get everything settled.' She reiterated that she believed what she had done was right and that she was 'entirely unconcerned about the result of the trial'.[5]

---

1. MEPO 3/2169
2. *Ibid*
3. *Ibid*
4. *Ibid*
5. *Daily Mirror* 14 November 1940

Members of the public using Aldwych Underground Station as
an air raid shelter during the blitz, 1940

The medical officer expressed his opinion that she was unfit to
plead. Mr Justice Wrottesley ordered her to be 'detained until
His Majesty's pleasure be known'. Ida Rodway was committed to
Broadmoor, where she died on 25 April 1946.

A case in a similar vein was also heard at the same sessions,
that of City of London air raid precautions (ARP) worker James
Miller (45) of Durant Street, Bethnal Green. He had been taking
his mother, Elizabeth Miller (75), to underground stations and
other shelters and claimed that what he had seen as a rescue
worker preyed on his mind. He said he had become worried
about her not getting any sleep and was concerned that her
health would suffer if she kept on sleeping on the steps of tube
stations. So he decided to strangle her with a length of wireless
aerial, then went around to Old Street Police Station and
handed himself in.[6] Miller admitted he had killed her because
he thought he was relieving her suffering, telling police, 'I did
it to save her being dragged around to the shelters.'[7] Mr Miller

6. *Daily Herald* 1 November 1940
7. *Daily Mirror* 19 October 1940

was found guilty but insane and was also detained 'during the King's pleasure'.

The Bath Chair Murder (Rayleigh, Essex 1943)

This story was not actually committed during a blackout. However, you may well have read books entitled *Murder by Gaslight* or similar; not all the murders in those books were committed by gas light but they all were committed during the time of gas lighting and reflect something of those times too. The case of the Bath Chair Murder is most certainly one peculiar to its time because of the particular device used; in fact it is unique in the annals of British criminal history.

Archibald Brown (47) had been born into the successful flour milling and corn merchant family who had owned Rayleigh Mill, near the Essex town from which it took its name for more than a generation. He lived in the fine family home known as 'Summerfield' close to the mill on London Hill with his wife, Dorothy, and two sons Eric (19) and Colin (16). Life had been good for Archibald until he suffered a motorcycle accident when still in his twenties which left him in constant pain and with a progressive paralysis of the spine. In 1942 he lost all movement in his legs, making him reliant on the use of a bath chair for mobility and hired nurses who tended to his needs. The condition also attacked his brain. His family would admit that Mr Brown had always been 'of very difficult temperament' and although not extremely violent he would hit out and had been harsh on his boys as they grew up, particularly Eric. In recent years his irritability had become more marked, and he made the lives of his family a misery through constant bullying and verbal abuse. On one occasion he even attempted to strangle his wife in a fit of rage while she was feeding him.[8] Dorothy Brown tried to be understanding of her husband and stood by him, but even she would admit that, when in a mood, his strength seemed greater than usual and 'he had a fair amount of strength in his right hand.'[9]

Archibald Brown took to spending most of his time in bed but would be taken out for 'constitutionals' in the fresh air, in his bath chair, by one of his three nurses who worked on a rota looking after him. On the lovely summer afternoon of 23 July 1943, nurse Elsie Mitchell was on duty and wheeled his bath

8. *Chelmsford Chronicle* 5 November 1943
9. Totterdell, G. H., *Country Copper* (London 1956)

chair to the back door of the house. Mr Brown remained in his pyjamas and wrapped up in his dressing gown as nurse Mitchell placed two pillows on the back of the bath chair, helped him into it, covered him up with a travelling rug and blanket and tucked him in. They then set out on one of their regular routes along the Hockley Road. They got about a mile away, and were near a house called 'Gattens', when Mr Brown wanted to stop and smoke a cigarette. Nurse Mitchell lit his cigarette, straightened the blankets and moved to the back of the wheelchair and pushed on. Within a dozen paces there was a sudden explosion, and she was thrown to the ground.

She had been fortunate that the frame and the cushions she had diligently placed in the bath chair had absorbed enough of the blast to save her life. Elsie would later recall that she heard Archibald Brown's body parts falling around her immediately after the explosion before she lost consciousness. When she regained consciousness she said:

> I could smell my hair burning and a terrific heat came up from somewhere ... I saw the head and shoulders of my patient in front and I think I saw a leg in a tree. My own legs were pumping blood badly. Small pieces of metal were embedded in them. I received treatment in a house and I was admitted to hospital.[10]

Mr Brown had indeed been dismembered in the explosion; his lower extremities had been blown apart and the upper trunk of his body carried upwards and backwards onto the road by the force of the blast. The police examination of the scene found his left leg had been flung more than 30ft away and was hanging 15ft off the ground on a nearby tree. His right leg was discovered some 48ft away in the front garden of a house. The bath chair had been reduced to an horrific tangle of twisted metal and human remains on the road.[11]

Fragments of the device that had caused the explosion were recovered from the scene. These were confirmed by army experts to be from a Hawkins No.75 anti-tank grenade. The device was designed so that when a tank or armoured fighting vehicle drove over the grenade it would compress the pressure plates, which in turn would crack the ampoule containing acid inside the grenade, releasing the fluid onto a sensitive chemical and detonating the explosive. In the case of Archibald Brown, the police were of the

10. *Chelmsford Chronicle* 5 November 1943
11. Totterdell, *Country Copper*

opinion that the pressure plates of the grenade had been modified so the lesser weight of Mr Brown would be sufficient to trigger the explosion. This he had done when he shifted his weight after feeling for a packet of cigarettes in the pockets of his dressing gown.

When she was well enough to be interviewed by the police, Nurse Elsie Mitchell said that the bath chair was usually stored in the air raid shelter outside the house, but when she had gone to collect it at about 1.45pm on 23 July she had discovered the shelter door had been bolted from inside. She rattled the door but after getting no response went to see if Mrs Brown could help.

The twisted remains of Archibald Brown's bath chair after the explosion of a Hawkins grenade with him sat in it, Rayleigh, Essex 1943

As they walked back to get the chair the Browns' eldest son, Eric, was coming out of the shelter. Rather than exchanging pleasantries, it had struck her how irritated and evasive he had been when his mother asked what he had been doing inside the shelter to have bolted the door.

Eric had been called up in September 1942 and was serving as a private in 8th Battalion, Suffolk Regiment based in Spilsby, Lincolnshire but was at home having been given compassionate leave from the army to help with the family business. Eric had been trained in the assembly and use of anti-tank mines. There were 200 of them stored on his base, 144 of which were operational and checked every month; the rest were used for training purposes and were not checked.[12] Eric was brought into Rayleigh Police Station. Despite initial reticence he soon opened up and admitted he had purloined the grenade from the training stock at his army base – it had not been missed – brought it home and hid it in a tool box he kept in the air raid shelter. He removed the top plate to make it more sensitive and placed it under the cushion of his father's bath chair. He also explained his reasons for doing it:

> I decided the only real way in which my mother could lead a normal life and for my father to be released from his sufferings was for him to die mercifully. I therefore decided to cause his death in a manner which would leave him no longer in suffering. My father is now out of his sufferings. His death was in real truth a great shock to me but what I did I am not afraid to answer for.[13]

Brown was arrested, committed for trial for murder at Southend County Petty Sessions and tried before Mr Justice Atkinson at the Essex Assizes held at the Shire Hall, Chelmsford on 4 November 1943. The young man had displayed signs of mental illness for some time. Colleagues from a previous employer, Barclays Bank in Rochford, said that while he appeared to be a promising young man, he would suffer 'brain storms' during which he would throw his hands in the air and bring his clenched fists down on the desk. Sometimes he appeared quite unbalanced and had conducted some strange transactions, and although no criminal intent was believed to be intended, the manager had asked him to tender his resignation. While in custody Brown attempted to cut his throat.

---

12. Totterdell, *Country Copper*
13. *Aberdeen Press* 22 September 1943

At his trial Brown pleaded not guilty.[14] Nervous diseases specialist Dr Rowland Hill was called as an expert witness. He had diagnosed Eric with schizophrenia and expressed his opinion that the young man did not have 'a normal perception of the difference between right and wrong, he would have a wholly distorted idea of what he was doing.'[15] The jury agreed and a verdict of guilty but insane was returned and Eric Brown was ordered to be detained 'during the King's pleasure'. He was finally released in 1975 after thirty-two years in an asylum. After the national media attention surrounding the case evaporated, his mother Dorothy lived the rest of her life in quiet obscurity and died in Southend in September 1981.

Sledgehammer to Crack a Nut (Leicester 1944)

There is an old army song written by Irving Berlin in 1918 that would be sung again with much the same feeling about army routine, and those responsible for it, in the Second World War. Entitled *Oh! How I Hate to Get Up in the Morning*, its initial curse was aimed at the bugler, but on the march it would be sung in rounds, each time finding a new target, among them:

> One day I'm going to murder the sergeant, one day they're going to find him dead. I'll amputate his reveille and step upon it heavily and spend the rest of my life in bed.

Private (Pte) Raymond Howard Bushell (18) was one for whom the song had especial meaning. Born in Australia, Bushell had moved with his family to England when he was just a year old. When he turned 18 in 1943 Ray had volunteered to join the Australian infantry to do his bit for king and country. Problem was he was not placed with a regiment to train for frontline fighting on active service abroad. The army had decided that, as he had worked previously as an electroplater's assistant and sheet metal worker, he should be sent to the Royal Electrical and Mechanical Engineers based at an ordnance depot in the North Midlands.

Bushell didn't want to be stuck in that backwater for the war and put in for transfer on two occasions, and both times they were not approved. The man he suspected of blocking his

---

14. Totterdell, *Country Copper*
15. *Chelmsford Chronicle* 5 November 1943

transfers was Staff Sergeant Thomas Albert 'Gibby' Gibbs who ran one of the depot workshops. For some reason Staff Sergeant Gibbs and Pte Bushell never hit it off. Bushell felt he was being victimised by Gibbs and held him responsible for the pursuance of charges of absenteeism and failing to obey orders. On one occasion, for example, Gibbs had reprimanded Bushell for idling, and as this was the second time Gibbs felt he had cause to reprimand Bushell for idling again, he asked the section corporal Frank Whitehead to charge him with being absent from work.[16] Four charges had been upheld against Bushell and he had been punished with spells in military detention.

Bushell would claim in a statement to a DS Jones:

> He [Gibbs] was victimising me in the shops [workshops]. He told me the first time he got the chance to railroad me back to detention he would do so.[17]

On more than one occasion Bushell's comrades said he would recount stories of being reprimanded by 'Gibby' in their barrack hut, and having told his tale Bushell would spit out the words 'I'll do him.'[18] Bushell was at the end of his tether. Was he young, angry, frustrated and foolish and had access to weaponry to be young and foolish with, or did he snap in November 1943?

Everyone at the depot was looking forward to the Armistice night dance on 11 November. However, Bushell was determined to use the opportunity, not to make merry, but to take matters into his own hands, as he recalled later:

> I knew he [Gibbs] was bound to be at the dance, so I went to the ammunition dump. I picked the lock with a pair of pliers and a nail and took a 36 grenade, cleaned it, and put the detonator in. I waited until about eleven o'clock and proceeded to the dance. I put the grenade behind a case where no-one would notice it. I went into the dance, had a few drinks, and kept my eye on him. I lost sight of him in the dance hall, then went outside and waited at the bottom of the shed. Gibby comes down with his girl and I followed.

It was about 12.20am when Gibbs and the woman left the dance hall. At the same time, Bushell recovered the grenade from its

---

16. *Leicester Evening Mail* 8 December 1943
17. *Leicester Chronicle* 29 January 1944
18. *Leicester Evening Mail* 8 December 1943

hiding place and followed the pair up the road. He said: 'I gave them about 28 to 30 yards distance, waited till the girl got in front of Gibbs, so the blast would not kill her. I gauged the distance and let throw.'[19]

The grenade exploded, inflicting fatal injuries on Staff Sergeant Gibbs. His female partner, Iris Alice Turner, was uninjured. Later, as she recalled what happened, she said she had heard a 'very loud click' behind them and both had turned to look at where the noise had come from. She saw a flash and heard a bang then, as she turned to Gibbs and asked, 'What was that Tom?', he collapsed at her feet. Miss Turner immediately shook Gibbs but upon seeing his injuries screamed for help and ran back to the dance hall to summon the police.[20]

Iris had not seen who had thrown the grenade but a passer-by had spotted *someone* in the shadows. Bushell heard them shout 'Hey!', so he fled back to the dance, merged with the crowd in the dance hall and eventually went to bed as if nothing had happened. Police and CID were soon on the scene and rapidly began their investigations. A number of those connected with Staff Sergeant Gibbs were aware of the animosity between Gibbs and Pte Bushell so he was taken from his bed for questioning at about 3.30am. Sergeant Raymond Bullimore would recall that when they passed the body of Sergeant Gibbs covered by a tarpaulin. Bushell had remarked, 'None of the boys will be sorry about that.'[21] Once in the hands of the police Bushell freely confessed 'I did it' to DS Jones and gave a full and frank statement.[22]

The inquest for Staff Sergeant Gibbs was opened on 13 November and was attended by Gibbs' wife of ten years, Agnes Lilian Gibbs. Lieutenant William White Black of the Royal Army Medical Corps stated that death had been due to multiple injuries, with extensive damage to the brain caused by a piece of metal which had entered the skull by the right eye. He was of the opinion that death would have been instantaneous. Captain Ernest Riley who had been Gibbs' company commander since 1942 was also called as a witness. When asked by Mr H. K. Barker, who was appearing for Bushell, 'Was the sergeant very strict?', the coroner interceded and said, 'I think this is not the time for such a question.' [23]

---

19. *Leicester Chronicle* 29 January 1944
20. *Nottingham Journal* 9 December 1943
21. *Ibid*
22. *Halifax Evening Courier* 13 November 1943
23. *Leicester Evening Mail* 13 November 1943

Bushell was tried on a charge of murder before Leicester Assizes on Wednesday, 26 January 1944. Despite claiming that he had waited until the girl was in front of Gibbs 'so the blast *would not kill her*' [my italics] Bushell would claim in his defence that he intended only 'to scare' Gibbs and 'not to injure him.' [24]

Any trained soldier would know Pte Bushell had been playing an extremely dangerous game with a potentially fatal outcome. One of the thunderflashes commonly used on army exercises to simulate grenade and mortar explosions in battle would have easily done the trick. If Bushell had only intended to frighten Gibbs he was using a sledgehammer to crack a nut.

There was, however, a twist to the tale. In response to Bushell's defence of his actions with the grenade Mr Paul Sandilands KC for the prosecution put it to Bushell: 'But you had another weapon ready for him... . You had a Sten gun hidden by the cemetery on the sergeant's route.'

Bushell replied matter-of-factly, yet again: 'I intended to use the gun to frighten him.'

After deliberating for nearly an hour the jury, clearly impressed with Bushell's candour, his youth and perhaps convinced by his naivete, found Pte Raymond Bushell not guilty of murder but guilty of manslaughter. Passing a sentence of ten years penal servitude the judge, Mr Justice Charles, commented that, 'the jury have taken, as they were entitled to, an extraordinarily lenient view of your case'.[25]

After the jury returned their verdict a police officer read out Bushell's history. He had one conviction for theft as a juvenile. After leaving school his employers described his character at work as 'poor' and he was also described as a 'very poor soldier with four convictions against him'.[26]

Were Bushell's military misdemeanours the result of some petty vendetta pursued by Gibbs against a disillusioned soldier, or was he really as bad as he was painted? Much was made in court of how Bushell had shown the grenade to his pal, Pte John Wells, when they were out walking together on Armistice afternoon. Bushell had said: 'I'm going to give Gibby a Christmas box but not the type you think.' It was put to the court by Bushell's defence, 'Would a man who intended to blow up his staff-sergeant show

---

24. *Leicester Chronicle* 29 January 1944
25. *Leicester Evening Mail* 27 January 1944
26. *Ibid*

the grenade to his mate?' It is, perhaps, telling that Pte Wells did not warn Gibbs nor his officers of Bushell's intentions.

Bushell himself appears to have served his time, got married, settled down and had a family. He died in 1999.

The Leeds Axe Murder (Leeds 1945)

At approximately 8.10am on the morning of Sunday, 30 April 1945, just days before the end of the war in Europe, electrician Bill Whitaker was walking home from work when he spotted a man lying just inside the gates and behind a black Morris 10 saloon car on the driveway at 176 Beeston Road, Leeds. Mr Whitaker told a *Yorkshire Post* reporter:

> I saw a person on the ground... . At first I thought it was a man fixing a jack under the back of the car but I was attracted by the stillness of the body and making a closer examination, I saw a patch of red which proved to be blood. I realised that something unusual had happened and I crossed the main road to a telephone booth and informed the police, waiting there until the arrival of the police ambulance.[27]

Police were called to the scene and soon ascertained that the body, which was lying in a large pool of blood, was that of the homeowner Dr David Walker Dewar (42).[28] He had been hacked to death, with eleven separate wounds inflicted upon his head by a hatchet which had shattered the skull into many pieces. The fatal blow was believed to have been the one that cut through the upturned collar of his overcoat, penetrated the lower part of his skull and lacerated his brain. Police surgeon Dr Hoyland Smith was of the opinion that Dr Dewar's body had been lying there for seven or eight hours before it has been discovered.

Such a serious and violent crime demanded the presence of the most senior police officers, and the chief constable and chief of the CID, Supt Frank Swaby, personally attended the scene and led the investigation. A police appeal, including a description and the number plate of the doctor's car (DNW 625), was circulated to the press. Dr Dewar's movements on Saturday night were soon ascertained, up to shortly after midnight when he attended a patient at a public house near his home. He was

27. *Yorkshire Post* 30 April 1945
28. *Ibid*

Leeds pictured shortly before the outbreak of war, a city shocked
by an axe murder in 1945

last seen alone in his car on Beeston Road at 12.40am and was
believed to have been killed shortly afterwards.

When Dr Dewar's body was examined at the scene he was
found to be holding the ignition key for his car, and because one
of the double gates of his driveway was closed it was suggested
he had just driven his car into the yard, got out and was bending
down and fastening the gates when he was attacked. The blackout
was still in force and there is a good chance he would not have
seen his assailant before he was attacked, and may not have even
had time to cry out before the fatal blow had been delivered.[29]
His Chilean-born wife Elizabeth Gemmell Izaat Dewar had gone
to bed before midnight and was unaware anything untoward
had happened to her husband until the alarm was raised in the
morning. Neighbours also heard nothing suspicious during the
night. There was no indication of robbery or attempted robbery;
in fact there was no apparent motive for the killing and despite a
close search of the allotments and fields in the area the murder
weapon was not recovered.[30]

The public face of Scot Dr David Dewar was one of
respectability. Educated at Wishaw Public School, he qualified at
Glasgow University in 1930 and after being in practice in Glasgow
and Sheffield he had settled in Leeds about twelve years earlier,

29. *Yorkshire Post* 30 April 1945
30. *Shields Daily News* 30 April 1945

after taking over the Beeston practice of the late Dr Crawford. He also held the position of factory medical officer for a Leeds firm of optical instrument makers and took a keen interest in the Medical Practitioners Union. He was a popular man with a wide circle of friends

He was also quite a lothario and was having affairs with a number of local women while their soldier husbands were away serving king and country. Among them was Mrs Laura Walker (27) of Lady Pit Crescent, Beeston Hill, Leeds. Laura had worked as a tailoress specialising in hand lining but had taken up work as a wood-cutting machinist for the war effort. She worked long hours, but was determined to enjoy her social life. Dewar had been her family doctor since 1933 and she had been flattered by the attention he had paid her in recent years, and they had often been seen out together in his car and visiting pubs. Investigating officers did wonder if this could be a case of a jealous husband finding out about his unfaithful wife on his return from the war, but Laura's husband, Arthur, was still abroad serving in Italy and he had not been home on leave at the time of the murder. However, unknown to the police, there was Thomas Eric Richardson (28), a surgical-implement maker who lived on Harlech Road, Beeston, who was also on intimate terms with Laura.

On 28 April, Mrs Walker had what newspapers covering the story in 1945 would quaintly call 'a social appointment' with Dr Dewar and she had informed Richardson that she was going for a drink with him. Richardson did not want her to go. He was suffering from boils on the neck and he wanted her to dress them. Talk about showing a girl a fun time on a Saturday night.

Laura agreed to see Richardson again that night but only after she had been out with Dewar. She suggested that Richardson could come and see her at her home around midnight.[31] Dr Dewar and Laura visited a number of bars that night and he dropped her back home around 12.30am. She had not been in long before Richardson arrived looking tired and was very morose. Laura dressed his boils and he left about 5.00am.

On 20 May, Laura told Richardson she had been worrying about the murder of Dr Dewar and that she had been questioned by the police. She obviously felt the finger of suspicion was being pointed at her. Richardson asked if she had mentioned his name and she assured him that she had not. It was at that moment Richardson said, 'I can tell you who killed Dr Dewar.' She begged him to tell her so she could be cleared. Richardson clearly loved every moment

31. *Northern Daily Mail* 8 June 1945

of having that power, and Laura recalled the moment of his reveal when Richardson said: 'The fellow that did it had a reason. I did it. I was not going to let him ruin your life.'[32] He also told her later that he had killed Dewar with a hatchet.

Laura Walker went to the police with the revelatory information and Richardson gave a statement to Supt Craig. In it he admitted that he had been 'friendly' with Laura for the two years since her soldier husband had been away and continued:

> I was annoyed and grieved when she went with Dr Dewar. I had a carbuncle and everything was whizzing round in my head. I began to have nightmares. I could see Laura's face all night. I don't know what I was doing as I was ill and my mind was in such a state.

Richardson also admitted that he had thrown the axe he used to kill Dr Dewar into the river.[33]

Richardson's trial opened at Leeds Assizes on 16 July 1945. When he appeared in the witness box he wore a smart suit and had the appearance of an intelligent man with a quiet disposition. He appeared cool and answered almost all the questions put to him in a calm and confident manner. He denied everything, claiming he had met Mrs Walker but had gone home and went to bed because he was nursing a bad carbuncle, was feeling ill and did not wake up again until 8.00am the following morning. Richardson's father Harold was called as a witness and was 'practically certain' his son was in the house overnight on the night in question. Richardson's defence also pointed out that no blood stains had ever been found on his hands or clothing.[34]

The trial ended on 19 July. After hearing the final summing up, the jury retired and took one hour and thirty minutes to reach a unanimous guilty verdict. Mr Justice Hallett passed the sentence of death upon Richardson[35] and Thomas Eric Richardson was hanged at Armley Prison, Leeds, by Thomas Pierrepoint, assisted by Herbert Harris, on 7 September 1945. It appears that Mrs Laura Walker's shenanigans during the war did not result in divorce when Arthur returned and the couple remained married for the rest of their lives.

---

32. *Northern Daily Mail* 8 June 1945
33. *Ibid*
34. *Bradford Observer* 18 July 1945
35. *Northern Daily Mail* 19 July 1945

CHAPTER 3

Bogeymen

When a child doesn't come home in the country you go round asking at Grandma's or Auntie's, assuming everything will be all right. But when a child is missing in the city it pays to suspect the worst straight away.
Detective Chief Superintendent Edward Greeno

If, like me, you are one of the generation born in the 1960s or '70s, you probably think back to the things you used to do when you were a child and consider how much has changed. We would regularly go and play in the woods and fields and cycle for miles around our local area. Kids would still play on streets and back alleys and in spooky empty buildings where they had been told not to go. Even though it had been illegal to sell tobacco products to children in Britain under sixteen years of age since 1908, many youngsters were regularly sent by Mum or Dad on an errand to pick up an evening paper and a packet of cigarettes. Tragically, there have always been cases of child abduction, assault and murder but as media has evolved and become more accessible, thanks especially to cheaper televisions becoming a feature of every home, high-profile coverage of infamous cases such as the Moors Murders committed by Ian Brady and Myra Hindley in the mid-1960s and the murder of Holly Wells and Jessica Chapman in 2002, changed our attitudes and highlighted the need for greater child protection.

Some folks who grew up in the 1930s and '40s recall a safer, more neighbourly Britain where children would play out on the streets and bombsites (although they were not meant to). In fact it was so safe you did not need lock your front door. Parents in those times would often be aware of a 'funny' man (perhaps someone rumoured to have a past conviction for indecency or known for behaviour with children that made parents uncomfortable) in the local area and would warn their children not to go near him. Children were often warned that if they were naughty or strayed to places out of bounds, that 'the Bogeyman will get you'. What he would actually do if he got a child was often not explained in detail, the threat of capture and the rest being left to the child's imagination was usually enough. Most kids got the message and learned to keep their eyes open for what would become known in later years as 'stranger danger'. The problem was in the 1930s and '40s, children were more naïve and tragically, for some, the Bogeyman really was waiting in the blackout.

Every Parent's Worst Nightmare (Waterloo, Merseyside 1940)

Fifteen-year-old schoolgirl Mary Hagan was a happy, home-loving child who lived with her parents James and Mary Hagan, and her little brother John, at 15 Brookside Avenue, Waterloo on Merseyside. She was popular at Seafield Convent School and was known to neighbours as a quiet child who only mixed with girls of her own age. Just like thousands of other teenagers at that time she would often run occasional errands for her parents and not give it a second thought.

On the evening of Saturday, 2 November 1940, Mary's dad asked her to pop down to the newsagents to get him an evening newspaper and a packet of papers for hand-rolling cigarettes. With a two-shilling piece and a penny in her pocket Mary left the house at 7.00pm, but she didn't return. Her parents wondered if she had bumped into some friends, but as time ticked by their concerns mounted because Mary was not the sort of girl to stay out longer than expected without letting her parents know. Her father walked round to some of her friends' houses to see if she had visited them, but none had seen her. As more time passed Mary's parents organised a search party and informed the police.

More people soon joined in what turned out to be five-hour search carried out by neighbours, police officers, wardens and members of the Home Guard. It ended when family friend, Richard Brown of Brookvale, and air raid warden Sydney Williams, looked in the entrance of an unlit blockhouse situated about 300 yards from Mary's home. The area inside the entrance was two or three inches deep in rainwater. Richard Brown spotted what he thought was a sack, but closer investigation revealed it was in fact young Mary Hagan. Mr Brown and Mr Williams thought Mary still showed some signs of life and so the two men, and local nurse Mrs Bazendale who had arrived on the scene, took it in turns to render artificial respiration for about twenty minutes. But Mary could not be revived.[1]

---

1. *Liverpool Daily Post* 4 November 1940

Detective Chief Superintendent (DCS) Peter Gregson, head of Lancashire Constabulary CID and Detective Inspector R. C. Floyd of Seaforth took charge of the investigations and called in the aid of the Forensic Science Laboratory at Preston. The post-mortem examination was carried out by Home Office pathologist Dr James Matthewson Webster. It had been clear from the scene of the crime that Mary had fought hard for her life, but she had been overpowered and her clothes disturbed. Medical examination confirmed she had been strangled and revealed she had been raped. The findings of the pathologist also proved that when Richard Brown discovered her, he had been mistaken in thinking he had detected signs of life; death had taken place about 7.30pm.[2]

The police appealed in newspapers and over BBC radio for assistance in their enquiries as to Mary's movements after she left home to go to the shops and issued a description, describing her as being 'rather tall and well-built for her age', and that she had been wearing a coat of a rusty shade of brown with a fur-trimmed collar and brown shoes. She had not been wearing a hat.[3] Numerous witnesses came forward in response to the appeal and police were soon able to build up an accurate picture of Mary's movements.

She had been seen visiting three newsagents in Sandy Road and Lawson Road but apparently no one had seen her after she left the last shop. On her return journey, Mary would have crossed over Brook Vale railway bridge, skirted some barbed wire and then have passed the blockhouse where her body had been found.

Over the following days police received several reports of a soldier in battledress and side cap, but no greatcoat, spotted loitering on Brook Vale railway bridge and near the blockhouse in the days before and in the early Saturday evening of Mary's disappearance.

As the police pressed on with their investigation the Hagan family, friends and the whole Waterloo community came together to mourn Mary's death on 7 November 1940. Thousands lined the streets of Waterloo as her funeral cortege wound its way to the church of St Thomas of Canterbury where Requiem mass was said for Mary followed by an interment at Ford Cemetery.

More police appeals were made in the local press and as the word spread more witnesses came forward. One woman, on her way home from work as a waitress, said she had been stopped by a uniformed soldier asking for directions to the nearest barracks as she was walking along Sandy Road, Seaforth, at about 11.45pm

---

2. *Liverpool Echo* 11 February 1941
3. *Liverpool Daily Post* 4 November 1940

Some of the shops visited by Mary Hagan on Sandy Road, Seaforth, Merseyside

on the night of the murder. He even walked along with her in the direction of Crosby, and when they reached her house he asked if he could come in and wash his face because he claimed to have 'met with an accident'. She noticed his face was scratched, and she made her excuses and went inside leaving the soldier on the street.[4] It is likely this young woman had a very narrow escape. Her description of the soldier with the scratched face was very similar to the descriptions of the soldier who had been seen hanging around the blockhouse, and the description given by an Anne McVittie of a soldier who had assaulted and robbed her as she cycled along a canal bank at Ford on 4 October. This attack had taken place just a mile or so from where Mary had been killed.

Police enquiries at Seaforth Barracks threw up a promising suspect – Samuel Morgan (27), serving with the Irish Guards at the barracks, had fallen under suspicion for the McVittie robbery and was currently absent without leave (AWOL).

Detectives on the McVittie robbery case discovered Morgan had been hiding out with relatives in London and he was arrested by Metropolitan Police on 13 November and held at Streatham Police Station. The following day, DI Floyd travelled to see the suspect for himself and personally brought him back to Seaforth, formally charging him with the murder of Mary Hagan by Liverpool County Magistrates' Court in Islington on 19 November.

---

4. *Liverpool Daily Post* 5 November 1940

Soil samples taken from Morgan's uniform were found to match soil taken from the blockhouse; his boots matched an impression of a boot heel that had been found on muddy ground near Mary's body, but the clue that would that provide a vital link between Morgan and Mary was an army field dressing stained with zinc ointment.

As Mary fought off her attacker, the dressing had come off her killer's injured thumb and was recovered from the murder scene. There was no DNA back in those days, but when Morgan had been arrested it was noticed there was a healing scar on his thumb. Morgan said he had cut himself on barbed wire and had treated the wound using his own field dressing and zinc ointment.

Police enquiries would reveal that two days before the murder, he had been staying with his brother Tommy and sister-in-law Mildred Morgan on Molyneux Road in Seaforth. Two hours after Morgan left on the morning of 31 October, he had returned with a nasty cut on his thumb that was bleeding badly. He produced his own field dressing and Mildred helped him bandage the wound. Only a portion of the dressing's gauze had been used and Morgan told her she could keep the rest of the material. On the morning of 1 November Morgan had said he was going to Seaforth Barracks, and before he left his sister-in-law re-dressed the cut on the thumb using zinc ointment and more of the field dressing. He returned the next day, and stayed in his brother's house until 4.00pm. He then went out and was next seen by some hoardings close to Brook Vale railway bridge. Several witnesses positively identified Morgan as the man they had seen loitering in that area between 30 October and 1 November.[5]

When police called at Morgan's brother's house during the course of enquiries, Morgan's sister-in-law handed over the remaining pieces of the field dressing that had been used to dress his wound. Forensic examination confirmed the parts of the dressing from Morgan's house matched with the dressing found at the murder scene. A chocolate bar wrapper found at the murder scene also had traces of the same zinc ointment. Mary's autopsy revealed that she had eaten the chocolate bar.

Morgan's trial before Mr Justice Stable opened at Liverpool Assizes on 10 February 1941. On 14 February, Morgan spent four hours in the witness box. He admitted to being on the bridge on the evening of the murder but said he had not been there after 6.15pm. He admitted to having a cut thumb dressed with a field

5. *Liverpool Echo* 11 December 1940

dressing but said he had not lost it that night. He also claimed he had not seen Mary Hagan, nor did he know anything about her murder.[6] It took the jury fifty-five minutes to return a guilty verdict. Samuel Morgan was executed at Walton Prison by Albert Pierrepoint, assisted by Herbert Morris, on 4 April 1941.

The 'Babes in the Wood' Murder (Buckinghamshire 1941)

On Wednesday, 12 November 1941, two little girls, Kathleen Trendell (6) and Doreen Joyce Hearne (8), went missing as they were walking home from school to their respective homes on Hazlemere Road in the idyllic rural village of Penn in Buckinghamshire. The two friends lived just a few doors apart – the Hearne family at 3 Burke's Cottages and the Trendells at 2 Laburnum Cottages. When the children did not return home a search party went out, and as the hours passed the girls' mothers Minerva Trendell and Louisa Hearne visited family and friends seeking news of the girls and their whereabouts. When they could search no more they sat up throughout the night, waiting for news. Doreen's dad, William Hearne, a bricklayer by trade, searched the countryside until 2.00am. Kathleen's dad, Ralph Trendell was serving overseas with the Royal Artillery in India.

With no sign of the girls Mrs Hearn told reporters:

> I am frantic with worry. To think of my little one out in the cold last night. I knew Doreen often went with other children for little rides in lorries but neither she nor her little friend have ever been far way. Kathleen is only a little mite and does not look her age. She only weighed three and a half pounds when she was born, but she is an intelligent child for her age and I am sure she and Doreen would have been able to ask their way home.[7]

Hundreds of police, wardens, boy scouts, members of the Home Guard, neighbours and volunteers joined in the search. After three days of hell for the families, the bodies of two young girls were found by two 10-year-old schoolboys on Saturday, 22 November 1941. They were about 40 yards apart on either side of a cart track running through a beech wood at Mop End near Amerham, about 7 miles from their homes. The bodies were soon identified

6. *Liverpool Daily Post* 15 February 1941
7. *Daily Mirror* 21 November 1941

The beech wood at Mop End where the bodies of Kathleen Trendell (6) and Doreen Hearne (8) were found in November 1941

as Kathleen and Doreen. Both bodies had been partially covered by falling leaves, and the press would soon dub the murders 'the Babes in the Wood tragedy'. Police searching the area for clues found a child's gas mask in a black metal box, a khaki handkerchief and a child's sock hanging from a low branch of a tree.

Scotland Yard was called in by Buckinghamshire Constabulary and Chief Inspector George Hatherill was dispatched, post haste, to Amersham Police Station. Detective Sergeant Albert Webb picked up Home Office pathologist Sir Bernard Spilsbury and followed on. Spilsbury conducted the post-mortems at the local emergency hospital; his examination revealed that both girls had suffered partial strangulation sufficient to induce unconsciousness, but had actually died from multiple stab wounds to their necks inflicted with a weapon with a blunt point.

In a statement to the press, Dr Thomas H. Cattrall of Chesham who had assisted Spilsbury in the examination, commented that the girls had lost a considerable amount of blood before they died. There was no evidence to suggest they had been sexually assaulted. The lack of blood on the ground where the girls were found suggested they had been killed elsewhere then dumped there. By the time they were found, it was estimated Kathleen and Doreen had been dead for forty-eight hours.[8] On Thursday

8. *Manchester Evening News* 15 January 1942

27 November, a joint funeral service for the girls was held in the tiny church of St Margaret in the neighbouring village of Tylers Green. Thousands attended and the church was packed for the funeral service and a special service for the children of the village school to say goodbye to their friends was held immediately afterwards.

As for the perpetrator, investigating officers did have a lead. People in the area kept a weather eye on the comings and goings, and residents on the road leading to Penn reported that they had seen the two little girls in an army lorry on the day in question at about 4.30pm. No one worried unduly as local kids were often given a ride home from school by army drivers. The lorry was spotted later, when it passed the children's homes, and was seen to turn sharply and mount a grass verge to take the road to High Wycombe on the fringe of the woods.

Brenda Teasdale (12) of Tylers Green had left school just after 4.00pm and walked with two schoolmates to Potters Cross where she saw an army lorry coming towards her. She could see Kathleen and Doreen get very excited when the lorry drew up and they asked the driver for a ride. She saw them get into the lorry and never saw them again. Brenda could remember some of the number plate and noticed the driver was wearing steel-rimmed glasses. Norman Page (13) was a young lad who had an avid interest in army lorries. He recognised that the truck the girls had climbed into was a Fordson. He had also noted that the lorry was camouflaged and had numbers on a red and blue background. There was also a poppy on the front of the truck. He provided police with a drawing of the lorry he saw, complete with identification markings.

The boy's recollection was superb and police were able to trace the markings and the lorry to a Royal Artillery field regiment which had been based in nearby Amersham at the time of the murders but had moved to a new camp with headquarters at Ralph's Mill in Westleton near Yoxford, in East Suffolk.[9] Young Norman Page had been right. The truck he described was found and when tread on its tyres was compared with casts taken near the scene of the murder, it proved to be an exact match. There was even a Haig poppy in the mesh on the radiator.

The driver of the lorry was identified as soldier Harold Hill (26). Soldiers were paraded in the guard room with Hill, and brave little Irene Jacques picked him out. Other children were also able to identify Hill as the man who picked up the girls. His kit was

---

9. Fairlie, Gerard, *The Reluctant Cop* (London 1958)

The army lorry identified by local children that led to the capture of the 'Babes in the Wood' murderer

examined and, despite still being damp after being hastily washed, his spare uniform had bloodstains on it. Crucially, a portion of fingerprint found on the black metal gas mask belonging to Doreen Hearne matched Hill's left middle finger.

Hill's trial at the Old Bailey lasted for four days in March 1942. He attempted to evade the gallows by pleading insanity. Dr Hugh Grierson, senior medical officer at Brixton Prison was unequivocal, stating that he had found no evidence of any disease in Hill's mind. His condition, however, was typical of sadism. Once Hill had been taken down after sentence had been passed the judge reassured the jury by saying, 'It may be some satisfaction to you that the sentence I have passed is never carried out on any person about whom the smallest question of sanity has been raised without independent medical investigation.'

The murdered children's mothers sat behind Hill in court as the sentence of death was passed upon him. They listened unmoved throughout.[10] Harold Hill was executed at HM Prison Oxford on 1 May 1942. There was never any doubt about his guilt but the legacy of this tragedy lingered in the memories of everyone involved. Hill never confessed, nor offered any indication of his

10. *Daily Herald* 6 March 1942

motives. The families, investigating officers, and the community were never given any answers, and were for ever left wondering why Hill had killed the girls.[11]

Doreen Hearne and Kathleen Trendell were buried together and share a double headstone. The inscription simply records their names, ages and date of their deaths. It has but one epitaph, which comes from 'St Matthew's Gospel' in the *New Testament*: 'Suffer the little children to come unto me.' Flowers are still occasionally left on their grave.

The Girl in Green (Lewisham 1942)

By 1942 air raids on London had become far less frequent, clearing up was going well and there was a great feeling of hope that the worst of the war on the capital was over. Children began to return to their families after being evacuated to safe areas in the countryside. Two of these children were Sheila Margaret Wilson (11) and her little brother Derek (8) who had been evacuated to Dorset and had returned to their mother, Edith Wilson, at their home at 67 Leahurst Road, Lewisham. Before the war Mr and Mrs Wilson had worked together as street-trading greengrocers, but as more men were required for National Service, Richard had been required to 'do his bit' as a demolition worker and was working away in Wiltshire.

Even though there had been a few horrific attacks on children during the war, such events were often forgotten by those not directly involved and parents were simply happy to see their children playing with friends on local streets again.

In the early evening of Wednesday, 15 July 1942, Sheila Wilson was playing with friends outside on the street where she lived. When her mum got in from work at 7.55pm, she gave Sheila a shilling to get a penny lemonade for herself and her little brother at the corner shop. When they returned Sheila told her mother someone – she did not say whom – had given her two pence to run an errand to buy a paper. Sheila ate her supper and then off she went again to fetch the paper. Before she left, Edith reminded her that it was 8.35pm and it would be bedtime at 9.00pm. It was the last time she would see her alive.

When she did not return by 8.45pm, her mother was not unduly concerned; she just thought she was playing with the other children in the street. Sheila's brother Derek had seen her

---

11. Fairlie, *Reluctant Cop*

running down the street and thought she was going to play with friends, but he did notice she paused and spoke to a man who was lounging against a window sill outside 19 Leahurst Road.[12]

The house was home to Rose Hyder, a part-time barmaid, her children, and a lodger, Patrick William Kingston (38). Edith went there to ask the three children at the house if they knew where Sheila was, or if she had gone to buy the paper for the lodger. All the children said they had not seen her. Later that evening, Edith returned to number 19 twice but received no reply. At 11.00pm she went back with two other women and knocked again. Kingston slowly made his way to the door and, thinking it was probably his landlady, called out, 'Is that you Rose? Haven't you got your key with you?' Another blank was drawn.

Edith then went to Lee Road Police Station to report Sheila missing and a search of the area was soon underway. When, the following day, there was still no sign of the child, the police appealed to local and national newspapers for members of the public to come forward if they thought they had seen her. The police description that was circulated described Sheila as 4ft 5ins tall, of slight build with fair hair, rosy cheeks, blue eyes and a scar on her right ankle. She had last been seen wearing a green check dress with white shoes and socks, and the press soon dubbed her 'The Girl in Green'. Her mother commented to a reporter: 'I know she would not have gone with anyone she did not know well. She was a very sensible girl.'[13]

Divisional Detective Inspector (DDI) Bill Chapman headed the search. He instigated house-to-house enquiries, the River Quaggy, near to where Sheila lived was dragged, local volunteers helped search farm buildings and land all around, and ARP workers undertook a search of bombsites in the area. When Sheila did not turn up Scotland Yard was informed and DCI Ted Greeno soon joined DI Chapman at the scene of crime.

When police had called at 19 Leahurst Road to ask Patrick Kingston for a statement the day after Sheila's disappearance, he seemed reasonably calm and lucid. However, when they returned their suspicions were aroused as Kingston was found to have departed. An initial search of the property, its garden and air raid shelter revealed nothing suspicious but DCI Greeno decided they should return for another look. A lot of houses in the area had a trap door under the hall floor. Police had previously taken up

12. Greeno, Edward, *War on the Underworld* (London 1960)
13. *Daily Mirror* 17 July 1942

the lino and opened the trap door and looked inside but nothing appeared untoward, there was just some rubble in the crawl space. This time Greeno set two constables, who were on probation with CID, to scrape out the rubble. They had cleared the majority away when they uncovered a child's arm and when other bricks were removed there was poor little Sheila. She had been strangled and was found with a cord wrapped three times around her neck, before being tied off. A cord of exactly the same type was found in a dresser in the house. A post-mortem examination also revealed that Sheila had been raped.[14]

A police announcement was sent to the press to say the national search for 'The Girl in Green' could be called off. It was, however, added that police were now anxious to hear from Patrick Kingston. He was a short man of slight build who was made distinctive by the fact the tip of the second finger of his left hand was missing. He also walked with a limp, and with the aid of a stick, after being injured by bomb splinters while working as an ARP stretcher bearer in November 1940.[15]

Police maintained a constant watch on Kingston's lodgings at Leahurst Road after Sheila went missing. After eight days, on 23 July, he returned and was promptly arrested and brought into custody at Lee Road Police Station. When interviewed by DI Chapman, Kingston was asked to account for his movements between the hours of 7.00pm and 11.00pm on 15 July, to which he replied, 'I know. It is terrible. I strangled her and then I got scared and went away.' Told he would be charged with murder Kingston said, 'I did it; I am sorry and I don't know why I did it.'[16]

The inquest into the death of Sheila Wilson was held on 24 July before the coroner, Major W. H. Whitehouse. Edith Wilson attended to give evidence dressed in mourning black. When the coroner asked her if Kingston was a lodger at the house down her road Edith replied that he was 'a murderer – not a lodger'.

An intriguing note on the background of Patrick Kingston was that seven of his siblings were killed during a Zeppelin air raid on Hither Green, Lewisham on the night of 19–20 October 1917. Kingston had only escaped because he was out of the house, having been sent some time previously to an industrial school for wayward children. Throughout his adult life he went from job to job, continually dismissed for dishonesty and theft. As early as

14. Greeno, *War*
15. *Belfast Telegraph* 20 July 1942
16. *Ibid*

1926, at Marylebone Police Court, where he was being sentenced to six months hard labour for a string of burglaries and stealing jewellery, he was described as being 'of a depraved mind'.[17] When Kingston was tried at the Old Bailey on 14 September 1942, he pleaded guilty. Assured by Kingston's defence counsel that he understood the meaning of the guilty plea Mr Justice Hallett passed the sentence of death. In reply Kingston muttered, 'Thank you.'[18] The entire trial lasted less than five minutes. Patrick Kingston was executed by Albert Pierrepoint at Wandsworth on 6 October 1942.

17. *The Scotsman* 20 May 1926
18. *Belfast Telegraph* 14 September 1942

CHAPTER 4

The Blackout Ripper (London 1942)

*In the pitch-like darkness of the blackout which enveloped London in
February 1942 terror stalked through the shattered streets of our city.*
Chief Superintendent Fred Cherrill

The year 1942 saw two extremes in the world conflict. In
February, the people of Britain were shocked by the
defeat of British forces defending Singapore but would be
jubilant to learn of the decisive victory for Monty's 8th Army of
'Desert Rats' at the Battle of El Alamein in November. It was also
a year when some of the most horrific crimes were committed on
the British home front; notoriously a series of gruesome murders
which captured the imagination of the British public like no
other during the war years, committed by the killer who would be
dubbed 'The Blackout Ripper'.

As the people of London woke up on the morning of Monday,
9 February 1942, they would have seen that the ground had
been covered by a fresh layer of snow. At about 8.40am, plumber
Harold Batchelor and his mate William Baldwin were on their way

A busy evening at a Lyons Corner House during wartime

The body of Evelyn Hamilton in the doorway of the air raid shelter with her broken torch and turban hat in the foreground, 9 February 1942

to their first job. They had walked through Dorset Street across into Montagu Street towards Edgware Road. As they were passing through Montagu Place in Marylebone, their eyes were drawn to a broken torch lying between two brick-built surface air raid shelters. There was also a green woollen turban-style hat, a box of matches and a small tin of Ovaltine tablets lying nearby. Then, they spotted a woman's leg protruding from the doorway.

Batchelor telephoned the police and PC 437 John Miles arrived at 8.51am. Upon seeing the lifeless body of the woman lying on her back in the gutter of the walkway that ran through the centre of the street shelters, PC Miles reported in, secured the scene and

The body of Evelyn Hamilton photographed from inside the Montagu Place air raid shelter, 9 February 1942

awaited the arrival of senior officers.[1] DDI Leonard Clare arrived shortly before 9.00am, followed soon afterwards by Divisional Surgeon Alexander Baldie.

It was noted that the woman's clothing had been 'disarranged' and her skirt pulled up to her thighs. The body was removed to the Paddington Green Mortuary where a post-mortem examination was carried out by Home Office pathologist Sir Bernard Spilsbury. His report confirmed that the woman had been killed by manual strangulation. Her underclothing had been torn on her chest and her right breast had been exposed. She had suffered a number of abrasions to her upper body including a group of small abrasions

---

1. Crim 1/ 1397

to her exposed right breast. The lower part of her clothing had been disarranged but she had not been raped.

Blood was found in and around her vagina, which had also stained her knickers and one of her stockings. She had been left with her legs wide open in the doorway of the shelter. Police were of the opinion that she had been deliberately posed and left in that humiliating position by her killer. Her handbag had been taken, and with it her money and all her identification papers. (The handbag was discovered by PC Miles later that morning on the pavement a short distance away in Wyndham Place; it had clearly been rifled and nothing of value was left inside.) Nobody living nearby had heard or seen anything untoward the previous night.[2] Scotland Yard fingerprint expert Supt Fred Cherrill also examined the body and handbag. No fingerprints could be found from the woman's killer but the bruises left on her neck suggested he was left-handed.[3]

With her identity card stolen and no clues to her name forthcoming, police issued a description of the murdered woman in the hope someone would recognise her. On 10 February, Kathleen Rosser Jones, the manageress of The Three Arts Club at 76 Gloucester Place, saw the press reports of the murder. The description of the victim tallied with that of a female guest, Evelyn Hamilton, who had arrived on 8 February and had been due to depart the following day. She had not returned to her room, nor had she taken her baggage with her. Miss Jones' fears were proved correct and she identified the body as that of her missing guest. Evelyn's family, who lived in the Newcastle upon Tyne area, were contacted and Evelyn's sister, Kathleen, a registered nurse who lived at Denton Burn, made the journey to London and formally identified her sister at Paddington Green Mortuary on 11 February. Evelyn's Newcastle dentist, Jack Abrahams, was also able to supply dental records which helped to confirm her identity.[4]

Born in Ryton on Tyne, Evelyn Margaret Hamilton (41) was described by her local district nurse as 'a very quiet but a very nice girl, most reserved'. She had been a student at Sunderland Technical College Pharmacy Department and studied chemistry at Edinburgh University, graduating in October 1928. She had worked steadily in a number of pharmacies and she was

---

2. MEPO 3/2206
3. Cherrill, Fred, *Cherrill of the Yard* (London 1954)
4. *Newcastle Evening Chronicle* 11 February 1942

spending her birthday weekend in London before travelling up to Grimsby where she would be taking up a new position as a pharmacy manager. Police enquiries into her movements on the night of her death revealed that the last person to see her alive was waitress Betty Witchover at the Lyons Corner House in Marble Arch. She saw her late in the evening and also recalled seeing her drinking a glass of white wine shortly before midnight on Sunday 8 February. She noticed her because the woman had been alone; she had seen her raise the glass in a solo toast and felt sorry for her.

The location of where Evelyn's body was found suggested to police that she had either taken a wrong turn, or had been persuaded to divert to Montagu Place, rather than walking back directly to her room at The Three Arts Club. On Tuesday 10 February, as many of the provincial daily newspapers carried the story of the (at that time) unidentified woman found strangled in Montagu Place air raid shelter, the evening editions reported that another woman had been found murdered in her flat at 153 Wardour Street, Soho.

Charles Fuelling and George Carter were doing their monthly rounds to take readings and empty the money from the prepay electricity meters in the flats on Wardour Street when they knocked on the door of number 153. They were let in by Ivy Poole, but when they knocked at the door of the girl who had the flat next door to Ivy there was no reply. Certain that she would be in, Ivy tried the door, found it unlocked and they walked inside. There, they discovered the body of Evelyn Oatley (34) lying dead on her bed.[5] Fuelling and Carter rushed onto the street to summon the police and found Inspector John Hennessey, who returned with them to the flat. Hennessey described what he saw in his report:

> I flashed my torch and saw a woman (believed to be Evelyn Oatley) on her back on a divan or single bed, in a transverse position. Her head was pointing north and was hanging over down the side of the bed. She was naked except for a slender garment which covered her breasts. I saw that her throat had been cut and a hand torch was wedged in her private parts. A tin opener was lying near the torch and her legs were wide apart.[6]

Supt Fred Cherrill was brought in to examine the scene for fingerprints. What he saw clearly left a lasting impression on the seasoned Scotland Yard officer who would recall: 'She was a

5. CRIM 1/1397
6. MEPO 3/2206

Evelyn Oatley aka Leta Ward

ghastly sight. She had been the victim of a sadistic attack of the most horrible and revolting kind.'[7]

The murdered woman had been killed in the flat she rented and was soon formally identified as Evelyn Oatley. She had been born and grew up in the country town of Earby on the Lancashire and Yorkshire border and, like many other girls in her local area, had gone to work in a local weaving mill. Evelyn had married a poultry farmer in 1936, but was drawn to the bright lights of London and had started living in the capital, apart from her husband, before the war. Her dreams of being a stage-show sensation never materialised so she had worked as an exotic dancer. She told her husband she had performed at The Windmill Theatre, but no evidence has been found to support this. She did dance, but not in the best gentlemen's clubs. She worked as a nightclub hostess

7. Cherrill, *Cherrill*

Shaftesbury Avenue c1942. On the left is The Monico Restuarant, where Evelyn Oatley was last seen alive on the night of 9 February 1942

and supplemented her income with prostitution under the name of Nina or Leta Ward. By 1939 she had become a full-time prostitute.

Evelyn walked the streets of the West End seeking clients and was last seen outside the Monico Restaurant on Shaftesbury Avenue at 11.00pm on 9 February. Her post-mortem revealed that she had been beaten and strangled to unconsciousness and had then suffered extensive sexually motivated mutilations, inflicted by the killer using a safety razor, curling tongs, a corner fragment of broken mirror and the tin opener. She had also been violated with a battery torch which had been left inserted inside her vagina. The fatal wound was a 5 ½ ins long cut to her throat from a 2 ins razor blade which severed her carotid artery. Evelyn had also been posed, her legs splayed open and her genitalia exposed by her killer.

Supt Cherrill recovered fingerprints from the mirror fragment and can opener used to inflict some of the injuries. Again these indicated her killer had been left-handed, but a check of fingerprints held on file found no matches.[8] Investigating officers commented on how strange it was that the rest of the

8. Cherrill, *Cherrill*

room showed no sign of struggle or disturbance. The only
thing that had been forced was the lock on her wardrobe; her
handbag had been removed and the contents rifled through.
Her killer left her bank books and just took her silver cigarette
case engraved with the initials LW, with a precious photo of her
mother inside. Evelyn's neighbour Ivy Poole, who slept the other
side of the thin hardboard wall, had not heard a thing because
Evelyn had been with a noisy client earlier in the evening so she
had turned her radio up to cover the sounds from next door,
then put in ear plugs to sleep.[9]

As the police and Londoners were still reeling after the news
of a second horrific murder, Margaret Florence Lowe (43) was
killed in her home, flat 4 on the ground floor at 9/10 Gosfield
Street, Fitzrovia (north of Soho) in the early hours of Wednesday
11 February. She was not discovered until the afternoon of
13 February when her 15-year-old daughter Barbara came to visit
her. When she received no reply from knocks at her door, Barbara
spoke to a neighbour who said they had not seen Margaret for two
or three days and a parcel had sat outside her door for that amount
of time.

Margaret Lowe had been living in Southend-on-Sea, where her
husband Frederick had a fancy goods business, and they ran a
boarding house together. All was well until her husband, who was
eighteen years her senior, died in 1932. After his death, Margaret
was stricken with grief and found solace in drink. Life spiralled
downwards and she lost just about everything. Her only child,
Barbara, was sent to boarding school and Margaret relocated to
London where her daughter visited her every third weekend. In
her younger life, before marriage, Margaret had been convicted
of soliciting. Although officially she was working as a domestic
cleaning woman, she had returned to her old ways and was
earning most of her money from prostitution using the alias Peggy
Campbell or Peggy Burkett.

Many of the street girls in the West End knew her by sight and
nicknamed her 'The Lady', because of the way she dressed and
the fact she spoke so well. The few who knew her well enough
to talk to, knew she hated having to sell herself for money – she
referred to it as her 'dirty piece of work'. But she was caught in
a vicious circle of using alcohol to numb her depression, and
prostitution was an easy way to earn the money she needed to
fund the purchase of the alcohol.

---

9. MEPO 3/2206

With no answer to her knocks at the door and with her mother not being seen for days Barbara telephoned the police. Detective Sergeant Leonard Blacktop, from West End Central Police Station on Savile Row, arrived outside the flat at 4.30pm. Using his initiative, he found a spare key under the door mat. When he entered the flat, he found the blackout curtains were still up so he switched on his torch, but as he swept the beam around he saw all was quiet and nothing was out of place in the sitting room. As he walked past the kitchen he could see what appeared to be the contents of a handbag strewn across the kitchen table. The only door left was the one to Margaret's bedroom, it was locked but with Barbara's permission Detective Sergeant Blacktop forced entry.[10]

What he saw was horrific. Making sure Barbara was kept away from the scene, Blacktop reported in and the case was escalated to DCI Ted Greeno of Scotland Yard. Margaret had been found naked and the wounds inflicted on her body were worse than any of the previous victims. She had been hit about her head and face with a fire poker with such force that her jaw was shattered and the poker had snapped. She had been strangled with one of her own stockings (this would prove to be the fatal assault as the killer tightened the stocking until it dug deep into her neck, tying it off with a knot). The killer had used a variety of implements including a razor blade, potato peeler, table knife and a poker to cut, slash and mutilate her body. A large, serrated bread knife was left protruding from a deep wound near her groin. A wax candle had also been inserted into her vagina. The extent of her injuries moved pathologist Sir Bernard Spilsbury to describe it as the work of 'a savage sexual maniac'. Fingerprints recovered from the scene by Supt Cherrill pointed again to the killer being left-handed and the injuries on Margaret Lowe's body left little doubt in Spilsbury's mind that they had been inflicted by the person who had mutilated and killed Evelyn Oatley.[11]

On Thursday, 12 February, the killer headed into the West End again. Margaret Mary Theresa Heyward, known to her friends as Greta, was another girl who loved to escape to the excitement and gaiety of London from her home in Kingsbury in north-west London. She was early when she arrived to meet her date, and with over an hour to kill, she was in the Brasserie Universelle around

10. Crim 1/1397
11. MEPO 3/2206

8.00pm when a smart airman said to her, 'Excuse me, are you waiting for someone?' Greta replied, 'Yes, I have an appointment.'

He asked the time of her appointment and she said between 8.00 and 9.00pm, so he asked if she would like to have a drink with him while she was waiting. She agreed. He then said: 'Why do you come down here? You are a very nice girl, I have been looking at you for some time. You should not come down to a place like this. It is not very nice down here.'[12]

He offered to buy her supper at the Trocadero and she accepted, on the proviso she got back in time to keep her date. Once inside, they went to the Salted Almond Cocktail Bar and the aircraftman became more suggestive, asking, 'Are you a naughty girl? Can't you take me somewhere?'

Greta told him, 'No, I don't do that sort of thing', to which he replied, 'Well I am not broke, I will just show you something.' He then took his wallet out and showed her twenty or thirty £1 notes.

Greta pointed out she was not a prostitute and said she wanted to get back to meet her appointment; she left the Trocadero with the airman following close behind. Back outside it was a very dark night and Greta took out her torch. The airman said, 'You don't want that torch', took it from her, put it in his pocket and said he would walk her back. After walking for a while she realised something was amiss and said to her escort, 'You are taking me away from the brasserie.' He replied, 'Well you must let me kiss you good-night.' He then asked Greta if she knew if there were any air raid shelters nearby. Greta retorted, 'I don't know of any and in any case I would not go in one with you.' The airman then grabbed Greta and forcibly pulled her into an unlit doorway at No 1 St James Market. Later, she recalled in a statement:

> He tried to pull my clothes up and I said, 'You must not do that.' Then he put his hands up to my face as if he was going to kiss me. He got hold of me by the throat and he pressed. After a little while I lost consciousness. He was muttering something like, 'You won't. You won't.'[13]

Night porter John Shine (24) was walking through St James Market when he saw a torch light in a doorway of the Express Wine Company. As he got closer he heard the sound of a scuffle, noticed the torch light flicker and saw a pair of women's legs sticking out from the doorway. He shouted 'Police!' and the torch

12. Crim 1/1397
13. *Ibid*

Piccadilly Circus, heart of London's West End, 1942

and its carrier went off round the corner to St Albans Street.
Shine struck a match and saw Greta laying on the floor with her
head propped against the wall. He also found a service respirator.
Meanwhile, a woman with a torch came over and an usher from
a nearby cinema came across. Shine helped Greta up and they
sought out a policeman in Piccadilly Circus. They found War
Reserve Police Constable (WRPC) James Skinner at the top of
the Haymarket who took them to West End Central Police Station
where Shine handed the respirator to Detective Sergeant Thomas
Shepherd.[14]

An hour later the airman picked up flame-haired Irish prostitute
Catherine Mulcahy (22), known on the street as Kathleen King;
she was loitering in the doorway of Oddenino's restaurant, near the

14. *Ibid*

corner of Regent Street and Piccadilly Circus. The pair travelled
by taxi back to her flat at 29 Southwick Street. Once inside they
both undressed but Catherine kept her boots on. The pair were
on the bed, with the airman straddling Catherine and, thinking
he had her pinned to the bed, put his hands around her throat
and attempted to strangle her. She managed to get his thumbs
off her throat and kick him in the stomach. Despite being naked,
bar the boots, she ran out the flat and banged on the doors of
her neighbours, Agnes Morris and Kitty McQuillan, screaming
'Murder' and 'Police!' The two women answered Catherine's
call for help but the airman, who had followed her out, did not
appear to be flustered in any way; he lit a cigarette, apologised to
Catherine, gave her five £1 notes and walked off into the night.

Doris Jouannet had only recently moved to London. Born
Doris Elizabeth Robson in the Lemington district of Newcastle,
her early life had not been easy. Her mother was not married when
she fell pregnant and she died shortly after Doris was born due to
medical complications. Doris was then raised by her two maiden
aunts in Hartlepool. All she ever wanted to do was find some way
to escape the impoverished life she had known, so like the other
women who had fallen prey to the killer, she had come to London
to see if she could make a new life for herself and find the man who
would keep her in the style of which she had always dreamt. Doris
took to prostitution as an easy way to earn money as she sought
out her wealthy husband. Just months after arriving in the capital,
in August 1935, Doris (25) met French-born Henri Jouannet
(60). Jouannet was an Eastbourne hotelier with a big bank balance
and a Rolls Royce and he showered Doris with expensive gifts of
jewellery and furs. Three months later they were married.

The couple lived the high life of parties, fine dining and a
home with domestic servants. However, a series of bad business
deals, costly legal wrangles and gambling debts saw the trappings
of their wealth fritter away. Henri was no longer the employer, he
had to find employment, and when he was appointed manager of
The Royal Court Hotel in Sloane Square the couple moved into a
ground-floor flat at 187 Sussex Gardens, Paddington.

Doris hated being in reduced circumstances after such a
vibrant, wealthy lifestyle. Henri worked long hours at the hotel,
regularly staying overnight, and Doris returned to prostitution
offering flagellation among her services (she claimed to have
many classy clients who paid her well for such services).[15] Tall,

15. MEPO 3/2206

well dressed and willowy with striking features, on the streets she called herself 'Olga'. On the night of 12 February she had been to the Piccadilly Circus area, and after meeting up with two female friends and having a drink she headed home, but at some point on this journey she picked up a client and took him back to 187 Sussex Gardens. It was the airman who had attacked Greta Hayward; he had just been kicked out by Catherine Mulcahy.

Henri slept at his hotel on weekday nights, but he would pop home every evening, between 7.00 and 9.00pm, for dinner. When he arrived home shortly after 7.00pm on Friday 13 February, the dirty plates from the previous night's meal were still on the table. More disconcerting was the fact that when he tried the bedroom door it was locked. Henri called out to Doris to see if she was inside but there was no answer. Something was not right so he went to Paddington Green Police Station and returned with PC William Payne and PC Cox. They forced the door open and when they turned on the light, they saw two single beds had been pushed together in the corner of the room. PC Payne wrote what he saw in his report:

> there appeared to be the shape of a body under the bed clothes. I pulled the bed clothes but slightly and revealed the head of a woman. I pulled the bed clothes of the other twin bed and saw the apparently lifeless body of a woman naked except for a dressing gown.... A tight bound stocking was round the neck, a circular cut ran round under the left breast, and the private parts appeared slashed.[16]

Constable Payne went next door to telephone Marylebone Police Station and DDI Leonard Clare arrived about 8.00pm.

The killer had used a stocking to subdue and strangle Doris and a razor blade to cut deep gashes on and around her breasts and genitals. A number of rubber contraceptives were lying around the room – two appeared to have been used. The killer had taken money, a gold watch from her wrist and a black fountain pen engraved with her married initials DJ, and then disappeared into the night.[17]

DCI Ted Greeno was put in charge of the entire investigation and established his operational headquarters at Tottenham Court Road Police Station. The murders were so frequent and the injuries

16. MEPO 3/2206
17. *Ibid*

so sadistic he knew it was only a matter of time before the killer would strike again. He began a systematic tour of Paddington and Soho, making enquiries among prostitutes, asking whether they had been attacked or if they knew anyone who had. A manhunt for the killer, who would soon be dubbed 'The Blackout Ripper' was instigated. Police patrols were on alert, door-to-door enquiries were carried out and women police officers in plain clothes were being used as decoys in an attempt to draw out the killer.

Clues leading to the identity of the murderer had been unreliable until the attack on Greta Hayward. Greta had seen her attacker close up, she could describe him to the police and was confident she would be able to identify him if she saw him again. At a time when it was feared poison gas would be dropped during air raids, all service personnel had to carry gas masks at all times in their issue respirator bags. Greta's attacker had taken off his service respirator in its bag and left it at the scene in his haste to get away when John Shine had raised the alarm. Shine handed the respirator and bag over to police investigators and Greta confirmed it was the respirator bag that was being worn by the man who assaulted her.

Detective Sergeant Shepherd examined the respirator bag and noted the service number 525987 was stamped inside. A call to RAF records revealed there was a leading aircraftman of that number who was a cadet training to fly fighter aircraft at the Air Crew Receiving Centre, 14/32a (St James' Close) Abbey Lodge, Regent's Park. Detectives were soon on their way to find the possessor of that number, Leading Aircraftman Gordon Frederick Cummins (28), and bring him in for questioning.

At this stage Cummins was only being investigated for the assault on Greta Hayward. In his statement, he claimed he had been drinking with another corporal at The Volunteer pub on Baker Street and only had a hazy memory of events as he was very drunk. He was immediately arrested and charged with causing grievous bodily harm. As the police made further enquiries, they discovered there was a culture among the RAF cadets where he was staying of vouching for each other and filling in the billet passbook and no-one could honestly provide an alibi for Cummins on the nights in question. Some had observed that he had not returned until the following morning on a number of nights the preceding week.

A police search of Cummins' possessions turned up a number of the trophy objects that had been taken away by the, as yet unidentified, Blackout Ripper. They found Evelyn Oatley's silver cigarette case engraved with LW, which still contained a photograph of her mother, and Doris Jouannet's pen engraved

Gordon Cummins
'The Blackout Ripper'

with her initials. When brought in for an identity parade, both Greta Heywood and Catherine Mulcahy were able to confidently pick out the man who had attacked them.[18]

The case of The Blackout Ripper had received huge media attention and long queues waited outside the entrance to Bow Street Magistrate's Court to catch sight of handsome Cummins when he appeared on remand charged with the murder of Oatley, Lowe and Jouannet.

Gordon Cummins was born on 18 February 1914, the first of four children for Jack and Amelia Cummins at 9 Western Terrace, New Earswick in North Yorkshire. His father had been an assistant master in an elementary school in York but made a career of running government approved schools and homes for delinquent boys. In 1939, Jack was warden and Amelia was matron at Macgregor House on Tulse Hill in Streatham, south London. Cummins' family photographs show them to be an ordinary lower-middle-class family, smiling and enjoying good times together.

Cummins received a private education at Llandovery Inter-mediate County School in Carmarthenshire. He was an average student, remembered as someone who preferred to socialise rather than study. He had moved with his father to Harlestone, Northampton and Northampton Town and County Secondary

---

18. MEPO 3/2206

School for Boys, progressing to Northampton Technical School where he was awarded a diploma in chemistry.[19] He then went from job to job in the chemical and leather-tanning industries, but never lasted very long in any of them. He eventually came to London and worked in the lab at Messrs Reptile Dressers Ltd in Swiss Cottage as an assistant tanner and research assistant. Seeking to live a far racier life, he became a Walter Mitty character, claiming to be of aristocratic blood. He adopted a cultured accent, hung out in West End hotels and bars, and styled himself the Honourable Gordon Cummins.

In 1935, he joined the Royal Air Force. He progressed well through training, but his high-and-mighty accent, coupled with the lies and hollow boasts he had spouted on civvy street, did not make him popular among his comrades and he was given the nickname 'The Duke'. Cummins also boasted about his sexual conquests (no doubt more lies but he did have a way of making women trust him and feel comfortable in his presence). He met Marjorie Stevens at an Empire Air Day in May 1936, and after a seven-month courtship the couple married at Paddington Registry Office on 28 December.

Mrs Marjorie Cummins attended every day of her husband's trial. He swore he was innocent, and despite seeing and hearing all the evidence presented against him she claimed she was convinced he was innocent too. His father, Jack Cummins, also maintained a blind faith in his innocence. Members of the public, seeing photographs of good-looking Cummins in newspapers, would comment somewhat sceptically, and even with some disappointment, that 'he doesn't look like a monster'. But then such killers seldom do. Some even said they were struck by how handsome he was.

Cummins' trial at the Old Bailey ran from 24 to 28 April 1942. The expert witnesses, fingerprints, objects from victims found among his possessions, and the all-important respirator bag, made a robust case for his conviction. The jury retired for just thirty-five minutes and returned a verdict of guilty of murder. A *Daily Mirror* reporter was in court and observed Cummins as Mr Justice Asquith pronounced the death sentence:

> This handsome young murderer, whose strong, flexible, well-kept hands have done to death four women and to have attempted to kill two others, received his sentence with a calm which amazed the court. Gripping the front of the dock,

---

19. *Ibid*

he said in a cultured voice: 'I am absolutely innocent.'[20]

When the murder of the woman – later identified as Evelyn Hamilton – first appeared in the press, several newspapers mentioned two unsolved murders within the past six months. Cummins was touted as a likely suspect for the killings of Maple Churchyard (19), whose body was found in a bombed house on Hampstead Road just to the east of Regent's Park on Monday, 13 October 1941. She had been strangled with her own knickers. Four days later, Edith Eleanora Humphries (48) was found bludgeoned and stabbed to death in her home on Gloucester Crescent, north east of Regent's Park, just a few streets away from where Maple Churchyard's body had been found. Officially, these two murders remain unsolved.

Cummins was hanged by Albert Pierrepoint at Wandsworth Prison on 25 June 1942. Ironically, his execution was conducted during an air raid. Cummins swore his innocence to the end. He never offered any confession, leaving criminal psychologists, criminologists and crime historians to ask *why* did this apparently

---

20. *Daily Mirror* 29 April 1942

British railway stations in wartime were places of fond farewells and thankful homecomings

Paddy and Margaret Rice on their wedding day, April 1942

ordinary man from an ordinary family commit those horrific crimes at all?

The Final Farewell (Newcastle upon Tyne 1942)

Leonard and Margaret Liell had been so proud when they saw their pretty daughter Margaret Mary (24) smartly turned out in her Women's Auxiliary Air Force (WAAF) uniform for the first time. Margaret, of Wedens, Wintry Park, Epping in Essex was a personable, bright and efficient young woman and was soon promoted to corporal. She had also met a fine young Royal Artillery officer, Second Lieutenant Patrick 'Paddy' Rice and the pair had married in April 1942.

With both of them serving in the forces – Margaret in Newcastle and Paddy in Woolwich – they had hardly seen each other since the wedding, and it was only when Paddy received a forty-eight-hour pass for 'embarkation leave' before going to serve abroad that he was able to come up to see Margaret in June. Time was so precious in wartime, and it really had been wonderful for them

The ground opposite 22 and 23 Claremont Road, Newcastle upon Tyne, where the body of Margaret Rice was discovered

to see each other, but time had flown so quickly. Paddy bade farewell to Margaret at Newcastle Central Station, caught the 12.56am train on Friday, 12 June 1942, and advised his tearful wife to get a taxi back to her billet at Kenton, but Margaret told him she wanted to walk back and clear her head.[21]

Margaret's body was found by Henry Kelly, a milk-delivery boy on the grass verge at the edge of the Town Moor opposite 22 and 23 Claremont Road, Newcastle, at around 8.40am. Police were of the opinion the attack must have taken place between 1.25am and 1.55am. The killer was thought to have struck her and seized her as she walked along Claremont Road, and then dragged her behind a large cast-iron water pipe on the grass verge where he inflicted more injuries, violated and robbed her.

Margaret had been horrifically assaulted; all of her lower clothing had been ripped off and she had been left on the street naked from the breasts down, aside from a brassiere and silk vest which had been pulled up round her neck.[22] She had suffered extensive head injuries; there were numerous lacerations and a depressed fracture to her skull. She had been beaten to death with

21. *Newcastle Journal* 15 June 1942
22. *Sunday Mirror* 14 June 1942

a jagged instrument, but the weapon was not found immediately. There was also evidence she had been raped. Her purse had been taken and the engagement and wedding rings had been torn from her finger. The coat she had been wearing was discarded nearby – it still retained the Royal Artillery sweetheart brooch she wore for her husband.

None of the police officers who patrolled the area had heard a scream or seen anything untoward. Initial enquiries in the area drew blanks so a manhunt was rapidly instigated. Police notices were put up in public places, and in newspapers, offering a £100 reward for information leading to the arrest and conviction of the killer. Police notices made no bones about who they were looking for and what sort of person they thought had committed the crime:

> Any man in or out of uniform who may have suspiciously returned to lodgings, billets of lodging houses after 1.55am should be subject of a communication to the police. THE MURDER IS THE ACT OF A SEX MANIAC, ROBBERY BEING INCIDENTAL.
>
> Women who may have been recently frightened by the approaches of suspicious men should supply descriptions.[23]

With the so-called 'Blackout Ripper' case fresh in the minds of the public, news of this murder spread like wildfire through the streets of Newcastle and its suburbs and became even more gory and dramatic in the retelling. The frenzy shown in this murder, combined with the suspicion it had been the work of a maniac, meant investigating officers thought they could be dealing with the first in another string of murders. Local women were suddenly a lot more wary when they stepped out into the blackout. Many would not go out alone, some chose not to go out at all, and the streets were markedly quieter.

Less than forty-eight hours after bidding a fond farewell to his wife, Second Lieutenant Paddy Rice was placed on compassionate leave and was back in Newcastle to help with the search for her killer. Margaret's father also came up to identify her body. The investigation was led personally by Newcastle Chief Constable Frederick J. Crawley.

William Ambrose Collins (21), a Merchant Navy apprentice who lived at Framlington Place (not far from where Mary's body had been found) came forward of his own volition, at 6.35pm on

---

23. *Newcastle Journal* 15 June 1942

13 June, to talk to Police Sergeant (PS) Hogg who was on duty near the murder scene. Collins claimed he had been advised by 'fellows in a public house' to talk to the police because he had been in Claremont Road at 1.30am, but had not seen or heard anything suspicious. A short while later a police officer at the murder scene recovered some broken fragments from the vulcanised grip of a revolver.

Collins concerned PS Hogg so much that he took him to be interviewed at the police station. There, he let something slip about a revolver and police were soon at his residence, where a bloodstained revolver was found, from which the vulcanised grip was entirely missing. Half the grip was later found in his room, and the fragments recovered from the murder scene were confirmed as coming from the other half. Blood was also found on a shirt hidden in a suitcase. The blood on the revolver and his clothes was identified as belonging to Margaret Mary Rice. Collins was arrested, charged with murder and remanded at Newcastle Magistrates on 16 June. Collins was a keen amateur actor and the first published photographs of him were in costume when he was appearing in *The Taming of the Shrew*.[24]

On the afternoon of 16 June, the funeral of Corporal Margaret Rice took place at the Newcastle upon Tyne Crematorium on West Road. Her father, mother and husband were all present; her coffin was draped with the Union Flag and escorted by officers and members of the RAF and WAAF. Margaret's ashes were scattered in the Garden of Remembrance and she was commemorated on the Commonwealth War Graves memorial to the members of HM Armed Forces that was erected in the cemetery after the war.[25]

Police investigations revealed that on the night of the murder, Collins had spent the evening with Edward Morgan who had sold him a revolver for thirty shillings. They then went to a dance hall and later to the Central Station in Morgan's car and had something to eat and drink in the refreshment room. They would have been there at the same time Margaret was saying farewell to her husband. The pair left before Margaret, and Morgan dropped Collins off on Claremont Road. Was it by devious plan or tragic coincidence Mary was walking up the road at the same time? Either way Collins attacked Margaret with his fists and beat her to death by pounding wound upon wound on her head using the butt end of the revolver.

---

24. *Daily Mirror* 20 June 1942
25. *Newcastle Chronicle* 16 June 1942

Collins' defence was that he committed the murder while in an alcohol-induced frenzy. He was observed and examined at length by Dr Bartholomew G. Derry, the medical officer at Durham Prison, who found him to be not only of sound mind but also 'a man of quite superior intelligence'.[26] He agreed that alcohol could produce a state of frenzy which might result in acts of extreme violence, and the person would not be conscious of what he was doing. He did take pains to add that frenzy induced by alcohol was rare and he did not consider Collins a susceptible individual.[27]

Collins' trial took place at Northumberland Assizes 26–27 August 1942. It took the jury just twenty-two minutes to return a verdict of guilty of murder. When passing the sentence of death, Mr Justice Cassels described Collins' actions as 'a wicked crime'.[28] William Collins was hanged at HM Prison Durham by Thomas Pierrepoint, assisted by his nephew Albert, on 28 October 1942.

26. *Birmingham Mail* 27 August 1942
27. *Ibid*
28. *Newcastle Chronicle* 28 August 1942

CHAPTER 5

'Perfect' Murders

Who was it? How had it got there? Was it murder? These questions
were obviously going to take a lot of answering.

Professor Keith Simpson

The Blitz Butcher (Kennington, London 1941)

'If you go digging in graveyards you are going to find bodies' is a saying as blindingly obvious as a 1970s public information film. Yet this is exactly the sort of work that had to be done to clear up the bombsites of London in the days, weeks and even years after they'd been reduced to rubble. Tragically, the bodies of those who had died as a result of explosion, fire or the collapse of buildings – as well as the body parts of those who had been blown to pieces by bomb blast – had become a familiar sight amongst the rubble. In a city where there are so many ancient churches and burial grounds that also suffered in the indiscriminate bombing, it was sometimes a difficult matter to discern which bones were old and which were new.

The Vauxhall area of London had suffered along with the rest of the capital during the blitz of 1940. On Kennington Lane there had been twenty-one air raid incidents between September 1940 and March 1941. On the fateful night of 15 October 1940, there were 104 fatal, sixty-nine serious and sixty-four minor casualties in the area but local authorities were confident that all local residents had been accounted for after the attack. On that night, numerous properties were badly damaged including the Vauxhall Baptist Chapel on Kennington Lane. Sadly, more raids would follow and more damage would be caused. Clearing up after the raids was a long and laborious process.[1]

On 17 July 1942, a gang of demolition workers was clearing the damaged Vauxhall Baptist Chapel when one of the men, Benjamin Marshall, who was working in the cellar, drove his pickaxe under the end of a heavy stone slab set across the north end of the floor,

---

1. *Daily Mirror* 19 November 1942

prised it up and set it on end. As the stone was lifted, a number of human body parts loosely covered with earth and a strange yellow powder were revealed. Could this be another tragic victim of the air raids on London? Even to the untrained eyes of the men who had worked on the demolition squads they had seen enough bodies to know this one looked odd. The head lay loose, parts of the arms and legs were missing and there were signs of burning to the head, hip and legs. The police were called to the scene, the body was removed to the public mortuary at Southwark and the coroner Hervey Wyatt requested an examination of the body by pathologist Dr Keith Simpson.

Dr Simpson arrived the following morning, 18 July, along with DDI Hatton and DI Keeling. Since body after body was being found on bombsites, they assumed it was going to be another air raid victim. However, something about this discovery was not sitting right in their minds.

Simpson's examination concluded the remains were indeed recent, about twelve to eighteen months old, and were those of a woman. A lot more work would be required to learn more about the body, particularly the cause of death, so Dr Simpson obtained permission to have it removed to the Department of Forensic Medicine at Guy's Hospital, a place far better equipped to take these investigations forward. Detailed examination revealed that the body had not been blown to pieces. It had, in fact, been deliberately dismembered, after death, by someone who demonstrated no trained surgical skill or particular knowledge of human anatomy.

Efforts had also been made to remove the flesh and tissues of distinguishing parts of the body, such as the scalp, hair, face, eyes, lower jaw, hands and feet. None of these were ever found but Simpson did note that these parts 'might be disposed of by fire with ease'.[2]

And what of the yellow powder that appeared to have been sprinkled over the body? Samples were sent to Home Office analyst Dr J. H. Ryffel who reported back that they were calcium soaps. These would occur as a natural result of the interaction of slaked lime with body fats over months in conditions of moisture such as under the stone slab where the body had been found. There was no natural way for the body to have been caked in the powdered

---

2. Simpson, Keith, *Rex v. Dobkin: The Baptist Church Cellar Murder*, Medico-Legal & Criminological Review 132 (1943)

slaked lime as it was found – it would have had to be done by human hand.

The killer had also made a fatal mistake. It was known that the use of quicklime on bodies speeded up decomposition; it was often used on the burial of executed felons and mass burials during epidemics. However, the slaked lime used by builders and in this instance the killer, had rather different properties. Instead of accelerating the destruction of the body, it had little or no destructive action, indeed in this case it *preserved* the soft tissues of her neck and trunk from decomposition by bacteria and vermin. The soft tissues of the throat, in particular the voice box, had been perfectly preserved and upon careful examination localised bruising and a fracture of the horn of the wing of the thyroid cartilage were discovered. This very specific injury is consistent with numerous cases of fatal manual strangulation. Her uterus was also found to have contained a fibroid tumour.[3]

The question that remained was how to identify the corpse? The body parts were assembled and Simpson assessed that the woman had been in her late 40s and had a height of about 5ft 1in. From the hair, it was ascertained that she would have been dark brown going grey. Aware that her death was the result of foul play, DI Keeling suggested a possible candidate from his knowledge of missing persons. Her name was Rachel Dobkin (48), the wife of a fire watcher employed at the premises of a firm of solicitors next door to the chapel at 302 Kennington Lane. Mrs Dobkin had been separated from her husband for years and had been reported missing by her unmarried sister, Mary Dubinski, with whom she lived at 47 Cookham Buildings, Old Nichol Street, Bethnal Green, back in April 1941. Rachel's description was held on file among the police records of missing persons and had been published in the 'Missing from Home' column of the *News of the World*. She was also known to be suffering from a uterine fibroid tumour.

The description of Rachel Dobkin was a good match for the body, and she had been missing for a period of time consistent with the decomposition of the corpse. The hands had been removed so there were no fingerprint clues, but there were still teeth in the skull. Rachel Dobkin's dentist, Barnet Kopkin of Crouch End N8, was traced. When he compared the remaining teeth left in the upper jaw of her skull they not only matched with

---

3. Simpson, *Rex v. Dobkin*

Yard of the chapel with cleared cellar on right and back of 302, Kennington Lane in middle background

Rachel Dobkin's skeletal remains were discovered under the arch at the back of the chapel cellar

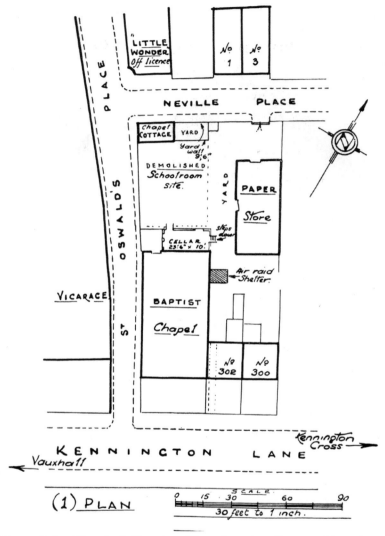

Plan of the Vauxhall Baptist Chapel and cellar on Kennington Lane where the body of Rachel Dobkin was discovered

the record of extractions and features of her mouth he had noted, he recognised his own work when he saw the fillings in her teeth.

Facial reconstruction is a relatively new addition to forensics, but the technique of superimposing the skull of a murder victim on a photograph of the person's face had been developed in the 1930s. The process had been used to great effect in the case brought against Dr Buck Ruxton. In 1935, Ruxton murdered his

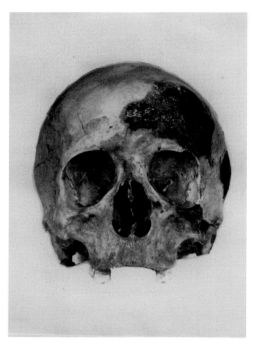

The skull recovered from
the cellar of the Vauxhall
Baptist Chapel

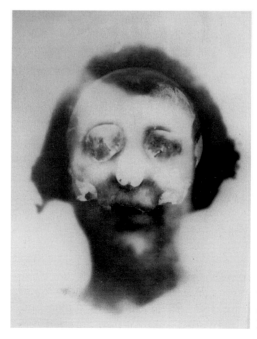

An x-ray of the skull
found in the chapel
cellar superimposed
on a photograph of
Rachel Dobkin by
Mary Newman of
the photographic
department of Guy's
Hospital

wife and their housemaid and then used his medical knowledge to cut off as many of their features as possible in an attempt to prevent them from being identified. The skull from the body thought to be Mrs Ruxton was superimposed on a photograph of her face, and numerous points of similarity could be discerned from this.

A portrait photograph of Rachel Dobkin was obtained and Mary Newman of the photographic department of Guy's Hospital achieved superimposition using an x-ray negative of the skull they had found in the chapel cellar, and a positive of the photograph of Mrs Dobkin. The result was compelling and matched superbly with her facial features on the photograph of her in life.

Having ascertained the identity of the body and the cause of death, police wanted to find out who killed her. Most investigations into the murder of a husband or wife begin with questioning the surviving partner, and in this case it was the fire watcher from next door, Harry Dobkin.

Dobkin had been born Harris Dopkin in Udan, Yakutia in Russia in 1890 and had been brought to Britain with his parents, Marks and Yetta Dopkin, two months later when they emigrated to London. Harris had grown up in the Whitechapel and Spitalfields area of the East End which had become infamous as the territory of Jack the Ripper in 1888. He had six younger brothers and sisters (some of whom died while they were still young). Known as Harry since he was a boy, he was educated at Berner Lane School and adopted the full anglicised version of his name – Harry Dobkin – in later life.

Like his father, mother, brothers and sisters, Harry began work in the family business of manufacturing and selling aprons from their home at 21 Navarino Road, Dalston. The family was Jewish and, according to custom, when Harry was 29, a marriage was arranged for him via a *shadkhan* (matchmaker), and his wedding to Rachel Dubinski (27), was performed at Bethnal Green Synagogue in September 1920. Sadly, the match did not prove a good one and Harry left Rachel just three days later. Others would claim the marriage lingered for a total of about three weeks. Harry may have hoped that he could turn his back and get on with his life again, but nine months later, in June 1921, the couple was blessed with a son, Stanley.

Harry Dobkin was a very absent father and was not keen on paying anything for the upkeep of his son, so Rachel had no other option than to apply to Old Street Police Court for a maintenance order. Even then Dobkin's payments were irregular and he ended up serving several terms of imprisonment for default. On more than one occasion Rachel had cause to track

Harry down at his market stall, or on the street, and try to obtain some payment from him. Harry regarded her at best as a pestering nuisance, but sometimes he lost his temper with her and resorted to physical violence.

Nothing much had changed by 1941. Stanley had grown up but Harry Dobkin had never paid the arrears he owed for maintenance. Times were hard for Rachel as she had been incapacitated; she was suffering with her fibroid tumour in her uterus, had been unable to work and was now living with her sister Mary Dubinski. The money owed to her by Harry could have been a big help.

A curious story was told to a newspaper reporter, at the time of the trial in 1942, about Rachel's other sister Pauline 'Polly' Dubinski and how she and Rachel had attended a séance on 8 April 1941. At the time, blackouts made the nights long and there was an uneasiness of not knowing what was going to happen. So many people had loved ones serving in the armed forces, with many killed or missing in action, and there was constant fear due to regular air raids, that visits to spiritualist mediums in the hope of contacting the dead or being able to foresee the future became very popular.

At this particular gathering, the medium asked if there was anyone among those present who would provide an object which they could hold to perform psychometry. Rachel offered her wedding ring. Entering a semi-trance state the medium told her, 'You are planning to go and meet someone. Don't go. I see sadness for you.'[4] On 11 April 1941, Rachel admitted to Polly that she had made an appointment to meet Harry Dobkin at Shoreditch Church. She did not tell her sister why she was meeting him but Polly had assumed it was about the maintenance payments.

Rachel left at 4.30pm and was seen with Dobkin having tea at a cafe on Kingsland Road, Dalston at 6.30pm. She was never seen alive again. Polly became more concerned as each hour passed, but she thought she had probably met up with friends or popped over to see family. But after more than twenty-four hours, with no sight or word from Rachel, Polly could stand the worry no more. At 5.00pm on Saturday, 12 April ,she made her way to Commercial Road Police Station to report her sister missing and relate her fears that she had come to some harm.

Unknown to Polly, little more than an hour before she had reported her sister missing, Rachel's handbag containing her precious paperwork such as identity card, ration and rent books

---

4. *Daily Mirror* 24 November 1942

was found lying on the floor of Guildford Post Office in Surrey. It was such a crowded place that nobody witnessed how it got there.

Polly was so concerned about what the medium had said, and she was so worried about her missing sister, she went to see the medium again on 14 April, taking with her a scarf and jumper that had been worn by Rachel. The medium went into a trance and, as she did, she began desperately clutching at her throat as she experienced a strangling, choking sensation.

Now deeply worried by what she had seen, Polly sought out another spiritualist. While in her trance this medium declared, 'There is a passing out, a sudden death', and would later go on to describe a motor car, 'a very small hot room', she saw Rachel Dobkin in her husband's arms 'and she saw her head fall down.'[5]

Such stories appearing in newspapers long after the event should be taken with a pinch of salt; however a strange occurrence did take place on the night of 15–16 April. There had been no enemy bombers over London, yet a mysterious fire occurred at 302 Kennington Lane. Firewatcher Dobkin was on duty and would claim the fire started about 1.30am but the fire service was not summoned until 3.23am, almost two hours later, and then had been reported by PC Moore, who had spotted the fire while he was on his beat.

The fire was extinguished. It was clear that it had started in the cellar under the level of the floor of the church vestry. At 5.00am, Pastor Herbert Burgess arrived to inspect the damage caused to his church. When he went down to the cellar he saw the charred remains of a straw mattress, which appeared to have been ripped open, and small heaps of the straw had been strewn across the floor. He went to report his concerns to the fire brigade and returned about 2.00pm. It was then he noticed a garden fork in the cellar and signs someone had been there in his absence.[6]

In his account of the case published in the *Medico-Legal & Criminological Review* (1943), Dr Keith Simpson suggested a possible scenario whereby Dobkin had been destroying Rachel's distinguishing body parts by fire and had prepared the rest of her body to burn when the fire caught a lot quicker than he anticipated. It had then caught the eye of the policeman. Disturbed in his dark business by the fire crews, Dobkin had hidden the dismembered body parts of his wife in a large wooden trunk in the cellar. While Burgess was away reporting his concerns to the fire brigade,

---

5. *Daily Mirror* 24 November 1942
6. Simpson, *Rex v. Dobkin*

Harry Dobkin
'The Blackout Butcher'

Dobkin took the opportunity to lift the slab, move the body parts there, shovel over some slaked lime and lay the slab back down again.[7]

On 16 April, police officers investigating the disappearance of Rachel Dobkin approached Harry Dobkin about the matter. He made a statement in which he claimed that they had discussed living together but he had refused. He claimed she had then made the threat, 'If you don't make peace with me, I will make trouble for you.'[8] He said on the day she was last seen alive, they left the cafe together, he saw her board a bus to Shoreditch and he had not seen her since. A description of Rachel Dobkin as a missing woman was circulated on the police information sheet of 23 April 1941 and her photograph was published in the *Police Gazette* of 2 May. Newspapers ran the story, but no new witnesses or information were forthcoming and the police missing person investigation fizzled out ... until the demolition men made their grim discovery over a year later.

---

7. Simpson, *Rex v. Dobkin*
8. *Ibid*

When DDI Hatton asked Dobkin to accompany him to Southwark Police Station for further questioning he exclaimed, 'What! What you found my wife?' When he was informed that human remains had been found in a cellar at the chapel next door to where he had been a firewatcher Dobkin replied:

> I don't know what you are talking about. I don't know of any cellar at the chapel and I have never been down there. In fact, I don't believe it is my wife, but you tell me it is so, I suppose I must accept it.

No mention had been made of how Rachel's body had come to be there but just minutes later Dobkin asked for a pencil and paper and wrote:

> Dear Divisional Inspector,
> Dear Sir, In respect of what you say that my wife has **been found dead and murdered** [my bold], and that you say I know something I am holding back from the police...[9]

Dobkin's written message rambles on, but he had done the damage to himself in the opening lines. Despite being confronted with strong forensic evidence against him and witnesses that gave accounts of his ongoing and at times violent disputes with his wife, his suspicious activities around the time of her disappearance and more than one witness who had actually seen him in the cellar under the chapel, Dobkin continued in a similar vein of complete denial and accused all except the expert scientific and medical witnesses of being liars throughout his trial in November 1942. A typical scenario was when he was told that a policeman had seen him enter the chapel on 4 August. Dobkin grew excited and demanded, 'Show him to me, the liar, show him to me!' PC Wakely was brought into the witness box and when asked to point out the man he had seen entering the chapel, he pointed at Dobkin said, 'That's the man. I've spoken to him several times at Kennington Lane about lights he has shown. I know him well.' Dobkin replied with the outburst, 'That's a lie! I have never seen him before and I wasn't there. He's lying. He's lying.'[10]

The jury took just twenty minutes to find Dobkin guilty. While sentence of death was being passed upon him by Mr Justice Wrottesley, the powerfully built Dobkin stood erect in the dock

9. Simpson, *Rex v. Dobkin*
10. *Ibid*

looking straight ahead and showing no signs of emotion.[11] He was hanged by Albert Pierrepoint at HM Prison Wandsworth on 27 January 1943.

Rachel was buried quietly at the Edmonton Federation of Synagogues Cemetery. Her headstone describes her as a deeply mourned mother, daughter, sister and friend. Her son Stanley lived a good long life; he did marry and although both he and his wife have now passed away they lived to celebrate fifty years together.

When a search of 302 Kennington Lane, the premises where Harry Dobkin had been employed as a firewatcher, was conducted, it revealed that the builder who had been working there shortly before Rachel Dobkin's disappearance, had left a sack of slaked lime behind. Had this careless act, and Dobkin's limited knowledge of lime, been the spark for his devious plan to rid himself of Rachel once and for all?

Whether Dobkin had always intended to bury Rachel under the slab, her body caked with lime, in the hope her remains would be dissolved to the degree that they were unrecognisable, or he had thought of making Rachel appear to be another tragic air raid victim, but was disturbed in the act, we'll never know for sure. Perhaps if he had not dismembered her, or bothered with the slaked lime and just killed her with a deft blow to the head with a brick, and left her among the rubble of a bombsite he might have got away with it. Dobkin's crime, and the newspaper coverage it received, made people wonder just how many old scores had been settled and murders had gone undetected because they had been successfully disguised as casualties of the blitz.

The Luton Sack Murder (Bedfordshire 1943)

Early in the morning of 19 November 1943, employees at Vauxhall Motors walking to work along Osborne Road at Luton in Bedfordshire may have spotted a large, partly submerged sack near the bridge over the River Lea, which ran by the outskirts of the town. Perhaps the bundle was hidden by the fog that had hung in the air that morning. If any of them had seen it they could not have considered it anything more untoward than rubbish or, at worst, the dumped body of a dead dog, and thought nothing more about it. At 2.15pm two Luton Corporation sewer men checking the water levels in the river found the sack in about 4–6ins of water about 4ft from the bank. It appeared that the

11. *Derby Daily Telegraph* 23 November 1942

A stake with a white rag on top marks the spot where the body in the sacks was found in the river Lea near Luton

bundle must have been rolled down the bank from a public footpath that ran beside the Vauxhall works.

The men decided to open what turned out to be four sacks, and to their horror they discovered the body of a naked woman who had been tied up with rope. Her face had been beaten almost beyond recognition.

They immediately called police who swiftly attended the scene and 'at once scenting a murder of unusual substance'[12] called in Scotland Yard.

The following day, Chief Inspector W. Chapman and Detective Sergeant W. Judge were put in charge of enquiries, and after a preliminary visit to where the body had been discovered, Home Office pathologist Dr Keith Simpson examined the body at

---

12. Simpson, Keith, 'The Luton Sack Murder' (*The Police Journal* October-December 1945)

Luton Hospital. When briefing the officers from Scotland Yard,
DI Thomas Finch of Luton CID suggested that the crime had
taken place somewhere else and the body had been taken to the
river by means of some conveyance. There were initial hopes that
tracks found near the bridge may have been the vehicle involved,
but these were traced to a milk van which passed daily and was
proved not to have been involved in the crime.

The sacks that the body had been wrapped in – one for soda,
one for sugar and two for potatoes, one of which was marked
MFD, the other with the name of Frank Redman a local dealer –
were widely used in the area and could not lead the inquiry closer
to the killer.

Dr Simpson's examination of the body was written up in a
report which described her as:

> a young, well-proportioned woman, 30-35 years old, dark bob
> haired, brown eyes, 5ft 3inches in height. Lineae gravide scars
> lay over the lower abdomen to show she had borne a child or
> children and examination subsequently showed she was again
> 5½ months pregnant at the time of her death. An appendix scar
> was also present and, most unusual feature of all, there were no
> teeth. Slight thickening and chafing of the gums suggested she
> had worn dentures.[13]

The woman's injuries were noted as:

A. Being gripped across the neck by a right hand from in front –
   struggling to free herself but being pinned on her back to a wall
   or floor.
B. Sustaining a most violent single blow across the left side of the
   face from chin to ear from the edge of some blunt weapon...
C. Being felled by this, striking the head in falling.

Her head would have been bleeding profusely. The violent blow to
her head would have rendered her unconscious, but the woman
was not dead when the rope was tied around her legs and thus
it had caused bruising. The rope around the trunk of her body
had been applied post mortem. Simpson formed the opinion that
death had taken place during the trussing process.[14]

Death was believed to have taken place twelve to twenty-
four hours before the body was found. The problem was there

13. Simpson, 'Luton Sack Murder'
14. *Ibid*

was no jewellery, no tattoos, no really distinguishing marks or deformities, or any ordinarily visible features that may have led to the identification of the woman, and no local woman had been reported missing over the last few days. Full face and profile photographs were also taken. The image of the woman's beaten face was not deemed palatable for public circulation but the profile, which was believed to show less deformity and injury, was used on posters displayed around the town and was carried by officers making door-to-door enquiries. It was also shown, via a lantern slide, to local cinema audiences in the hope of finding someone who recognised her.

Chief Inspector Chapman also had casts made of the woman's jaw in the hope a dentist would be found with records of dentures he had made for it. Her fingerprints were also taken, and her feet removed and preserved in the hope that shoes might later be found.

A number of the reports in national and provincial newspapers over the days immediately after the discovery erroneously claimed that the woman recovered from the river had been shot in the head.[15] Some reportage even described the case as:

> An attempt at the perfect murder... . The crime bears all the marks of having been well thought out in every particular, save in the manner of the actual disposal of the body. Even the woman's teeth had been removed in an attempt to defy identification.[16]

Once Luton Police and Scotland Yard officers got to work on the case, newspaper coverage improved a great deal. Over the next two months, detectives appealed to the public via newspapers, posters and even BBC radio for their help in identifying the body in the sack. Some 250 lorry drivers who had called at the Vauxhall works around the time of the murder were traced and questioned, and more than 404 women who had been reported missing over recent months were either traced or excluded. Yet as the months passed, every lead petered out. After the initial publicity, almost forty people came forward and viewed the body. Nine people claimed to be able to identify who she was, but all these proved to be wrong. When all these leads dried up, the body of the unidentified woman was buried.[17]

---

15. *Lincolnshire Echo* 20 November 1943
16. *Evening News* 22 November 1943
17. Simpson, 'Luton Sack Murder'

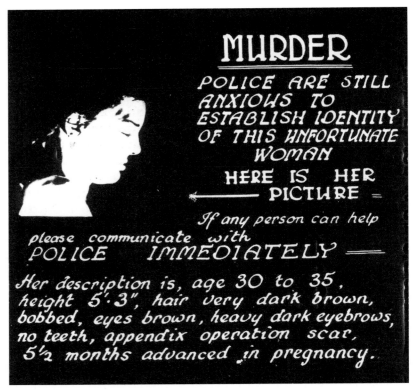

Slide shown to cinema audiences in Luton appealing for help establishing the identity of the body found in the sacks

However, the police were not going to just give up and they made a careful search of street and refuse dumps for clues, such as the clothes the naked woman would have been dressed in. During the Second World War there were salvage drives and collections for the likes of bones, paper and old clothes, which could be recycled in order to make items for the war effort. Rationing meant clothes became precious and once they wore out people were encouraged to mend them or make something else out of them, *not* throw them away. So when detectives saw any discarded clothing they would have bagged it for closer examination.

Despite the searches, nothing turned up. As the investigation was drawing blanks, in February 1944 it was decided that all the material should be gone through again, in minute detail, in case something had been missed. It was during this second search that a piece of a black coat was found with a dyer's tag still attached. It was traced to a local dyeworks office and when the tag was checked against their records, it showed the coat had been brought in to be dyed black by a Mr Manton of Regent Street in March 1943. If Mr Manton had brought in a woman's coat to be dyed, police investigations wanted to find out the current whereabouts of *Mrs* Manton. A few discreet enquiries with neighbours revealed that there was a Mrs Manton but she had not been seen since 18 November.

It was still a bit of a long shot but Chief Inspector Chapman went to the Manton residence at 14 Regent Street and knocked on the door. It was answered by the Mantons' daughter who informed Chapman her father Bertie was out and her mother was away at the moment. He asked to see a photograph of her mother, Irene Caroline Seagrave Manton (35). She duly obliged and Chapman noted that the young girl bore a striking resemblance to her mother. Chapman also felt he had seen that face before; indeed he was confident that he had finally put a name to the woman in the sack.

The girl's father, Bertie Manton, was traced to the National Fire Service (NFS) station where he was questioned by Chapman. Manton flatly denied that the woman in the sack was his wife and told the police they must be mistaken. He did, however, admit that he and his wife had not got on well of late and they had quarrelled. Mrs Manton had taken him to task about his long hours at the fire station and the time he was spending at a local pub in the company of a barmaid. He had retaliated, complaining about her association with soldiers. Manton then claimed his wife had 'slung her hook' and was staying with either her mother in Luton or her brother in Grantham. He produced letters he claimed he'd received from his wife since she'd been away.

Chapman asked Manton if he was sure the four letters were in Irene's handwriting and Manton was happy to confirm that they were. Chapman then dictated a few lines for Manton to write from one of the letters. Chapman had chosen one in particular in which he noticed the misspelling of Hampstead as 'Hamstead' on more than one occasion. When Bertie's copy was examined, he had repeated the same mistake. The Manton family dentist was also consulted. After being shown the plaster casts that had been made of the dead woman's jaw, his records confirmed they matched that of his former patient. The link to the body was also confirmed by the discovery of a fingerprint on a pickle jar at the Mantons' home. When checked against the prints taken from the corpse, there was a match. Bertie was arrested and charged with the murder of his wife. Rather than prolong matters, he confessed soon after.

Bertie had forged the letters to appear as if they had been sent by Irene the previous Christmas, to her children, in an attempt

Bertie Manton 'The Luton Sack Murderer'

to allay any fears over her continued absence. How long he could have carried on the charade is not clear. Perhaps Bertie would eventually tell them their mother had gone off with another man. It was almost a 'perfect murder', but more by luck than design, but Bertie had sealed his own fate when he tore up Irene's clothes and threw them away in the dustbin instead of burning them.

Bertie Horace William Manton (40), who in his younger days had been a keen amateur boxer, had lived with his wife Irene since they were married in 1926. Before the outbreak of war, Mr and Mrs Manton and their four children lived at 52 Trent Road, Biscot. Bertie was a heavy works driver employed by the local ARP organisation as an ambulance driver and later by the NFS as a fire engine driver. With emergency call outs becoming more and more frequent, Bertie needed to be closer to the vehicle depots so he moved with his family to the more conveniently situated mid-terrace house at 14 Regent Street nearer Luton town centre.

Bertie accused his wife of associating with soldiers and she had left him for four months in 1942 when she went to live with her parents. After a few months of reconciliation, Irene Manton informed her husband that she was pregnant with their fifth child. Irene was last seen alive on the morning of 18 November 1943. When their children returned home in the afternoon Bertie told them their mother had gone to visit her brother in Grantham.

It did not strike them as odd because their mother had spent time away before.

In the weeks and months after the discovery of the body in the sack, the Manton children had all seen the posters but did not recognise their own mother, even when they were shown the post-mortem profile photograph by the police during house-to-house enquiries. It was later claimed two of her sons had seen the image on a poster in a shop window and felt there was a likeness, but all the children were convinced their mother was having an extended break away and did not worry unduly.

Bertie gave a statement in which he explained that he and Irene had argued about her 'keeping bad company' with soldiers, as well as her drinking and smoking. On Thursday 18 November, he was on four days' leave and the couple seemed to have started the day on good terms. After their three teenage children Ivy (17), Ron (16) and Roy (14) had gone to work and daughter Sheila (10) had gone to school, they had a cup of tea and it was then Bertie claimed Irene threw the contents of her teacup in his face. He described what happened next:

> I lost my temper, picked up a very heavy wooden stool and hit her about the head and face several times. She fell backwards towards the wall and then on to the floor. When I come to and got my sense again I see what I'd done. I saw she was dead and decided I had to do something to keep her away from the children. I then undressed her and got four sacks from the cellar and tied her up in them. I then carried her down the cellar and left her there. I had washed the blood up before the children had come home to tea. I hid the bloodstained clothing in a corner near the copper. After it was dark [and their children had gone to bed] I brought the wife up from the cellar, got my bike out laid her across the handlebars and wheeled her down to Osborne Road. I laid her on the edge of the river bank and she rolled into the river.[18]

Bertie took the bloody clothes and her dentures, which he had found in a glass of water, and burned them in the copper the following day. When the family home was examined by police, his story was corroborated by forensic evidence. Splashes of blood were found on wallpaper in the living room, a ceiling plaster and on a door jamb. A bloodstained envelope was also found near the top of the cellar stairs. The blood type was found to match

---

18. Simpson, 'Luton Sack Murder'

Irene Manton's. The bicycle lay dismantled in the front room. The wooden stool, which had split and had been mended before the assault on Irene, had been broken again in the attack but could not be found. Apparently, Manton had instructed one of his sons to break it up for firewood and burn it.[19]

Manton concluded his statement: 'If it hadn't been for the children I think I would have given myself up. I had to study their happiness. I shan't worry about anything else as long as they are looked after.'[20]

Bertie Manton was tried and found guilty of the murder of his wife at Bedford Assizes and was sentenced to death on Saturday, 20 May 1944. He received a lot of public sympathy at the time of his trial because his wife was known to have consorted with soldiers, and photographs of Manton had shown him in uniform doing 'his bit' as a fireman. A reprieve from the death sentence was granted shortly before a petition of over 26,000 names was handed in to the Home Secretary. Manton's sentence was commuted to life imprisonment. He died while being held at Parkhurst Prison on the Isle of Wight in November 1947.

19. Simpson, 'Luton Sack Murder'
20. *Aberdeen Evening Express* 23 March 1944

CHAPTER 6

Notorious

Nobody was troubling to pursue so insignificant a case in the middle of a daily massacre.

The Ministry of Fear, Graham Greene (1943)

Reg Christie of 10 Rillington Place and John Haig, the 'Acid Bath Murderer', are without doubt two of Britain's most notorious serial killers. However, it is often forgotten that they committed their first known murders during the Second World War using wartime conditions, displaced persons, fractured society and an overstretched police force to their advantage, and the blackouts to cover their dark deeds. In fact it would only be years *after* the end of the war that their murders eventually came to light.

Christie (Notting Hill, London 1943 and 1944)

John Reginald Halliday Christie, known to family and friends as 'Reg', was revealed as one of Britain's most notorious serial killers after a chance discovery in March 1953 in the kitchen of a house where Christie had rented rooms with his wife at 10 Rillington Place, Notting Hill, North Kensington.

Rillington Place contained a terraced row of down-at-heel three-storey Victorian houses, in what was at the time a poor and socially deprived area of London. Built at the height of the housing speculation boom in the nineteenth century, many of the properties in the area were classic 'jerry-built' terraces that had been erected quickly and many corners were cut. By the 1950s they were suffering from rotting woodwork, damp walls, mould and crumbling plaster, the latter which had often been papered over for years and years with multiple layers of wallpaper. Conditions were often squalid and walls, mattresses and furniture were all prone to infestations of vermin and parasites. In March 1953, Christie had vacated 10 Rillington Place. Fellow tenant Beresford Brown, who lived upstairs with his wife, was left to clear out the rubbish and papers that had accumulated in the Christie's former kitchen which the landlord had recently permitted him to use.

On 24 March 1953, Mr Brown was looking for a good solid wall to mount a radio. In such dilapidated old houses, it was advisable to test the walls before attempting to put anything up and, as he tapped along, he came across an area that sounded hollow. The paper covering it was of the damp-proof, tarred variety; it was dirty and tattered so he tore away the corner of the paper. This revealed a hole with a void beyond. Fetching his torch, he shone it into what was soon revealed to be an alcove cupboard. To his horror, as he moved the beam, it illuminated what appeared to be the back of a naked body of a woman.

Beresford Brown called another tenant, Ivan Williams, to go and telephone the police. PS Leslie Siseman was one of the first to attend the scene and would later testify in court: 'I looked through the opening made by paper having been removed and I could see the body of a woman in a sitting position, back to the opening with her head and shoulders hunched forward.'[1]

Beyond the hunched-over figure were what looked like another two bodies which had been wrapped in blankets and propped against the wall.

The case received coverage in local and national newspapers and rapidly became a sensation as readers reeled at the horrors and avidly followed the case, which attracted additional controversy when it emerged that these were not the first murders there. Only a few years previously, in 1949, the bodies of Beryl Evans (20) and her baby Geraldine had been discovered hidden in the wash house at the back of 10 Rillington Place. Both mother and daughter had been strangled. Beryl's husband, Timothy John Evans (25), had been hanged for the crime on 9 March 1950, and Christie had been the chief witness for the prosecution against Evans at his trial. The concern was if Christie was guilty of murdering the women discovered behind the wall, could he also have been responsible for the murder of Mrs Evans and her daughter? Had an innocent man been sent to the gallows?

Could there have been two killers residing at 10 Rillington Place at the same time? At his trial, Christie confessed to the murder of Beryl Evans but this was countered with the suggestion he was lying as he tried to up his kill count to enhance his insanity plea. The debate would go on for decades, with approaches and petitions made to successive home secretaries. A compelling case for a miscarriage of justice has been argued in several books, notably *The Man on Your Conscience* (1955), by barrister Michael Eddowes

---

1. *Sunderland Echo* 22 April 1953

and *Ten Rillington Place* by Ludovic Kennedy (1961), but it was the film adaptation of Kennedy's book, starring Richard Attenborough as Christie and released in 1971, that caught the public's imagination. A similar scenario was also presented in the 2016 TV drama *Rillington Place*, starring Tim Roth as Christie, which portrays Evans as wrongly convicted and Christie as the sole killer.

The debates will undoubtedly continue but with so much focus on the later history, trial, and aftermath of the Christie case, it is often forgotten that the first murders Christie admitted to were committed during the Second World War, and he had a long history of criminal activity before then.

Christie was born on 8 April 1899, in Black Boy House on Turner Lane, in the Claremount area of Halifax and would grow up with a total of five sisters and one brother. His father Ernest gave his occupation on the 1901 census as carpet designer. Like many households, the siblings had love-hate relationships and Christie's father was very much a man of his time and did not show very much affection to his children; he was a disciplinarian who would punish his children if they stepped out of line, even for quite minor things.

Christie was a bright lad and won a scholarship to Halifax Secondary School. He also sang in the local church choir but he was remembered by his childhood contemporaries as being rather withdrawn. The problem that began to manifest as he reached adolescence was that there was some dysfunction with his ability to engage in sexual intercourse. Word got out and he was taunted with nicknames such as 'Reggie No-Dick' and 'Can't-do-it-Christie'. The problem would remain with him for the rest of his life. The post-mortem report on Christie, however, noted that his genitals appeared normal so it is likely his issue had been psychological rather than physical. Identifying what exactly had caused Christie's affliction, which may well have been the root cause of the murders he committed, still eludes conclusive diagnosis and probably always will. Any subsequent analysis of his condition is muddied by statements he made while attempting to provide material for a plea of insanity at his trial.

Christie 'joined up' for military service during the First World War. He qualified as a signaller and proceeded to France with the 2/6th Battalion, Sherwood Foresters (Notts and Derbys Regiment) in the spring of 1918. He would later serve in a battalion of the Duke of Wellington's Regiment. During his frontline service, Christie claimed had been caught in a mustard gas attack and had been exposed to some of the deadly vapour, and as a result he spent over a month recuperating in a military hospital in Calais.

Christie's subsequent claims that he had been rendered blind and mute for over three years as a result of the gas attack and a shell blast, however, were far less believable.[2] There were, of course, many servicemen who genuinely suffered from various mental and nervous conditions as a result of active service during the First World War, but none of Christie's doctors, nor any of his old army comrades, came forward to substantiate these claims at his trial. It was well attested that Christie was softly spoken, and he blamed this directly on the injuries he sustained during the gas attack but, it has been suggested, this may also have been a long-term psychological response to the incident.

Christie married Ethel Simpson on 10 May 1920 at Halifax Registry Office, but his sexual problems, use of prostitutes and dishonest behaviour that lost him jobs and earned him a criminal record led to the couple separating after three years. Ethel went to work in Bradford and Christie worked in various jobs, mostly in the London area, when he wasn't serving time in prison. During the 1920s, Christie would serve three terms of imprisonment; two separate terms for larceny and one for obtaining goods under false pretences. In 1929, we see the first recorded manifestation of a serious outburst of violence by Christie when he was living with Mrs Maud Cole and her son in a flat at 6 Almeric Road, Battersea.

Things were not going well between the couple and Mrs Cole had asked Christie to move out. After lunch on 1 May, as Maud sat at the table, she felt a blow to her head that she described as feeling like an explosion. She was stunned, she blacked out and she tumbled to the floor. Christie had picked up her son's cricket bat and hit her hard on the head with it. As she came round she felt Christie's fingers in her mouth and he injured her lip. Maud Cole screamed. Neighbour Richard Boswell had heard the scuffle, saw Mrs Cole being pushed out of her door and heard the key in the lock turned from inside. Her head was bleeding profusely and her face was streaked with blood. Seeing her neighbour she pleaded, 'Don't let him get me. He's trying to murder me.' Mr Boswell took her into his flat and called the police.

When police arrived on the scene, Christie fled but was soon found, arrested and charged with causing grievous bodily harm. He was brought before South Western Magistrates' Court

---

2. *The Times* 24 Junes 1953

on Monday, 13 May 1929, for what magistrate Mr Campion described as a 'murderous attack'. He did not hide his disdain for Christie, describing him as a liar and a coward and sent him down for six months with hard labour in Wandsworth.[3] But Christie did not learn, and in November 1933 he was back in HM Prison Wandsworth for stealing a car.

After his release from this prison term, in 1934, Christie was reconciled with his wife Ethel and they started living together again. They first moved to Notting Hill and lived at a few addresses, usually renting just one room in a house. In 1937 the Christies moved into rooms on the upper floor at 10 Rillington Place, Notting Hill, and took over the ground-floor flat in December 1938. Reg appeared to be going straight (or was getting away with whatever he was up to), working as a foreman at the Commodore Cinema in Hammersmith. Neighbours remembered him as a well-dressed and politely spoken man who lived quietly with his wife. He dabbled a bit in photography. Most people knew Mr Christie as a nodding acquaintance and he was kind to local kids. He was not grumpy, as some would suggest in retrospect, he was known to share a laugh and a joke but in the main, he just kept himself to himself.[4]

As war loomed in 1939, the Metropolitan Police established the Police War Reserve of salaried constables to help fill the gap caused by the call-up of policemen still on the military reserve, and to assist with the additional duties brought about by wartime conditions. Recruitment was rapid; in wartime, corners were cut and background checks were not as thorough or were not carried out at all. This meant when Christie applied to join the Metropolitan Police War Reserve two days before war broke out on 1 September 1939, and did not declare he had a criminal record, he was accepted and was soon in uniform serving as WRPC 118 with X Division, based at Harrow Road Police Station, Kilburn. He was so proud of this achievement he even sent a photograph of himself in his police uniform to his family, even though they had distanced themselves from him over the years because of his criminal activities and convictions. Christie certainly looked smart but even then he could not tell the whole truth. Christie's medal index card shows he was entitled to a British War Medal and Victory Medal but in the photo he is also wearing the ribbon

3. *The South Western Star* 17 May 1929
4. *Kensington Post* 17 July 1953

'Reg' Christie in his Metropolitan PoliceWar Reserve uniform

Harrow Road Police Station where Christie was based as a War
Reserve Constable

of a 1914–15 Star which he had not earned and was *not* entitled to wear.

The standard training for WRPCs included a first aid course, Christie passed the exam and gained a proficiency certificate. During his four years' service, he also undertook plain clothes duties and received two commendations, one for the arrest of a man who was making false air raid warnings and the second for his work on a bicycle theft case. He was also congratulated by a magistrate for the manner in which he gave evidence at a court hearing. Christie became an utter martinet at Rillington Place. He made sure everyone was aware of his appointment on the Police War Reserve and he regularly took neighbours to task, at length, over the most minor lighting infringements, and even reported cars parked on the street. His neighbours soon nicknamed him 'Himmler' after the much-loathed leader of the SS. Christie didn't care, he had authority and power for the first time in his life and he was revelling in it.[5]

WRPCs were also trained in police methods and had the opportunity to access information that would have provided invaluable intelligence for a predator like Christie. Despite being smart and efficient, some of his fellow police officers regarded him with some suspicion. Frederick Byers, who retired as a DI, recalled that although he could never quite put his finger on the reason why, he had never liked Christie.[6] Prison hospital officer Daniel Heaney, who was at Brixton when Christie was held there, said Christie had recounted how he made friends with a number of West End prostitutes and had come to an arrangement with them whereby he would turn a blind eye to their activities, and in return he 'could have a good time with them'.[7]

PC George Outram was stationed at Notting Hill at the same time Christie was a WRPC at Harrow Road. He recalled how Christie used to 'go out picking up prostitutes' on numerous occasions, a habit Outram knew Christie continued to do after he left the War Reserve.[8] He also related a telling story of one night on Westbourne Grove when he had been paired with Christie. Outram was going to arrest a woman he suspected of prostitution but Christie intervened before they moved in claiming that the woman was, in fact, his wife. Outram later discovered this was a lie.[9]

5. Lefebure, Molly, *Murder with a Difference* (London 1958)
6. Oates, Jonathan, *John Christie of Rillington Place* (Barnsley 2012)
7. MEPO2/9535
8. *The Times* 4 December 1965
9. Oates, *Christie*

Christie used his colleagues, and the authority, trust and good faith members of the public placed in the police uniform he wore, to his advantage. He found his victims by preying on the vulnerable, the disenfranchised and those who were struggling to make ends meet, those who, if they did happen to disappear, would not cause too much of a stir. In his statements and the testimony he gave at his trial, Christie speaks as if he meets the women he kills by chance but make no mistake, this inoffensive looking man was a murderous sexual predator who would deliberately seek out women in the Notting Hill area, in cafes, at tube stations and by loitering near newsagents windows that displayed cards offering rooms to let. His ploy was to open with friendly conversation, show he had a listening ear, then offer friendship and monetary assistance with no catches. To some he claimed he had medical training, and could assist with some medical conditions and even carry out abortions. His methods were well evinced by Mary Ballingall (20), one of the few who lived to tell her story.

Mary had been sitting in Ladbroke Grove Underground Station with her three-week-old baby and was about to light a cigarette when a match was proffered by what appeared to be a kindly gentleman who turned out to be John Christie. He engaged her in light conversation and helped her onto the train and then the bus at Hammersmith where he travelled with her to the offices of the National Assistance Board. He had looked over her shoulder as she was paid her allowance and commented: 'That's not very much to live on. I will give you a pound to help you along.' It was a kind gesture from the stranger and, feeling obliged not to rebuff him when he suggested they should go to a café, Mary went along. Christie bought her a cup of tea and twenty cigarettes and spun her a yarn of how he was very lonely, that his wife had been dead for some years and he would appreciate some company. He invited her to come round and visit and gave her his address. As they parted he said, 'Come along after dark. I don't want anyone to see you and don't tell anyone you are coming.'[10]

There was no pressure, no intimidation, and thinking there would be no harm in visiting this lonely man, Mary dropped by one evening and was welcomed into the kitchen. They chatted, he showed her pictures of his wife and told stories of his time in the police. Before she left he gave her £1 and asked her to pay a return visit. It seemed no hardship to call again, she did so on several occasions and each time he gave her a pound and a small

---

10. *Sunday Mirror* 28 June 1953

gift, such as a little bottle of whiskey. On another occasion, it was an old-fashioned handbag and then a lady's wallet. They were probably once the property of his 'dear departed' wife Ethel, who at that time would have laid buried under the floorboards in the bedroom. Only once did he press a kiss and attempt to embrace Mary but she resisted and said she would scream. He immediately apologised and gave her £1. Mary forgave him and visited Christie again but on this last occasion he did not put on the light in the kitchen and the fire was blazing. For the first time she felt worried and unsafe, so she told Christie she had a date with a friend that night and claimed she'd told them she was going to Rillington Place before meeting up with them. Upon hearing this, Christie became furious and told her to get out and never to return. Later, Mary reflected that 'He usually behaved like a gentleman. He spoke well and seemed to be very generous. Until that last night, I was never really suspicious. He always seemed kind and gentle and rather sad. I felt sorry for him.'[11]

Mary Ballingall could easily have become one of Christie's last victims; his methods had not changed since his first known murder back in 1943. Sadly, there is only Christie's account of the circumstances surrounding how he met Ruth Margarete Christina Fuerst (21).

Ruth's story is particularly tragic. Born in Bad Vöslau in Lower Austria in 1922, the daughter of the painter Ludwig Fuerst, she had done well at school and showed promise. After the Anschluss in 1938 the Nazis took over her country and, because one of her parents was Jewish, her family was forced to flee the country. Somehow, amid the turmoil, the Fuersts became divided and Ruth arrived as a refugee in England in June 1939. Shortly after her arrival, she became a student nurse but this did not seem to work out for her. During the height of the invasion scares in 1940 Ruth, along with all other 'enemy aliens' in Britain, was arrested and detained until her case was scrutinised and she appeared before a tribunal. The tribunal was satisfied that she did not pose a threat to the security of Britain and she was released.

Ruth spent June to December 1940 in a detention camp on the Isle of Man. As part of the terms of her release, she was expected to register regularly with the police, obey hours of curfew set for 'enemy aliens' and ensure police were informed if she changed address. In 1941, Ruth was in London and had found employment at the Mayfair Hotel during which time she

---

11. *Sunday Mirror* 28 June 1953

had a relationship with a Cypriot waiter which resulted not in marriage but a pregnancy. Ruth gave birth in a home for unmarried mothers in October 1942; the baby was taken away from her and was later adopted.[12]

The following year Ruth found employment making munitions at John Bolding and Sons Grosvenor Works and lived in a rented room at 41 Oxford Gardens, Notting Hill, just around the corner from Rillington Place. In the summer of 1943, while his wife was away visiting family in Sheffield, Christie was on police duty in plain clothes at David Griffin's Refreshment Room at the junction of Lancaster Road and Ladbroke Grove. While at the snack bar he struck up a conversation with Ruth Fuerst. Always appearing to be a caring sort of chap, Christie listened intently and showed genuine concern as Ruth explained how she needed ten shillings for her rent.

Christie offered to help her, of course, but he didn't carry that sort of money on him – if she would like to pop round to his home 10 Rillington Place, she could collect it. No doubt he told her to come after dark, not to tell anyone and he'd make sure his wife was out (he did not kill Ethel until 1952), so it was just their little secret. Ruth came round at the arranged time and Christie took her into the kitchen for a cup of tea and a chat. He claimed she had popped around to 'Number 10' (as Christie referred to his home) two or three times before he killed her.

At Christie's trial, his defence counsel Derek Curtis-Bennett asked him, 'What did you do to her?'

After hesitating, Christie replied, 'I must have strangled her. I seem to remember.'[13]

Christie claimed they had gone to bed together and he had killed her there by strangling her with a piece of rope. While Ruth was in the house, he received a telegram from Ethel letting him know she was returning home and would be travelling back with her brother Henry Waddington. Christie claimed he had killed her impulsively. Rather than sending the girl away, it appears that he wished to kill and hide her away instead. Christie wrapped her body in her leopard-skin coat and buried her under the floorboards in the front room. He knew brother-in-law Henry would be sleeping in there and was worried that he might suspect something was wrong. Clearly, Henry didn't notice anything amiss. The following day when Ethel was back at work, Christie

12. Oates, *Christie*
13. *The Times* 24 June 1953

moved Ruth's body into the outside wash house. He then dug a hole in the back garden. That night, under the cover of the inky blackout, he buried Ruth Fuerst and the rest of her clothes in the garden. Christie said later, 'My wife never knew. I told her I was going to the lavatory. The only lavatory is in the garden. The next day I straightened the garden up with a rake.'

In the garden, there was an old dustbin that Christie used for burning rubbish. One afternoon, while he was doing just that, he decided to dig up Ruth's clothes and burn them too. Christie would later recall:

> A few months later I was digging in the garden and I probably misjudged where I was. I found a skull and put it in the dustbin and covered it. I dug a hole in the garden and put the dustbin in the hole. The top of the dustbin was open and I used it for burning rubbish.[14]

Ruth's disappearance was reported by her landlady after she could not find her when her rent was due. On 1 September, the Friends Committee for Refugees and Aliens also reported Ruth as missing and her description was published in the *Police Gazette* of 16 October – not because she was missing, but because she had failed to register with the police as an enemy alien as per the terms of her release from detention.[15] There were no immediately apparent suspicious circumstances attached to her disappearance. With no family and few people she knew, let alone a close friend, Ruth was soon forgotten by authorities stretched to the limit in a country where there were already so many missing people.

Christie voluntarily left the Police War Reserve on 29 December 1943. The official reason was that he was released for employment in industry; in reality he was probably told to go after it came to the notice of Christie's superiors that he had been having an affair with a married colleague named Gladys Jones.[16]

He then went to work at the Ultra Electrics factory on Western Avenue at Park Royal, making military radios, where he met West Ham-born Muriel Amelia Eady (31) in the canteen in April 1944. Muriel's mother had died in 1918 and she and her brothers were all put into children's homes by their merchant seaman father. Muriel was taken on by her aunt in 1923, but as she grew up

14. *Sunderland Echo* 23 June 1953
15. MEPO 3/1744; *West London Observer* Friday, 28 August 1953
16. Kennedy, Ludovic, *Ten Rillington Place* (London 1961)

Muriel was expected to take on the role of carer and was not permitted boyfriends.

Muriel had been quiet, reserved and withdrawn for years but when she left that home and started living with her uncle and aunt, Albert and Martha Hooper, at 12 Roskell Road, Putney, her life began to change for the better. She had a job and was earning her own money, had friends, a social life and even had a date or two. When Muriel met Christie in April 1944 she met someone who appeared to be a nice, safe, married man and a former WRPC. He would no doubt have told her to call him 'Reg'. Christie soon invited Muriel over, with her man friend Ernest Lawson, to meet his wife for tea and cake, and she accepted. Muriel and Ernest visited a few times and on one occasion all four of them went to the cinema together.

'Reg' would have appeared to Muriel to be an inoffensive man; she had a brother called Reginald too, and it was easy to trust him. Muriel had been suffering from nasal congestion for some time, which she thought was persistent catarrh (she was suffering from inflamed adenoids). Christie convinced her that he had some medical training and would be able to alleviate the condition. Muriel left her uncle and aunt's home at 4.00pm on the afternoon of 7 October 1944. She told no one where she was going nor who she was seeing, but simply told her aunt she was going to do some shopping and would not be late back. Muriel had undoubtedly been told what Mary Ballingall would hear Christie say all those years later: 'Come along after dark. I don't want anyone to see you and don't tell anyone you are coming.'

Muriel probably did have a look around the shops and, as the night began to close in, caught the tube for the hour-long journey to Ladbroke Grove Station and found her way through the dark streets to 'Number ten', the last house on the left before the wall at the end of Rillington Place. After developing a friendship with Reg over several months she would have had no inkling that anything untoward might happen.

Christie later recalled:

On one occasion she came alone and I believe she was complaining about her breathing. She came by appointment when my wife was out. I mixed some stuff up with Friars Balsam. She was in the kitchen ... no it was in the bedroom. I had two holes in the lid and through one I put a rubber tube from the gas into the liquid. And through another hole, I put a rubber tube about two foot long. I had to put the second tube to get rid

John Reginald Halliday Christie

of the smell of gas. She inhaled the stuff from the tube. I did it to make her dopey. She became sort of unconscious and I have a dim recollection of getting a stocking and tying it around her neck. I am not too clear about this and am a little confused.[17]

If he was true to form, Christie would then have raped her unconscious and dying body as he strangled her. We do know that he put her body in the wash house, then dug a hole next to where he had buried Ruth Fuerst and put Muriel's body in the garden after dark the following evening. Muriel was reported missing on 4 November. Sadly, just like Ruth, no leads were forthcoming that shed any light on her whereabouts.

Christie would claim he did not commit any more murders during wartime, and it is chilling to think that if he had stopped

17. *Sunderland Daily Echo* 23 June 1953

killing there and then, he may never have been revealed as a murderer. However, the bones of his victims were not left undisturbed and he would murder again. He himself recalled that several years after the war he dug up a femur which was broken in half. Instead of burying it again quickly, he used it to prop up his fence. In 1949, fellow 10 Rillington Place tenant Timothy Evans handed himself in to the police and told them he had killed his wife Beryl Susanna Evans. A search of the property revealed that the bodies of his wife Beryl and their baby Geraldine had been hidden in the wash house. Both mother and baby had been strangled. The police also produced a document purporting to be a confession by Evans for the murder of his wife, which he later withdrew before accusing Christie of both murders.

After finding the bodies, the police did not thoroughly check the rest of the garden although, in fairness to them, there had been no allegations of any other murders there. It simply appeared to be a tragic killing of a wife and child by their husband and father. Such killings are rare but it would have been a scenario known to the police. The idea of a serial killer being on the loose, especially one who based his activities around his home rather than on the street, was such an alien concept at that time and it would probably not have occurred to them.

So without a thorough search, detectives did not spot the half human thigh bone Christie had dug up and used to prop up his fence. Christie would later say:

> It was about this time that my dog had been digging in the garden and I found the skull from the body of the woman Eady that I had buried in the nearest corner of the garden. I just covered it up with earth and later in the evening when it was dark I put my raincoat on. I went into the garden and got the skull and put it under my raincoat. I went out and put it under a bombed house. There was corrugated iron covering some bay windows and I dropped the skull through the window where the iron had been bent back. I heard it drop with a dull thud as though there were no floorboards.[18]

The bombed house that Christie had used to dump the skull was 133 St Mark's Road, Notting Hill, just a couple of minutes' walk from Rillington Place. It was discovered a few days later, 6 December 1949, by children playing on the bombsite. The skull was taken to the police and examined by pathologist Dr Edward

---

18. *Sunderland Daily Echo* 23 June 1953

Burnett. He suggested it was the skull of a woman approximately 33 years old, who had suffered from a condition affecting her adenoids. The coroner concluded it was the skull of an air raid victim from the bomb which hit the house in 1940 and ordered it to be destroyed.[19]

In 1953, when Christie's crimes were finally exposed after the discovery of the bodies of three women in the kitchen alcove behind the wall, a thorough search of the rest of the house was conducted by police. The body of Ethel Christie (54), who had not been seen alive since December 1952, was discovered under the floorboards in the front room She had been strangled. Police also searched the garden. Hour after hour they systematically dug out the earth and passed it through sieves. Thanks to their diligent work, almost complete skeletal remains of two women were recovered between 27 March and 30 April 1953. Dr Francis Camps examined the remains in detail. A tooth with a continental crown sparked an investigation that led to one set of remains being identified as those of Ruth Fuerst. A further four teeth, unconnected with that skeleton, were found to belong to someone closer to the age of the skull examined by Dr Burnett and this led to the identification of Muriel Eady.[20]

After the end of the war, and the end of the blackout, street lights were turned on again and blackout blinds and curtains no longer had to be drawn. Christie could no longer rely on the inky blackness to cover his nocturnal burials in the garden, so all his later victims would be hidden under the floorboards, in the wash house and in the alcove cupboard in the kitchen. As soon as Beresford Brown discovered the bodies behind the wallpapered alcove, Christie was soon tracked down. He stayed in a hostel for a few nights and then took to sleeping rough. His description was circulated to all police, and he was recognised by PC V400 Thomas Ledger who arrested Christie on the embankment near Putney Bridge on 31 March 1953.

The three bodies in Christie's kitchen alcove were identified as those of missing women Rita Elizabeth Nelson (25), Kathleen Maloney (26) and Hectorina Maclennan (26). They had been killed between 19 January and 6 March 1953, just weeks and months before they were discovered. Post mortems revealed that they had all been subjected to Christie's gas trick, before being strangled and raped.

19. *West London Observer* 28 August 1953
20. *Ibid*

A policeman stands beside the corner where the bodies of
Ruth Fuerst and Muriel Eady were buried in the garden
at 10, Rillington Place

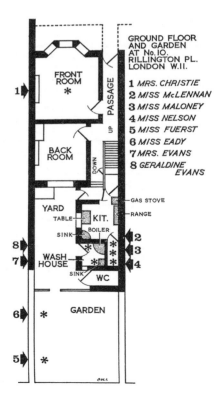

Floor plan of 10, Rillington
Place showing the locations
of where the bodies had
been hidden

After his arrest, Christie was given several psychiatric assessments and having been found fit to stand trial, proceedings opened at the Old Bailey on 22 June 1953 before Mr Justice Finnemore. The trial lasted four days, concluding on 25 June. The members of the jury were not convinced by the arguments that Christie was insane and they found him guilty of murder. The sentence of death was passed, no appeal was lodged and John Reginald Halliday Christie was executed at HM Prison Pentonville on 15 July 1953 by Albert Pierrepoint.

The impulses Christie exhibited, his lack of horror at what he had done and the calm, calculated manner in which he disposed of the body of his first-known victim Ruth Fuerst in 1943 do beg the question, had Christie killed before? There are no additional suspected victims mentioned in the files relating to the case, but modern criminal profiling studies on serial killers suggest Christie was apparently starting at quite a late phase of the progression pattern evinced in serial killers. His first-known murder also occurred more than a decade after his first-known violent assault on Maud Cole in 1929. Now in his trusted Police War Reserve uniform, displaced people, refugees, empty properties and bombsites would have provided a perfect combination of opportunities and cover-ups for the predator Christie. It is likely he did commit other murders, but there is nothing conclusive to date.

Christie did confess to killing all the people found at 10 Rillington Place, with the exception of baby Geraldine Evans, for whose murder her father, Timothy Evans, had been executed in 1950. Christie's testimony had been key to the prosecution of Evans, and as he was facing the death penalty for the other murders, it was hoped he would tell the truth once and for all. While Christie was awaiting execution he got in touch with Dennis Hague, one of his old army comrades and a fellow signaller in the Sherwood Foresters. They had last seen each other in 1918 and Hague was shocked to receive a letter out of the blue, but he agreed to meet with Christie in the hope he would tell him the truth about the Evans murders.

The man Hague saw in prison he described as lonely, broken and utterly dejected. Christie told him, 'I don't care what happens now. I have nothing to live for.' They reminisced about their times together during the war but in the final five minutes of their time together, Mr Hague asked Christie directly if he had murdered baby Geraldine. Christie replied hesitantly, 'I don't know. I don't remember. My mind is a blank.' On reflection, Hague did wonder if Christie had flashed a confession by signalling 'yes' in morse code by blinking his eyes.[21] As sincere as Dennis Hague may have been in his belief, it is doubtful that Christie did such a thing. Instead, he took the truth to his grave. Campaigns arguing for the innocence of Evans continued for many years afterwards and Timothy Evans was granted a royal pardon in October 1966.

Was Evans innocent? Over the years, a number of authors, such as Molly Lefebure, Conrad Phillips, John Newton Chance, Rupert Furneaux, John Eddowes and more recently Jonathan Oates, have all argued the case for two killers in Rillington Place and that it was Evans who killed his wife and baby. Beryl Evans' younger brother, Peter Thorley, has also researched the case and draws the same conclusion. Mr Thorley has memories of visiting his sister and witnessing the violent arguments that erupted between his sister and brother-in-law, usually over money. He also vividly recalls how, during these rows, Timothy Evans would threaten to kill Beryl. Thorley also remembered Mr and Mrs Christie as a couple who were kind to him, treating him to tea and sticky buns, and how protective 'Uncle Reg' had been of Beryl. Peter Thorley remains convinced it was Timothy Evans who murdered Beryl and baby Geraldine, not Christie.[22]

A macabre postscript to this story was provided by the discovery of a Lewis & Burrows 'Gees Linctus' Pastilles tin among the rubbish dumped in the garden at 10 Rillington Place. Inside were four clumps of pubic hair. Christie claimed one was from his wife and the other three were from the women found in the alcove. However, expert examination of the hair could not link any of the tufts to the bodies in the alcove, nor Mrs Christie. No hair had been removed from Beryl Evans. If two tufts of pubic hair came from Fuerst and Eady, two more remain unaccounted for.[23] The question is, did he cut these tufts of hair as trophies from those he killed and could they indicate that there are more, as-yet-unidentified-victims of Christie that he killed and disposed of elsewhere?

The Acid Bath Murderer (Kensington 1944 and 1945)

The case of John George Haigh, the 'Acid Bath Murderer', caught the public's imagination, achieving notoriety akin to that of George Joseph Smith the so-called 'Brides in the Bath' murderer in 1915 and even Jack the Ripper back in

---

21. *Daily Mirror* 2 December 1965
22. Thorley, Peter, *Inside 10 Rillington Place* (London 2020)
23. Simpson, Professor Keith, *Forty Years of Murder* (London 1978)

1888. When Haigh's murders were exposed in 1949, the most popular detective fiction books were written by authors such as Agatha Christie and Peter Cheyney, whose stories told of dastardly murders committed by devious killers by diverse and unusual means. Indeed, in Agatha Christie's *One, Two, Buckle My Shoe* (1940), a woman disappears from Kensington and Chief Inspector Japp wonders if she has been dissolved in an acid bath. The crimes of John Haigh and the method of disposal he used for the bodies could have come straight off the pages of those novels. Yet if those authors had resolved any of their stories with a denouement revealing the killer's motive had not been for financial gain but to quench his vampiristic thirst for blood, even their most loyal readers would be left feeling the story was simply unbelievable. Yet this is exactly what Haigh would claim, and when reflecting on the Haigh case decades after they covered the story, old press men would still shake their heads and say, 'You couldn't make this stuff up.'

As revelation after revelation appeared in the press the public was gripped, and lapped up the headline stories of the 'vampire' killer. What is often lost amid the maelstrom that surrounded Haigh's trial for the murder of his last victim, Mrs Durand-Deacon, in 1949, is that Haigh actually committed his first murders during the Second World War.

John Haigh 'The Acid
Bath Murderer'

By 1939 John Haigh was no stranger to crime and he had already served two terms of imprisonment for fraud and dishonest offences. He certainly had not been raised to be like that. Born in Stamford, Lincolnshire on 24 July 1909, his family moved soon afterwards and Haigh grew up at 112 Ledger Lane, Outwood, a suburb of Wakefield in the West Riding of Yorkshire. His father, John Robert Haigh, was employed locally at Lofthouse Colliery as engineer in charge of electrical installations while his mother Emily Haigh kept house. Both parents were staunch members of the Plymouth Brethren, a strict and highly moral Christian sect, and they instilled those values into their one and only child.

John Haigh, known to his parents affectionately as 'Sonnie', went to preparatory school and at the age of 11 he won a scholarship to Wakefield Boys Grammar School which he attended until he was 17. His teachers would remember Haigh as lazy and recall how he made little effort to master subjects that did not capture his imagination – but he did have notably good handwriting of a standard beyond his years. He also took an interest in science, was a member of the school science club, had a great love of classical music by popular composers and learned to play the piano and organ.

Those at school with Haigh – it could never be said that he had any close friends there – remembered that he never got involved in the rough and tumble of organised sports, nor high jinks in the playground.[24] Haigh himself would write about his youth (it should be borne in mind that what written material we do have was written at the time of his trial when he was angling for an insanity plea but there will be some elements of truth within it):

> As I grew up I realised, though imperfectly, that I was different from other people, and that the way of life in my home was different from that in the homes of others. Without being to explain the difference between us, or to measure the chasm which divided me from others, I realised its existence. This stimulated me to introspection and strange mental questions...[25]

Some of Haigh's peers at school did regard him as supercilious but said he also had a very good sense of humour, could take a joke and was mischievous. Haigh would play schoolboy pranks and the boys were aware that he had developed a cunning way to avoid punishment when he was caught for such transgressions.

---

24. Lefebure, *Murder*
25. *Ibid*

By gaining access to the punishment book by various devious means, he would forge the teacher's initials to show the punishment due to him, probably a caning, had already been carried out.[26]

Haigh was particularly remembered for always being fastidious about his appearance, be he in his day-to-day clothes, wearing his school uniform or the vestments he wore as a chorister at Wakefield Cathedral. He had charming manners and was blessed with an angelic face but as the barrister, Lord Dunboyne (Patrick Theobald Tower Butler), would later point out in his eloquent introduction to the volume relating to Haigh in his *Notable British Trials* book series, while Haigh was at school another of his lifelong characteristics became apparent:

> He became an inveterate liar; the habit developed as a matter of convenience because, as he put it, the truth often distressed his parents and he preferred to avoid trouble by inventing what he knew they wanted to hear.[27]

That said, those at school or those who worked with Haigh in the years immediately after he left school, were surprised when he was exposed for taking the criminal and darker paths in life. Most thought he was the sort of man who would do rather well for himself in business or politics. However, Haigh would write candidly:

> When I first discovered there were easier ways to make a living than to work long hours in an office I did not ask myself whether I was doing right or wrong. That seemed to me to be irrelevant. I merely said this is what I wish to do. And as the means lay within my power, that is what I decided.[28]

When considering Haigh's subsequent actions it is worth bearing in mind the comments of Professor Friedrich Loesel, director of the Institute of Criminology at Cambridge in June 2007, when the Haigh correspondence was given to the institute by Vivian Robinson, an alumnus of Sidney Sussex College, whose father had helped Haigh's parents cope with their son's criminality:

> The really interesting thing that emerges from the letters he wrote to his parents is that he rarely addresses the question of his

26. Lefebure, *Murder*
27. Dunboyne, Lord, *The Trial of John George Haigh* (London 1953)
28. *Ibid*

actual crimes… . There is also very little evidence he understood the emotional impact of what he had done; it is as if he hears the tone but does not understand the music.[29]

Haigh continued to reside in the family home after he left school and worked a few office jobs with links to the motor industry. The jobs were quite menial, clerking and advertising, but he seemed to have acquired three rather nice cars. Strangely, he did not keep them at home, and his day jobs certainly could not have paid for them. His friends just assumed his family had money and he didn't really need to work.

John Haigh may have looked successful but in reality he was getting by on swindling. This attracted the attention of Leeds CID as early as 1932 but no charges had been pursued.[30] Just a few years later Haigh met a pretty, petite blonde waitress, Beatrice 'Betty' Hamer (23). They married, after knowing each other only a short while, at the registry office in Bridlington on 6 July 1934, and moved into their own home together in Leeds. The marriage would not last long as Haigh was still up to his old tricks. This time it was conspiring to defraud a hire purchase company through fictitious motor car purchases.

To pull off the fraud, Haigh co-opted advertising contractor John Lambert (26) and telephonist Alice Rochead (21), and even duped a local solicitor to act on the fraudster's behalf. The case was brought before Leeds Assizes in November 1934 and it was clear from the evidence, and it was stated in court, that 'Haigh was the moving spirit in the fraud'. His co-defendant Lambert was fined, and both Lambert and Miss Rochead were bound over and ordered to pay towards the costs in the hope this incident would be a lesson learned and not ruin their futures. A less understanding judge may not have been so merciful. It was another example of Haigh using other people as a means for his own ends, people he considered to be disposable. Haigh also asked that a further six similar offences be taken into consideration.

The *Leeds Mercury* reported:

> Sentencing Haigh to 15 months in the second division, the Judge said Haigh seemed to have embarked on a career of forgery. He was responsible for landing the girl in the dock and also for leading on Lambert. He had no doubt that he had got the

---

29. University of Cambridge, www.cam.ac.uk/news/sealed-with-a-hiss-the-letters-of-the-acid-bath-murderer
30. Lefebure, *Murder*

greater part of the money and only his youth had saved him from penal servitude.[31]

Betty Haigh was pregnant with their first child when Haigh was sent down. When their baby was born, a girl named Pauline, Betty was alone and with no financial provision from Haigh, she could not cope so Pauline was put up for adoption.

After his release from prison in December 1935, Haigh did not return to his wife. Instead, he went into the dry cleaning business with a partner – Major Charles Plackett, the solicitor who had represented him when he appeared in court on the fraud charges. The business was doing well until Plackett was killed in a motor accident in Ashdown Forest. Claiming he was 'too stunned by this disappointment to attempt to go on',[32] Haigh abandoned the business and went to London to seek his fortune.

He responded to an advert for the post of manager of an amusement arcade and, as a result, was employed by the entrepreneur William Donald McSwan. Known as Donald or 'Mac' to his friends, he owned a small chain of pinball saloons 'Mac's Automatics'. Haigh, being the amiable and charming sort of chap he was, became friends with Mac; he was introduced to Mac's parents, Donald and Amy, and was a frequent guest at their home for supper.

A year down the road, Haigh had found his feet in the city, was living in Luxemburg Gardens in Hammersmith and had left McSwan on very good terms to start another business (in reality a swindle) on his own account. This time he set himself up under the name of a real solicitor from the Law List and offered shares from deceased estates at tempting prices. Once the cheques had rolled in and cleared he, of course, moved on leaving all those hopeful investors in the lurch.

When Haigh was brought to court for this fraud at Surrey Assizes at Kingston on 24 November 1937, he pleaded guilty to eight charges of obtaining and attempting to obtain money by false pretences. He also asked that an additional twenty-two similar offences that amounted to £3,172 4s 6d – a small fortune in those days – be taken into consideration. Haigh offered a statement in his defence, saying he had been acting as a clerk for another man and did not realise what he was being asked to do was fraudulent. When he tried to back out, he said the man had

31. *Leeds Mercury* 4 December 1934
32. Dunboyne, *Trial*

threatened to incriminate him. Haigh was sentenced to four years penal servitude.[33]

Haigh was still behind bars serving this sentence when war broke out, and was only released on licence on 13 August 1940. Not keen to serve king and country in any of the armed forces, he dodged conscription by becoming a firewatcher in Victoria, based at the Art Display Services on Lupus Street, Pimlico.[34] It came as quite a shock to have to actually engage with war work when the blitz on London began less than a month later on 7 September and continued for fifty-seven consecutive nights.

Haigh would claim:

> I was shocked in both mind and spirit. The ghastly sights after two land mines [dropped by parachute] had wiped out a block of buildings are fixed indelibly in my memory. On one occasion, while on fire watching duty I was talking to a Red Cross nurse at a wardens post. The sirens shrieked, bombs dropped and the nurse and I moved off to our places of duty. Suddenly, in a moment of premonition, I knew that a bomb would fall nearby. I dodged into a doorway and awaited the inevitable crash. It came with a horrifying shriek, and as I staggered up, bruised and bewildered, a head rolled against my foot. The nurse who, but a few moments before, had been gay, full of life, high ideals and sense of duty, had in one instant been swept to eternity. I was shocked beyond all belief. How could God allow it to happen?[35]

Haigh was soon in court again, this time at the County of London Sessions, on 11 June 1941, where he was found guilty of stealing five three-tier bunk beds and kitchen utensils worth £17 10s, 60 yards of curtaining and a refrigerator. Now Haigh considered himself very much a gentleman fraudster and a confidence trickster but most certainly not a grubby common thief. He was smarting from what he considered 'the gross injustice' of being found guilty of theft, and all because the woman he had sold it to had complained to the police because she was concerned he had charged her too little for it. Haigh was sentenced to twenty-one months with hard labour.

While serving his sentence at HM Prison Chelmsford, he regularly told fellow inmates, 'if you are going to go wrong [commit a crime], go wrong in a big way like me', and added that if there

---

33. Dunboyne, *Trial*
34. Oates, Jonathan, *John George Haigh* (Barnsley 2014)
35. Dunboyne, *Trial*

was no body, police would find it very hard to convict a murderer. He banged on about this so frequently some inmates nicknamed him 'Corpus Delicti'.[36]

Haigh may have had some knowledge of this legal term (meaning concrete evidence of a crime, such as a corpse), but he clearly didn't comprehend it. What Haigh failed to appreciate was that even if no trace of the victim's body was found, there might still be sufficient evidence to prove the killer's guilt.

Haigh completed his sentence at HM Prison Lincoln which he described as 'the worst prison I have ever known', and there he vowed, 'after this, there would be no more inside for me.'[37] While in Lincoln Prison, Haigh was employed in the tinsmith's workshop where sulphuric acid was in regular use, and in quite some quantity. He began to ponder the practical applications he could find for the liquid and began experimenting. He persuaded some of the outdoor workers to bring him back field mice, which he then immersed in jars of cold concentrated sulphuric acid stolen from the workshop. He found that in the space of just half an hour the body of a mouse dissolved into black sludge. Now that *did* get him thinking.

Haigh was released on licence on 17 September 1943. After a few weeks staying with his parents, he forged some impressive references and obtained an introduction to a light engineering firm, the Union Road Tool and Garage Company in Crawley, West Sussex. Adding a bogus BSc to his name, and claiming to be a graduate of Leeds University, he was employed by the firm obtaining orders and quotations on a commission-only basis. While Haigh got himself sorted out with accommodation, he was invited to stay at the home of the firm's owner, Allan Stephens, along with his wife Eveline and their pretty daughters Barbara Elizabeth, who (like her mother and father) had been born in Monmouthshire, Wales in 1928, and Jeanne who had been born in Buckinghamshire in 1932.

Despite Barbara being just 15 years old, and nineteen years younger than Haigh, she was soon smitten with this dapper, classy man. Before long, they were enjoying rides through the countryside in his sports car, meals out, classical music concerts at the Royal Albert Hall and piano recitals at Wigmore Hall. There was, however, no impropriety in the relationship, and the pair would continue to see each other for years after he left Allan Stephens'

36. Lefebure, *Murder*
37. Dunboyne, *Trial*

Lincoln Prison Gateway. Haigh began his experiments dissolving mice in acid while serving time here

The George Hotel, Crawley, where Haigh stayed regularly during weekend visits to see his young friend Barbara Allen

firm in 1944. Haigh claimed he had found employment in London with the Union Group Engineering Company. This was a credible sounding, but fictional company, created by Haigh that only existed on the letterheads and business cards he produced. He seemed to be doing well too; in March 1944, he began to stay regularly at the classy Onslow Court Hotel in Queen's Gate, Kensington.

Haigh continued to visit Crawley at weekends, usually staying at the historic half-timbered George Hotel on the High Street. On the surface it would have appeared he was making an honest living. Later, when Barbara was asked what Haigh had done during the war years she recalled:

> That was rather strange. All I knew was that he was a 'liaison officer'. I never found out quite what that meant. He was not in the services, he was an engineer. It was also difficult to tell what work he did. He was a sort of agent and could always get things.[38]

Haigh also caught up with his old employer and friend Donald 'Mac' McSwan. Mac had visited Haigh in prison and afterwards the pair picked up their friendship as if no time had passed and started meeting up and going out together. By that time Mac's business had expanded from three to thirty pinball saloons, and he had also expanded into light engineering and had a factory, McSwan Engineering, with a lucrative wartime contract to make aircraft parts. He owned four houses, which he rented out, and several rather lovely cars.

Beneath the veneer of a successful entrepreneur and man about town, Mac had his secrets. He had a conviction for minor thefts and was not keeping to the terms of his parole. There is evidence that suggests Mac was homosexual at a time when it was against the law; he was known to have lived in a house with other gay men, one of whom had a conviction for running rent boys. He had also been seen on several occasions with a boy of about 16 whom he referred to as his 'nephew', but Mac and his parents had been distant from their family for decades and this familial relationship seems unlikely. When he had been called up for military service, he had not reported for duty as required and needed to get away fast to avoid further action. Perhaps his trusted old friend Johnny Haigh offered to help him disappear? Perhaps Mac should have been more careful about what he wished for.

On 6 September 1944, Haigh took up occupancy of a basement he had rented beneath 79 Gloucester Road, South Kensington. Haigh stated that he'd hired the basement so he could undertake 'experimental work for a Government contract', thus ensuring there would not be too many questions. After all, 'there was a war on' and people were used to not prying into the affairs of those who were keeping the Germans at bay. On 7 September, Haigh placed

---

38. *Sunday Mirror* 6 March 1949

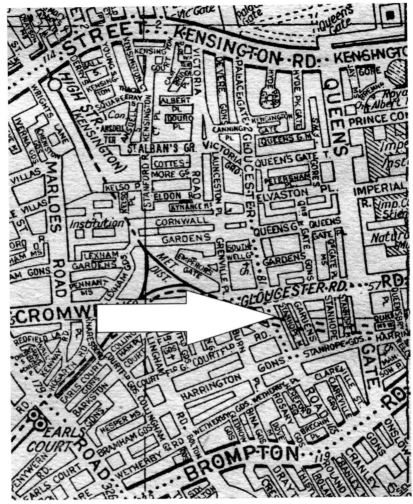

Arrow points to 79 Gloucester Road, South Kensington, where
Haigh dissolved his victims in acid

an order with East London chemical supplier Canning & Co, for
a Winchester of muriatic acid and twenty gallons of sulphuric
acid. He paid with a cheque, confirmed using his fictitious Union
Group Engineering Company letterhead, but gave his address as
the War Emergency Liaison Centre, Onslow Court Hotel, Queen's
Gate, Kensington SW7. Haigh signed it off with his name and
gave his position as technical liaison officer.[39]

---

39. HO45/23635, HO45/23636

Donald 'Mac'
McSwan

No eyebrows would have been raised, and with the motto 'careless talk costs lives' being drummed into the public few questions would have been asked upon receipt of this request at that time. Acid was needed in quantity for a wide variety of metal work, and factories large and small were opening all over the London area engaged in war work to help with the manufacture of components for aircraft, military vehicle engines and weaponry. The Winchester of muriatic acid and two ten-gallon carboys of sulphuric acid were delivered to Haigh's premises the following day.

On the evening of Saturday, 9 September, Haigh arranged to meet Mac for a meal and a few drinks at The Goat Tavern on Kensington High Street. A couple of hours later, the pair left the pub and strolled through the blackout to visit Haigh's new business premises. They did not enter from the street on Gloucester Road. Instead, Haigh guided his friend along the far quieter Stanhope Mews that runs parallel with Gloucester Road to the back door.

As the pair walked down the steps Haigh hit Mac on the head with a blunt instrument. In his statements, Haigh variously states he dealt the blow with a cosh, the leg of a pinball machine (an ironic weapon considering Mac's business) and a piece of lead pipe. One of the latter two is more likely than Haigh having any purpose-made offensive weapon at that time. Whatever the instrument, the result was the same, as Haigh would recall: 'He was dead within five minutes or so. I was appalled by the presence of a corpse on my hands, but experienced no sense of remorse.'[40]

In his account of what happened next, Haigh claimed he went home to bed and returned the following afternoon to deal with the body. He tried to make it appear as if he had acted impulsively, and with no premeditation, and that the question of how to dispose of the body had not been considered before the event. How fortunate then that he had gallons of sulphuric acid in the basement. Haigh also told a colourful story of stealing an old 40 gallon steel oil drum that had been kept in St Stephen's churchyard, where it was being used as a water butt for ARP purposes, and wheeling it back to the basement on a handcart he borrowed from a builder's yard.

When Haigh was finally brought to book, one of the questions that presented itself to the police officer interviewing him was how the slightly built man sitting in front of him had got Mac (and his other victims) into the barrel. Appearing rather pleased with himself Haigh said:

> It's quite simple. You put your barrel on its side. You then place the body with its head towards the mouth of the barrel. You then get the head and shoulders as far into the barrel as you can. Then you lift the legs of the body and as you do this the barrel comes up with the legs. When the barrel, or forty gallon drum, or whatever you are using comes upright, the body slumps into it, because naturally you start the disposal before rigor mortis sets in.[41]

Haigh's claims that this had been unplanned lack credibility, especially as a year earlier he had been carrying out experiments dissolving mice in acid in jam jars at Lincoln Prison. It is also worth noting that orders for his 'experimental work' for a non-existent government contract consisted solely of gallons of acid

---

40. Lefebure, *Murder*
41. Fairlie, Gerald *The Reluctant Cop* (London 1958)

and no other materials. However, when he got Mac's body into the empty oil drum, he realised he would not be able to lift a 20 gallon carboy of acid to pour it in and begin the process of dissolving his former friend. Haigh wrote:

> This was something else which hadn't occurred to me. I had to do it by bucket. Nor had I thought to prepare for the fumes. I was badly choked and had to keep going out for fresh air. Eventually the job was done... .
>
> Subsequently, I returned to find the operation completely successful and when the body disappeared I poured the sludge down the drain. If anything like teeth remained, they will now be down Barking Creek, or wherever it is the sewers of London flow into the sea.[42]

Fortunately, the evening shadows were falling and would have obscured anyone spotting Haigh as he kept popping out of his back entrance onto Stanhope Mews to gasp for breaths of fresh air, away from the fumes, as Mac's body bubbled and boiled as it dissolved. The mouse may have taken around half an hour to dissolve in acid at Lincoln but the body of William Donald 'Mac' McSwan (33), the first victim of the 'Acid Bath Murderer', would take two days. When it came to the final disposal of the sludge that had once been his friend, there was a drain in the floor of the basement. Haigh had taken the precaution of removing Mac's wristwatch and other personal effects, including his identity card, from his clothes before he put him into the oil drum. Haigh now had enough personal knowledge to take over much of his life. He informed Mac's parents that their son had gone into hiding to avoid conscription, just as Mac had told them he would do. His trusted friend John Haigh would look after his things while he was away. He even forged letters from Mac, to his parents, just to let them know he was alive and well. Haigh duly carried them up to north of the border to post them so they would have Scottish postmarks.

Haigh kept up the deceit for the best part of a year but after VE Day in May and with the war in the Far East coming to an end, Haigh realised the McSwans would be looking forward to seeing their son again. Donald McSwan (67) and his wife Amy (62) may have lived reclusive lives in their humble rented rooms, living off Donald's pension as a former employee of London County Council, but they had done so by choice. Between the

42. Lefebure, *Murder*

three McSwans, they owned several properties that they rented out, and Mr McSwan had thousands squirrelled away in savings. Not to mention that Haigh would never have been able to liquidate all of Mac's assets while his parents were still around. Haigh ordered three carboys of acid, having disposed of the drum he had stolen to dissolve Mac, and scrounged two old steel drums from a builder's merchant. The McSwans were last seen alive on 2 July 1945.[43]

The couple's landlady, Agnes Rethage, would later recall that she heard the McSwans moving around their room late on the night of 2 July and wondered what they were up to at such a late hour. Another lodger heard what sounded like a heavy trunk being dragged down the stairs. When the landlady used her spare key to enter their room (after Haigh came round to collect some items shortly afterwards, supposedly at the request of the McSwans), it looked as if they had left in a hurry.[44] Perhaps Haigh had duped the McSwans into leaving by leading them to believe they would be meeting up and going away with their son in secret, under the cover of the blackout. Presumably to minimise the risks of trying to murder two people at the same time, Haigh claimed, and it is probably true, that he killed Mr and Mrs McSwan separately – the husband first. Perhaps he picked up Mr McSwan and their luggage and then returned for his wife a short while later. Both the McSwans met the same fate as their son in the basement of 79 Gloucester Road. There is, however, a question over the murder weapon used. Haigh claimed he used a cosh again, but after his arrest in 1949 a Mr Marshall would recall that he had been given an axe by Haigh around the time of July 1945, and even Haigh would admit that when he killed Mr McSwan there had been much blood spilt.[45]

Haigh had learned his lessons of body disposal well and had purchased a stirrup pump with which he could fill the steel drums with acid from the carboys. He wore leather gloves and an old trench coat to protect him from acid splashes and fashioned a mask, 'out of a piece of tin, a strong tie and lint', to protect against the fumes. Two days later both Mr and Mrs McSwan had been dissolved to sludge and down the drain they went.

Estranged from their family, nobody missed the McSwans. Only after Haigh was apprehended, and the McSwans' names

---

43. MEPO 3/3128
44. *Daily Mirror* 4 March 1949
45. Oates, *Haigh*

were reported in all the newspapers, did William McSwan, a Renfrewshire grocer, come forward to say that the last he had heard from his missing brother was a letter written twenty years ago when he was living in Kent.[46] But it was to be a while before Haigh was caught. He had stolen the McSwans' pensions, cheques, sold their properties and made thousands of pounds which bought him suits and cars, and he became a permanent resident at the Onslow Court Hotel. Finally, he was living a lifestyle to which he thought he was entitled. The tenancy on the Gloucester Road basement ran out and Haigh relocated, along with the oil drums and empty carboys of acid, to a small workshop owned by his old employer, Allan Stephens, at 2 Leopold Road, Crawley.

The war was over and Haigh had enough money to last him the rest of his life if he was careful. Trouble was, Haigh was a gambler, and combined with his expensive lifestyle he was soon running short of money. He needed to find another couple to kill and rob. He became friends with Dr Archibald Henderson (52) and his wife Rosalie Mercy Henderson (41), known to friends as 'Rose', and the three began to see a lot of each other. Dr Henderson had been an army surgeon and it was from his kit, which he had stored at home, that Haigh purloined an Enfield No.2 Mk.1 .38 revolver, an envelope containing ten rounds of ammunition and a service respirator he would wear to protect himself from gas vapours when he dissolved the couple. On 12 February 1948, Haigh lured the Hendersons separately to the workshop on Leopold Road. When each arrived Haigh shot them in the head and dissolved their body in a drum of acid.

Haigh's final victim was Henrietta Helen Olivia Robarts Durand-Deacon (69), who resided, like Haigh, at the Onslow Court Hotel. Haigh took her to his workshop where he killed and disposed of her the same way as the others. Fortunately, Mrs Durand-Deacon had a friend who reported her missing to the police. After mentioning her acquaintance with Haigh, the police looked into his background and he was brought in to Chelsea Police Station where he gave a statement.

Despite giving direct and apparently satisfactory answers to the questions put to him, Haigh's involuntary swallowing during questioning implied nervous tension. Police looked a little closer into his background. They found his criminal record and detectives went to take a look around his workshop. A search revealed Mrs Durand-Deacon's coat, the Hendersons' passports and the

---

46. *Daily Mirror* 4 March 1949

McSwans' identity cards and ration books. The Enfield revolver and eight rounds of ammunition were also discovered in a hat box. Pathologist Keith Simpson investigated some sludge found at the workshop and discovered three human gallstones and part of a denture that was later identified as belonging to Henrietta Durand-Deacon.

Haigh was arrested and charged with her murder. When his room at the Onslow Court Hotel was searched, papers relating to the estates and assets of the Hendersons and McSwans were found. In his interviews with the police it soon become clear that Haigh was trying his utmost to go for a plea of insanity; he confessed to more murders than he was actually responsible and said he had a vampiric desire to drink human blood. It was far more likely that Haigh had killed the McSwans, the Hendersons and Mrs Durand-Deacon, not due to a thirst for blood, but from a desire to obtain money so he could lead a lavish lifestyle. Undoubtedly Haigh found the whole business unsavoury, but in his mind it was not murder, it was merely a means to an end. Detective Superintendent Albert Webb (who, as a Scotland Yard detective sergeant during the Second World War had worked on such notorious cases as the 'Babes in the Wood' and the 'Witchcraft Murder') recalled that Haigh had 'strongly objected to the use of the word murder. He never used it himself. What he did to his victims was "to dispose of them".'[47]

Fastidious to the end, Haigh's appearance at Horsham Magistrates' Court was described as follows: 'He wears a quiet suit, of immaculate cut, with a discreet tie. His hair is sleekly brushed, his nails well-kept and his handmade shoes glossy.'[48] The case was sent to the Crown Court and after being given a number of psychological assessments, Haigh was found to be of sound mind and fit to stand trial. Proceedings opened at Sussex Assizes in Lewes on 18 July 1949. Once the case had been heard the judge, Mr Justice Humphreys, cautioned the members of the jury that they should not find Haigh insane simply because he had committed several murders, and drew a poignant parallel with the 'Brides in the Bath' case where 'no one had ever suggested that the man who committed those murders was insane.'

The jury of eleven men and one woman retired at 4.23pm and after just fifteen minutes returned their unanimous verdict of guilty. Asked by the judge if he had anything to say before the sentence of death was passed, Haigh said he did not, and a faint

47. Fairlie, *Reluctant Cop*
48. *Daily Mirror* 4 March 1949

Crowds watch as the basement that had been rented by Haigh under 79 Gloucester Road is searched by police, March 1949

smile was noticed at the corners of his mouth.[49] Barbara Stephens, who was infatuated with Haigh although there was no evidence of a romantic relationship, described him as 'the most charming man I have ever met. In the five years that I knew him he was always kind and gentle, everything that a man of culture should be.'[50] She sat through the trial in the public gallery and appeared to be the only person in court, aside from Haigh, who was distraught upon hearing the death sentence. However, in a later interview, she said that if she had discovered Haigh's dark secrets she would have ended up in an acid bath too. In an interview published by the *Weekly Despatch*, Barbara's father Allan voiced his concerns about his former tenant: 'I was never sure of Haigh. We never had a row but I always felt he was a little too well-tailored.'[51] Barbara soon found a new love in Bernard Grimmett, a laboratory assistant at an aniline dye works. The pair were married at Horsham Register Office in 1951.[52]

Haigh spent his last days in the condemned cell at Wandsworth Prison and was hanged by Albert Pierrepoint on 10 August

---

49. *Bradford Observer* 20 July 1949
50. *Sunday Mirror* 6 March 1949
51. *Weekly Despatch* 24 July 1949
52. *Crawley and District Observer* 7 December 1951

1949. In one final conceit, on the day before his execution Haigh bequeathed the green suit, red and green tie, heather mixture socks, beige shirt and red handkerchief, all of which he had worn at his trial, to Madame Tussauds so that the figure they made of him could be dressed in his real clothes. He even sent instructions that the suit and figure must always be kept in immaculate condition, the trousers creased, the hair parted and one inch of shirt cuffs showing. Newspapers reported Haigh's figure was on display in the Chamber of Horrors within an hour of his execution.[53]

53. *Nottingham Journal* 12 September 1949

CHAPTER 7

Death on the Roads

*Leave your car outside in the street without lights and the police will
be down on you in a flash, but if you're murdering somebody at the
bottom of your garden, they'll never discover that.*

John George Haigh

During the first twelve months of the Second World War
road accidents in the nightly blackouts were the cause of
more civilian deaths than air raids. Throughout the war
years, the blackout would also provide the ideal cover for murder
on our highways and byways.

As the war progressed there were ever-increasing numbers of
young men from Britain, and allied countries, training for military
service in the UK. Many were away from their homes for the first
time and, fuelled by drink and bravado with their service pals,
fights and violence became more prevalent in the towns and cities
near military camps. The causes were various, from disputes over
a girl to inter-service rivalries and a host of petty matters were
blown out of all proportion by those under the influence of alcohol.
Playing cards or games of dice for money on military bases,
even if such gambling had officially been banned, were popular
pastimes for many servicemen.

Perhaps being young and foolish could excuse them to an
extent, but gambling can be addictive, and some got themselves
into serious debt with their comrades. Others took to drinking and
womanising but simply didn't have the money to support their
ardour. Some did all the aforementioned and got themselves into
a real mess.

The motives were various. There was a wartime attitude of
'live for today and hang tomorrow because we might be dead',
leading people to do things they would never do under any other
conditions. Incidents of violence increased manifold, and some of
those who had harboured thoughts of petty criminal activity, or had
struck upon the idea of an illegal get-rich-quick scheme, actually
had a go, sometimes with disastrous and even fatal consequences.
But do not be under an illusion that all of these crimes were

A wartime dance hall, always a popular venue for troops on passes and leave

simply opportunist or heat of the moment. Wartime conditions and blackouts provided an ideal environment for vicious predator criminals.

Two types of night worker – street prostitutes and taxi drivers – were particularly vulnerable to criminal attacks. By the nature of their work they both had to engage with complete strangers and assess very quickly if their prospective client posed a threat. They also carried their earnings about their person and would regularly go into dark and secluded places with their clients; places that were ideal for attacks and robberies.

Although there may have been rivalries, personality clashes and disagreements over what these workers considered to be 'their turf', they also kept an eye out for each other. They would watch who was picked up and spread the word about dodgy customers, but once the worker was away with the client, they would be pretty much on their own.

Wartime taxi drivers were kept occupied in the evenings by ferrying locally based uniformed-service personnel on passes, and those on leave, from pubs to theatres and dance halls and then back to their barracks, billets or hotels. Earnings for drivers could be good and assaults and robberies in taxi cabs became something of a phenomenon in the blackout. The two cases here ended in murder.

The Colchester Taxi Cab Murder
(Birch, Essex 1943)

The first taxi cab murder to hit the national newspapers in wartime Britain took place in Essex in 1943. Harry Claude Hailstone (28) was described by friends as an easy-going man who liked a laugh and was always joking. He had trained as a ladies' hairdresser but suffered an accident which left both hands with a deformity known as 'claw hands'.[1] One of his feet was also deformed and caused him to walk with a limp. Harry's injuries meant he could no longer continue hairdressing and nor would he be able to join the armed forces. He had been living with his parents, brothers and sisters on East Hill in Colchester until a bomb fell at the back of their house during one of the first air raids on the town in 1940. His mother, Gertrude Hailstone (57), suffered head injuries from which she did not recover and she died twelve months later. Tragedy rocked the family again when Harry's brother Roy, who had been an RAF Reservist, was killed while on active service in the Middle East in 1942. Harry worked for a while for an engineering company but changed career path in July 1943 when he became a taxi driver for local firm Blackwell's, later changing to William Bucknell of Parsons Heath Garage on Harwich Road.

Harry took up lodgings with Sidney and Mary Pearce at 127 Maldon Road, Colchester, where he got on well with his landlady who cooked and cleaned for him. Shortly after 11.00pm on Tuesday, 7 December 1943, Harry called at his lodgings to let Mrs Pearce know he would not be in for supper because he had 'two fares' to take to Birch. She asked Harry who he had in the car and he said it was two black American soldiers, an officer and a private, adding that he would be back in about half an hour.

Harry did not return that night but Mary Pearce did not worry unduly; she just thought he had picked up more fares or had even run out of petrol and had ended up sleeping in the cab. Knowing Harry, the latter was more likely. Harry had not been reported missing when his cab, registration number CPU 620, was discovered by PC 505 McCormack of Tiptree. The taxi had been found abandoned with its side lights and headlight still on, parked on the right-hand side of the road at Haynes Green Lane, just off the Maldon Road at Layer Marney. Looking inside, PC McCormack saw a jacket

1. Camps, Francis Edward, 'The Colchester Taxi Cab Murder', *Medico-Legal Journal*, vol. 17, no. 1, 1949

Colchester High Street as Harry Hailstone would have known it

Harry Hailstone

on the back seat which looked as if it had been pulled off in a hurry, as one of its sleeves was inside out. He also noted a raincoat with a bloodstained collar, that the leather upholstery had been badly scratched, the string parcel net had been torn down and Harry's personal papers, gloves and empty wallet were strewn over the floor. There were also several spots of blood spatter on the inside of the offside window and a clot of blood on the rear seat.[2]

Supt George Totterdell of Essex CID was alerted and sped off with DI Draper to the police station at Copford, where the clothes had been brought in by Sergeant Garrett after he had attended the scene. Harry's driving licence was in the pocket of the coat, with the address of his lodgings on it. Totterdell went to see Mrs Pearce to see if she could shed any light on Harry's whereabouts, but she could only tell him what she had seen of Harry the night before. It was thought something awful had happened to him. Perhaps he had been abducted, or beaten up and robbed and was lying in a ditch needing help somewhere? The experienced police officers knew the signs and feared he would not be found alive.

A wide and systematic search concentrating on the road leading to the five American army camps in the Birch area was made, involving both the police and locally based troops, to see if Harry could be found. On Thursday 9 December, a heavily bloodstained civilian mackintosh raincoat was spotted in the gutter of the main road near Tollesbury (about 6 miles away from where the taxi had been found abandoned), and handed over to the police. The question of what had become of Harry was answered when, shortly after noon that same day, his body was discovered by PC Snowling and PS Garrett. His lifeless body appeared to have been pushed over an embankment near Birch Rectory and had landed in brambles on the inside bank about 6ft from the main Colchester-Maldon Road. Essex County pathologist Dr Francis Camps noted:

> The body was photographed in its original position and I saw it later. It was fully clothed with the exception of a jacket, the head was pointing towards Maldon and the left side of the face showed bruising with much blood soiling. A provisional opinion of manual strangulation was based upon typical finger nail impressions and scratches on the neck with haemorrhages into the whites of his eyes. The position of the body and rivulets of blood were in keeping with the body having rolled down the slope after death.[3]

Harry's body was removed to Colchester Public Mortuary where Dr Camps performed a post-mortem examination. The inquest was opened by County Coroner Mr Reginald Proudfoot in the tiny

2. Totterdell, *Country Copper*
3. Camps, 'Taxi Cab Murder'

The embankment where Harry Hailstone's body was pushed over near Birch Rectory (*Essex Police Museum*)

Master's Room at St Albright's Hospital in Stanway on Monday 13 December.[4] During the brief hearing Dr Camps explained the findings of his post mortem, summarised in four points:

1. The man was healthy and of good physique (height 5ft 7inches) but had a deformity of both hands (claw hands) which would make him less able to defend himself. There was no evidence on the body that he had offered any resistance.
2. The left eye was bruised and also the left side of the nose, mouth and chin, indicating at least 3 heavy blows with some object such as a fist.
3. There were abrasions on both sides of the neck in front, these being more marked upon the right side but with underlying bruising more marked on the left side. There was a fracture of the left upper cornu of the thyroid cartilage.
4. The marks on the neck were characteristically those of a gripping hand, the fingers being on the right side with duplication due to slipping and reapplication of pressure.[5]

---

4. *Essex Newsman Herald* 14 December 1943
5. Camps, 'Taxi Cab Murder'

Camps confirmed the cause of Harry's death as asphyxia due to manual strangulation from behind with a left hand. There were also superficial grazes and bruises to his right knee and shins, which were consistent with them contacting the dashboard with force, probably from being pulled towards the back seat and kicking out while sitting in the front seat of the taxi. Camps also noted that Harry's clothing had yielded £2 18s 6d in cash and notes. If the motive for killing Harry had been robbery, all that money that Harry carried in his waistcoat for ease of access because of his deformed hands had been overlooked.

There were only a few clues for the investigating officers to work on. Firstly, Harry had told his landlady he was driving American servicemen to Birch. Secondly, the cab was found parked in a different location from where Harry had been killed, suggesting his killer had driven the cab himself, and because it was parked on the right-hand side of the road, this pointed to an American. The discarded raincoat, however, would contain the vital clue to tracing Harry's killer. The mac was of a type privately purchased for wear by Canadian officers; inside was a Canadian maker's label and, crucially, the name of the owner, J. J. Weber, was written in ink near the collar band.

Enquiries with Canadian Army headquarters in London revealed the owner was a Canadian captain who was, by the time police tracked him down, attached to the Canadian General Hospital at Cuckfield in Sussex. However, in early December 1943, he had been stationed at the 18th Canadian General Hospital at Cherry Tree Camp, Colchester. He remembered encountering a black American soldier dressed in the uniform of a sergeant at Liverpool Street Station. They got chatting and soon discovered both were travelling to Colchester, so they travelled back together in the buffet car. Weber then invited him back to his camp for a drink. The pair returned to a fellow officer's room in a barrack hut, chatted and had a few drinks from a bottle of whiskey Weber had provided. Weber left the room to visit the toilet and when he returned about ten minutes later his guest had gone, taking the bottle of whiskey and the officer's mackintosh with him. This was a coat, which not only contained the officer's gloves and torch but also £5 in notes and his Rolex watch! Weber reported the coat and its contents missing at the camp the following day, but had to leave soon after for Fleet in Hampshire.

Although Weber had never asked the American soldier for his name he was able to describe him as 'about 30 years old, height 5ft 10 inches, weight about 160lbs. Average build dark hair and eyes, dark complexion, slight thin strip moustache, straight nose, good teeth.'[6]

Weber was confident he would be able to recognise the man again if required to do so. The suddenly absent American had, however, left behind a gas mask with the name Hill inside. This was traced to Pte Solomon Hill of the 356th Engineer Service Regiment, whose camp was on the airfield occupied by 410 Bombardment Group United States Army Air Force (USAAF) at Birch near Tiptree. When interviewed by the police, he admitted it was his and informed them that he had loaned it to another soldier from his battalion, Pte George E. Fowler (22). When Fowler was questioned he initially denied all knowledge of the murder, but a search of his room found a sergeant's tunic stained with blood hanging up near his bed, and a pawn ticket for a Rolex watch, exactly like the one that had been stolen. Weber's coat was also recovered from Fowler's kit bag.

When asked to account for his movements, Fowler claimed he had gone to London on a pass with other soldiers. He had stayed at the Liberty Club on Euston Street until 4 or 5 December then could not say where he had stayed the night of 6 December when he claimed to have picked up a girl at the Florida Club and spent the night with her. He claimed he had little memory of getting back, saying he thought he had been very drunk, or had been doped, and could recall very little except being brought home by American soldiers and waking up in his bed at his camp at Birch wearing an American sergeant's shirt. Wilson should have returned to his camp by 3 December and had been punished for failing to do so. He denied meeting the Canadian officer while on leave. He also claimed his gas mask was on the floor under his bed back in his billet.

Despite Fowler's counter claims, his story failed to convince the police. Not only did he bear a likeness to the description given by Weber, but items reported stolen by Weber were connected to Fowler. He was held pending further investigations.

In a statement signed on 13 December 1943, Fowler changed his story. He began by admitting that he had been the soldier who had met and travelled on the train with Captain Weber, but claimed that once they got back to Cherry Tree Camp, Weber had got drunk, given the coat to him and then passed out on the bed in the room. Fowler then claimed he returned to London in the company of other soldiers. He confessed that he had found

6. Camps, 'Taxi Cab Murder'

Private J. C. Leatherberry   Private George E. Fowler
(*Essex Police Museum*)   (*Essex Police Museum*)

the items in the pockets, had not intended to return them, and got Charlie Huntley, also from the 356th Engineers and also in London with Fowler, to pawn the watch for him because he needed money.

While in London, Fowler claimed he had met Pte J. C. Leatherberry (21) from Crystal Springs, Copiah, Mississippi, who was also serving in the 356th Engineers – he was in A Company whereas Fowler was in E Company – and the pair travelled back to Colchester together. Leatherberry told Fowler he was desperately in need of money and was going to get it any way he could. Leatherberry suggested they rob the driver of the taxi they would be taking from Colchester Station back to their camp near Birch. Quite how he, or they, planned to subdue the driver or how much he, or they, actually expected to make out of the venture remains unclear. When they got off the train at Colchester Station Leatherberry complained he was cold and Fowler gave him the coat he had taken from Weber.

Stepping outside the station they hailed a taxi, the one being driven by Harry Hailstone. Fowler recalled that their driver stopped off on the way before they left Colchester (this would have been when Harry let his landlady know he would not be in for supper). Fowler claimed that when they were about 4 miles from Colchester he asked the driver to stop the cab because he wanted to relieve himself. His version of what happened next is quoted directly from his statement :

> The driver stopped the cab on the left-hand side of the road
> as we came from Colchester. As I was sitting in the left-hand
> rear seat I got out of the left-hand rear door to have a leak.
> He [Leatherberry] stayed in the taxi. While I was outside having
> a leak I heard a struggle and he called to me and asked me if
> I was going to help him and I did not answer.
>
> After I finished taking the leak I came back to the rear of the
> cab and he had the cab driver by the throat with his hand and
> was pounding him with the other hand. When I got completely
> into the cab the driver was limp.[7]

Leatherberry went through Harry's pockets and, at the same
time, told Fowler he was 'in this' just as much as he was and
told him to help him get the body out of the taxi, which he did,
and the pair carried it over the road and dumped the body in
the ditch. They wanted to move the taxi elsewhere so Fowler
drove the cab towards their camp and Leatherberry travelled in
the passenger seat for about a tenth of a mile. Leatherberry then
suggested they go to London instead, so they swapped places and
he drove to Maldon. There he even had the affront to park up,
walk up a street and ask a policemen what time the next train left
for London. Told there were no more trains that night, Fowler
drove back to a road near their camp. When they returned to
camp they handed themselves in to the guard tent for being a few
days late from leave.

Fowler claimed in his statement that they did not know the
taxi driver was dead when they left him in the ditch; he claimed
he thought he was unconscious. Leatherberry made a separate
statement the same day, in which he claimed he was staying
with friends he had made in London on the night of the murder
(7 December) and had not met Fowler until the following day
(8 December) at Morri's Cafe on Cable Street. When he was
detained his kit bag was searched and his uniform jacket, trousers,
shirt and vest were examined at the Police Laboratory. Human
blood was found on the uniform. There was enough blood on
Leatherberry's trousers to obtain a blood group. It was AB, one
of the rarest blood types, which is found in only one to two per
cent of the population. The same blood type was detected on
the stains on Weber's mac; it was the one that belonged to Harry
Hailstone.

Leatherberry declined to make any further statement. The
Rolex watch was recovered from the pawnbroker and positively

---

7. Camps, 'Taxi Cab Murder'

identified by Weber. Fowler also picked out Leatherberry from an identification parade as the man he had been with on the night of 7 December. The people Leatherberry claimed he had stayed with on the night of 7 December were quite clear that he had stayed with them on 6 December. Samples, measurements and photographs were also taken of both men's fingernails and it was noted that Fowler was left handed. Blood was also found under one of Fowler's fingers, whereas blood was found under all Leatherberry's fingers on both hands.

Fowler and Leatherberry were handed over to their commanding officer and charged with the murder of Harry Hailstone. They were tried in separate American courts martials, held in two different courtrooms, at Ipswich Town Hall, commencing on 19 January 1944. Fowler gave evidence against Leatherberry, and a demonstration of how the attack was delivered upon Harry from the back seat of the taxi was presented to the court. Fowler was then removed to the other courtroom to face his own trial. Both men were found guilty of murder but the court was impressed with Fowler's apparent candour, and he was sentenced to life imprisonment with hard labour to be served in the US Penitentiary Lewisburg, Pennsylvania.

Leatherberry was far less impressive as he tried to hang on to his story of being in London at the time of the murder. The rare blood type found on his hands and clothing, the blood type that belonged to Harry Hailstone, counted heavily against Leatherberry and he was sentenced to death. He was then removed to await execution at Shepton Mallet Prison in Somerset, which was being used by American forces as a military prison. Ten days before he was due to go to the gallows, Leatherberry wrote a confession in which he claimed it was actually Fowler who killed Harry Hailstone. If this really was the case, why did he not mention this sooner?

According to American custom, Leatherberry's execution would take place at 1.00am, and the appointed date was 16 May 1944. His executioner and assistant were uncle and nephew Thomas and Albert Pierrepoint. The sentence was carried out according to American regulations, in the presence of eight personnel and twelve witnesses. British execution suites were not very big spaces and it would have felt cramped for all present; no doubt they would have spread themselves around the walls. Unlike British executions, which were carried out seconds after the condemned was fitted with the rope and leg pinions on the gallows trap, in American executions the charges were read out (Albert Pierrepoint would later write of how he hated this delay in American executions[8]). The condemned would also be asked if they had anything to say. This question was even put a second and final time to Leatherberry by the chaplain when he was on the gallows. He replied: 'Sir, I want to thank you for being so nice to me and for everything you have done for me.'

Satisfied that was all Leatherberry had to say, the commandant gave a silent signal to Pierrepoint who then pushed the lever and the traps of the gallows fell. Leatherberry plunged through the opening with the rope noose around his neck. He was buried with other executed American servicemen in a separated section of Brookwood Cemetery in Surrey. By the end of the war, there had been a total of eighteen burials in what had been designated 'Plot X'. They were all exhumed in 1949, but only one was repatriated. All the others, including Leatherberry, were reburied with other dishonoured American service personnel at Oise-Aisne American Cemetery in France. Fowler was given parole and was released from prison in 1960 after serving just fifteen years of his 'life' sentence.

The Cab at the Cemetery Gates (Bradford 1944)

Harrison Graham, known to most as Harry, was born at Cross Gate Moor near Durham in 1886 and spent his youth in Durham and the Newcastle suburb of Byker. Just like thousands of other lads in the north of England, after a few years schooling he had gone to work 'down the pits' as a miner. In the First World War, Harry had served in one of the sturdy northern line infantry regiments, The King's Own Yorkshire Light Infantry. While fighting in France he had been badly wounded and had been given an honourable discharge. The psychological injuries from war had left him with a speech impediment.

Times were hard for many in the north in the 1920s and '30s. Pits closed and many unemployed men moved around the country as they sought work. Harry moved to Bradford in 1930. In 1939 he was living in North Wing and had been employed as a coal yard foreman, but his old war injuries and the labour-intensive work was beginning to take its toll. He decided it was time for a change, so as he and his wife Harriet already had some income from the North Wing cafe they owned at the front of their house, Harry decided he try his hand at taxi driving. He found employment as a driver for Claude Newton of Clayton.

---

8. Pierrepoint, Albert, *Executioner: Pierrepoint* (London 1974)

In July 1944, Harry took the plunge and decided to buy his own taxi and go into business as a self-employed driver. He secured the transfer of his licence on 1 September and obtained the written permissions to ply for hire on the rank in the London Midland and Scottish (LMS) Railway Station at Forster Square.

On the evening of Wednesday 6 September, Harry set out at 7.15pm for his night shift. His wife expected him home at around 3.00am the following morning. Instead, the police came to their home at 8.30am to relay some terrible news and Mrs Graham had to go the mortuary to identify the body of her husband. The grim discovery had been made when PC Joseph Pell looked in on a taxi that had been parked on Rooley Lane, opposite Bowling Cemetery gates, at about 5.30am on the morning of Thursday 7 September. Harry Graham's body was on the floor in the back of his taxi cab. There was blood spattered around the interior and he could see Harry had suffered a severe blow to his head. After carrying out a detailed post-mortem examination, Bradford's Chief Police Surgeon Dr Ralph Rimmer stated that the fatal blow had been so severe it had fractured Harry's skull, and it had been delivered using a blunt instrument such as a piece of iron, a spanner or a hammer.[9]

Despite a thorough search of the area, and men and equipment from the Corporation Cleansing Department being brought in to examine the contents of a number of drains in Rooley Lane, the weapon or object used to murder Harry Graham could not be found, and has never come to light. The police were also aware that, as in the case of the Colchester Taxi Murder, just because Harry was found in Rooley Lane, it did not preclude the possibility that the murder had been committed elsewhere and the perpetrator had driven the cab to the site. Finding a murder weapon in such circumstances was like trying to find the proverbial needle in a haystack.

When Harry's clothes and taxi were searched, all his takings were found to be gone and a blue case with silver lettering containing Harry's identity card, driving licence, insurance certificate and a permit from the LMS Railway company for him to ply for hire in the station was also missing. Perhaps his killer thought this was his wallet. The common misconception that taxi drivers carried large sums of money with them after a good night of fares was also raised, but Bradford taxi drivers who spoke to reporters in the aftermath of Harry's murder said it

---

9. *Yorkshire Post* 16 January 1945

would have been unusual for a taxi driver to have more than one pound in his possession. One said: 'We don't carry much about with us. We don't get the fabulous sums people imagine.'[10] Local taxi driver Albert Speight, who worked on the rank at Forster Square, spoke of having a number of uncomfortable experiences during recent nightshifts:

> Last Friday night I drew up in the station at 1.00am when two soldiers and a woman got into the taxi and one of the soldiers said, 'Get us to Halifax' and shut the doors. When they were inside one said get that light out and put his hand up to switch it off. I told him I would see to that and he then became abusive and told me to get going.[11]

Speight asked him for his fare in advance because he had previously had trouble with soldiers dodging their fare and running out on him after long journeys. He refused and became abusive and Speight told him to leave the cab. This he refused to do until a sergeant hauled him out. On another occasion Speight was paid 3s 6d by a soldier for a job which cost 6s. A week later Speight had the same man ask him to take him on another journey, Speight refused and the man slammed the cab door against his leg. Another Forster Square driver, George V. Earley, said the most trouble came from soldiers and he had received a punch or two in the stomach at a destination instead of the fare. Another driver had been given a black eye.[12]

DS John P. O'Hara of Bradford CID led the investigation into Harry's murder. From the word go it was clear that much would depend on the willingness of people who used taxi cabs late on the night of the murder to come forward and give information. Police appeals were made through the press, and public notices, for both civilian and military personnel who had waited for taxis in Forster Square around midnight on the night of the murder to come forward. Detectives were particularly keen to speak to a civilian man and a serviceman who had engaged a taxi which broke down at the junction of Bridge Street and Market Street. These passengers, who had asked to be taken to Bierley, alighted and it is thought they may be able to help with their enquiries.

City Coroner Raymond Selby Bishop opened the inquest into Harry Graham's death on 8 September. Mr Graham's widow and

---

10. *Bradford Observer* 8 September 1944
11. *Ibid*
12. *Ibid*

Forster Square, Bradford, in the 1930s

PC Pell were the only material witnesses asked to give evidence. It was rapidly adjourned at the request of the police to enable them to undertake further enquiries. Harry's body was formally released and his funeral took place on the afternoon of 12 September 1944. Harry's widow was accompanied by her son (Harry's stepson) Albert Hague. Four taxi drivers acted as pallbearers and a wreath from the Town Hall Square taxi stand bearing the inscription 'Hoping justice will be met' was placed in the hearse that carried Harry's body to Undercliffe Cemetery for burial.

In the aftermath, Bradford taxi drivers began to seriously consider whether they should apply for firearms certificates so they could buy handguns for self-protection, or perhaps have a mate with them in their vehicle at night. The murder brought a number of instances of violence and abuse to their minds. It had not been forgotten that only a short time previously, driver Joe Raynor had been attacked while driving a fare in the West Riding police area on 15 August, and there were fears among taxi men that the attacks may have been connected.[13]

A staff reporter from the *Bradford Observer* interviewed Joe Raynor and what he had to say provoked the question, was it purely coincidence that both Harry and Joe had been employed by Claude Newton of Clayton? In fact before working on his own account, Harry had previously driven the same taxi as Joe. Joe

---

13. *Bradford Observer* 8 September 1944

tried to remember what his assailants had looked like but it had been during the blackout and all he could recall was they were hatless and were wearing overcoats. He said:

> At 12.55am on Thursday 15 August, I was on the rank outside Bradford Town Hall when two young men, they looked like civilians asked if I would take them to Tong Lane. I said yes. When they were travelling up Birkenshaw Road one of the men said, 'That will do. Will you pull up here?' Just as I was putting the car out of gear one man said, 'Let him have it' and I was hit on the back and side of the head. I put my hands up to protect my head and was hit on the finger. The instrument with which they hit me seemed like a scythe stone. I jumped out of the car and ran to a police box. They must have seen what I was going to do and drove off in my car.[14]

The police took Joe to St Luke's Hospital where his head was treated for cuts. His car was found the other side of a military camp near Selby.

Police appeals for witnesses to Harry Graham's murder were kept up in the local press. Cinemas even showed slides announcing the murder, giving the salient facts and appealing to anyone with information to come forward. There were a few individuals the police were particularly keen to hear from. One was a man who had been seen to signal Harry's taxi by flashing a torch while crossing Canal Road near the YMCA at around midnight. Harry stopped his cab, got out, spoke to the man, and returned to his driving seat a minute or two later. He had a passenger, a local man serving in the RAF who was back in Bradford on leave. He did not hear what was said but the man with the torch did make a comment which so offended the airman he reported what had been said to the police.[15]

Despite all the high-profile appeals there was still very little for the police to go on. Specific requests for certain individuals had drawn blanks, or they were simply never identified, and not even the murder weapon had been found. The killing of Harry Graham was being branded the 'clueless murder' by local people and press. Then news of another tragedy rattled across the city. Jane Coulton (69), the licensee of the Nag's Head Inn in the Bradford suburb of Clayton, was found murdered, strangled with one of her own silk stockings, in her own bed on 21 September.

---

14. *Bradford Observer* 13 September 1944
15. *Yorkshire Post* 19 September 1944

Local newspapers wrote of the 'murder madness' pervading Bradford after two people had now been killed in less than two weeks.

It did not take much for Chinese whispers on the street to add additional stories of supposed recent murders such as 'a woman up Leeds Road' and 'a child behind a cinema' to spice things up as the stories got retold. The *Bradford Observer* commented:

> It is enough to say that there is not a vestige of truth in either of the rumours but nevertheless they provided conversation for hundreds of people in shops, streets, cafes, business premises and licensed houses. It is lamentable that people have the mentality to spread such stories.[16]

It is part of human nature for people to gossip and the press, police and local authorities have to be careful how they manage and contain such situations. Mass panics, where people start claiming they have heard of, witnessed or even been the victim of attacks, are no joke and can muddy the waters of a real murder investigation and waste hundreds if not thousands of police man hours. Just such a panic had occurred in the neighbouring city of Halifax over the supposed 'Halifax Slasher' attacks between 25 November and 2 December 1938.[17]

The killer of Mrs Coulton was swiftly identified as local army deserter Corporal Arthur Thompson (34). A manhunt was instigated and police were drafted in from across Yorkshire to assist. Thompson was arrested on 23 September, having aroused suspicions after attempting to sell some items of jewellery (that turned out to have belonged to the murdered landlady) to the landlord of The Globe Hotel at Overton.[18] His rapid arrest seemed to quell rumours and quench some of the grumbles about Bradford Police failing to capture Harry Graham's killer.

There had even been a suggestion that perhaps Thompson had also murdered Harry in his taxi, but DS O'Hara was quick to point out to reporters that the crimes were committed on opposite sides of the city and stated 'there is nothing to show the two crimes are connected.'[19] Instead, he renewed the appeal for witnesses for the Harry Graham investigation. He asked the

16. *Bradford Observer* 26 September 1944
17. *Halifax Evening Courier* 28 November 1938; *Halifax Evening Courier* 23 January 1939
18. *Bradford Observer* 21 October 1944
19. *Daily Herald* 22 September 1944

public to help track down a soldier they wished to interview, described as aged 25 to 30, 5ft 6 to 5ft 8 in height, clean shaven with a scar extending from the right cheek to the chin, who was wearing battledress uniform and a hat bearing the badge of the King's Own Yorkshire Light Infantry. He appeared to be 'under the influence of drink' and had asked two people in Market Street for money to pay his taxi fare to Bierley.[20]

DS O'Hara and his team also wished to speak to a man with a particularly deep voice who had engaged a taxi to drive him to Currer Avenue, Bierley, only a few days before the murder on 7 December. While on the way, he had questioned the driver about the amount of money taxi men were reported to carry with them, asked him if he drove for himself or for an employer, asked when he paid his fares and commented that it was dangerous for taxis to pick up passengers at night. Described as about 45 years old, about 5ft 11, medium build, wearing a fawn raincoat and a trilby hat, police were particularly interested in this man because of the questions he asked and because his destination had been about five minutes' drive from Rooley Lane where Harry Graham had been found.

Unfortunately, there was a lack of response, which frustrated the officers of Bradford CID. They were convinced that someone had key information but was not coming forward. DS O'Hara even said in a press interview:

> I am informed that there are persons in Bradford who could give information which might materially help the inquiry but that those persons are afraid their names will be disclosed to the public. Any person who has such fear can rest assured that his or her information will be regarded as confidential and I am prepared to see personally any person who has fears about coming forward.[21]

O'Hara was adamant that he was not going to call in Scotland Yard to assist with, or lead, the investigation. In early January 1945, he was still telling reporters he was hopeful the murderer would be brought to justice but when the inquest was resumed on 16 January a verdict of 'murder by some person or persons unknown' was returned. Coroner Mr R. S. Bishop commented that that did not mean the case was closed and he 'hoped someone

20. *Bradford Observer* 30 September 1944
21. *Northern Mail* 2 October 1944

might yet be brought to justice for the crime.'[22] On 31 January 1945, Arthur Thompson was hanged by Thomas Pierrepoint and Herbert Morris at Armley Prison for the murder of landlady Jane Coulton. The murder of Harry Graham still remains unsolved.

---

22. *Yorkshire Post* 16 January 1945

CHAPTER 8

The Blackout Bonnie and Clyde (Staines, Surrey 1944)

> *Jones and Hulten committed their murder to the tune of V-1, and were convicted to the tune of V-2 ... . Indeed, the whole meaningless story, with its atmosphere of dance-halls, movie-palaces, cheap perfume, false names and stolen cars, belongs essentially to a war period.*
>
> *Decline of English Murder,* George Orwell

One of the most infamous crime sprees of the twentieth century took place under the cover of the blackout in London and Surrey in 1944. It was perpetrated by a young American serviceman and a young woman, who apparently had no other connection than a shared sociopathic desire to live out a fantasy of him being a gangster and she being his gun moll.

Elizabeth Maud Baker was born on 26 July 1926 in the industrial village of Skewen in the county borough of Neath, Port Talbot, Wales. Elizabeth, known to her family and friends as Betty, would say she never received the attention or love she deserved from her mother, Nellie, because she gave the lion's share to Betty's older sister Gladys, who had a disability. Betty got on far better with her father Arthur, a railway worker who had wanted to give his family a fresh start in Canada when his daughters were still small. Sadly, after five years things were not working out and they came back, settling in a small council house on Coronation Road in Neath, Glamorgan.

Perhaps Betty inherited a sense of adventure and desire to escape from her father to whom she was close. When war was declared in 1939, he was called up as a sergeant in the Royal Field Artillery and was posted to Usk on the Welsh border. Betty, at that time aged 13, missed her dad terribly and ran away from home to try and join him on three occasions. Each time she was brought back by the police. Her desperation to be noticed led to her parents taking her to a juvenile court where they stated she was out of their control. Betty was sent to an approved school at Sale in Cheshire.[1]

---

1. *Daily Mirror* 24 January 1945

At the age of 16, in 1942, she left school, keen to start a new, exciting life. Just a few months after her sixteenth birthday, in November of that year, she married Gunner Stanley Jones (30). Whether there had been true love or not we will never know for sure; it was a wartime marriage and some would claim it was one of convenience. Betty would claim later that her husband had struck her on their wedding night so she left him after just two days and they never lived together. Stan had duties with his unit, 2nd (Oban) Airlanding Anti-Tank Battery, Royal Artillery. He was deployed abroad and killed in action on 26 September 1944, during the Battle for Arnhem, so he never had the chance to tell his side of the story.

What we do know is that Betty got the separation allowance money that was paid to the wives of servicemen, and she left for London to follow her dream in January 1943. New Betty, new name. She changed her old fashioned and rather prim sounding middle name of Maud to the more exotic Marina and, as she embarked on a career as a dancer, she chose a glamorous stage name befitting a budding screen starlet – Georgina Grayson.

Sadly the dancing work on the stages of glitzy West End theatres did not emerge, so she took on jobs that never seemed to last long, one to four weeks for one reason and another. She worked as a nursemaid, chambermaid, barmaid, usherette and waitress. She also accepted the bookings offered to her from shady nightclubs such as the Panama Club, Knightsbridge, and the Blue Lagoon on Carnaby Street, where she performed as a striptease dancer. The money she earned in the clubs was very good, but the work was far from regular so she worked as a waitress to supplement her small income from the separation allowance. In September 1944, Betty rented her latest room from Mrs Edris May Evans at 311 King Street in Hammersmith.[2] Betty was 18 years old and her London life was not proving to be quite the dream she had hoped.

However, Betty thought her luck was about to change on the evening of 3 October. She was in a cafe on Queen Caroline Street, just off the Hammersmith Broadway, when a friend of hers named Len Bexley – officially a coach trimmer by trade but actually a black marketeer and fence for stolen goods – introduced her to man dressed in an American army officer's uniform. Betty later recalled her first impression of the man: 'I thought he was a gentleman.' He told her his name was Lieutenant Richard John 'Ricky' Allen. His real name was Karl Gustav Hulten (22), and

---

2. CRIM 1/482

A cloud of smoke rises into the air after another V1 flying bomb crashes onto London, 1944

in reality he was a private in the 2nd Battalion, Service Company, 501st Parachute Infantry Regiment, US Army, and he was wearing an officer's uniform he was not entitled to wear. Betty also began their relationship with a lie: she told him her name was Georgina Grayson. And so began the adventures of Ricky and Georgie.

They had agreed to meet again that evening. Betty thought they had agreed to meet at the Broadway Cinema but Karl thought they were meeting in front of the cafe. When he did not show up, she started walking back to her bedsit, but Karl caught up with her as she was walking down King Street. He certainly made an impression as he rolled up in a two-and-a-half ton 6x6 US Army truck, which Hulten had taken without permission from his unit's motor pool at Reading a few days earlier when he had decided to go AWOL (absent without leave).

Karl and Betty would later give statements containing their own versions of the conversations they had, and the things they did together. The truth, as ever, is probably somewhere in the middle. Betty claimed that when they got talking in the truck, 'I told him I would like to do something dangerous, meaning to go over Germany in a bomber. I meant that but he got me wrong. He then told me what he was doing and showed me a gun which he pulled out from his inside pocket.' Karl claimed Betty had 'said that she

Elizabeth 'Betty' Jones
aka Georgina 'Georgie'
Grayson

Karl Hulten aka
Richard 'Ricky' Allen

would like to do something exciting like becoming a "Gun Moll" like they do back in the States.'[3]

It was then Karl informed her that they were driving a stolen truck. Betty claimed he told her he had been a gangster gunman with a mob in Chicago and was now the leader of a criminal gang operating in London. In truth, he had been born in Stockholm, Sweden, had moved to America as a young child and had grown up in Massachusetts. After leaving school he had worked at a grocery store, been a driver and a mechanic and had visited Chicago once. He was also a married man with a wife and child back home.

The pair drove to Reading, and, as they were moving, Karl showed Betty how to drive. At some point along the Great West Road it appears he decided to demonstrate to Betty he was not kidding about being a hoodlum. Shortly after overtaking a girl on a bicycle going in the same direction, Karl pulled up to the side of the road and stopped. He got out and waited for the girl on the bike to come along while Betty remained inside the cab of the truck.

When the girl came alongside Karl, he pushed her off her bicycle. He stepped forward and she screamed, 'Don't touch me!' He then grabbed her handbag from the handlebars and threw it to Betty, climbed back in the cab and drove off. He told Betty to sort through the bag with her torch. It was quite a large bag with a smaller handbag inside. Betty would recall that there were pyjamas and overnight things, a few photographs and a letter along with about nine shillings and some clothing coupons, which Betty kept for herself. Karl then threw both bags, and their remaining contents, onto the road as they sped along.

Betty claimed she was dropped back to her door at about 5.00am. Karl claimed he drove the truck to the Old Gaumont car park in Sussex Place, the pair walked back and he spent the night with Betty and would do so again the following night, but they did not go out.

Betty claimed she did not see Karl again until he called for her two days later at 5.00pm on the afternoon of Thursday 5 October. On that night they went to see a film at the Gaumont Cinema, Hammersmith, coming out at 8.30pm. They were going to a cafe on the Hammersmith Broadway but just as they got to the door the air raid sirens sounded so they sheltered inside and had something to eat. Three quarters of an hour later, when some couples might

---

3. CRIM 1/482

have thought they would go for a romantic walk by the river, this pair thought: 'We'll go and do another job.'[4]

Back in the 6x6 US Army lorry, they drove to Reading. Karl suggested breaking in to the White Hart Hotel to see if he could steal their takings but when they pulled up outside they both got jittery and thought they were being watched. They drove away and retuned to London by a different road, heading for the West End and then to Marble Arch.

In their statements, Karl and Betty each claim it was the other who suggested they should rob a taxi. They both agree Karl was driving; he followed the taxi for about ten minutes until they reached Cricklewood where it stopped and dropped off the passenger. Karl stopped the lorry about 400 yards behind, then the taxi turned round and passed them. Karl quickly turned his lorry around and followed the cab for another ten minutes until they were passing through a quiet and isolated area. Karl overtook and turned in front of the taxi, forcing it to stop. In his statement, he explained what happened next:

> I jumped out of the cab and pointed my gun at the driver and said 'Let me have your money.' He told me that he had just come out and that he didn't have any. I then noticed a man in a brown raincoat in the back seat. I ran back and got into the truck and drove away.[5]

Betty stated that the taxi followed them, but they managed to lose it and headed back to Marble Arch. According to Karl:

> I was driving on Edgeware Road and Georgina said, 'There is a girl, stop.' I had driven past the girl. I backed the truck up to where the girls was. I asked her where she was going and she said she was going to Paddington to catch a train. She said that she wanted to go to Bristol. I told her that I was going to Reading and that I would take her to Reading to catch her train. She agreed. She was carrying a brown suitcase tied with a rope.[6]

Karl claimed she gave him her case, he put it in the back of the truck, she got in the front sitting between him and Betty, and they drove to Windsor. As they were passing through Runnymede Park,

---

4. Crim 1/482 Statement of Elizabeth Jones 11 October 1944
5. Crim 1/482 Statement of Karl Hulten 12 October 1944
6. *Ibid*

Marble Arch and Oxford Street, one of the places Hulten and Jones cruised as they went in search of victims

Violet May Hodge, survivor of a callous attack by Hulten and Jones

he stopped the truck and informed Betty and their passenger that he had a flat tyre. Karl then asked Betty to ensure the girl had her back towards him. His statement continued:

> Georgina [Betty] gave the girl a cigarette and lit one for herself. Georgina told me that she thought the girl was wise. I told Georgina to get up in the back of the truck to see if she could set some blocks.

> When Georgina got up into the truck I hit the girl over the head with an iron bar which I had taken from the truck. The girl did not fall down. I grabbed her round the neck and we went down on the ground. She fell on her stomach and I knelt on the middle of her back. I had a headlock on her neck. The girl was waving her right arm around and I told Georgina to hold her arm. Georgina knelt on her right arm and went through her coat pockets. As I recall she had about five shillings.
>
> By this time the girl had ceased struggling. I picked up her shoulders and Georgina picked up her feet. We carried her over and dumped her about three feet from the edge of the stream.[7]

Betty's account of the attack in her statement is even more chilling. The woman they had picked up had heard Karl call Betty 'Georgie' and as he began to attack her, she pleaded directly with Betty saying, 'Georgie don't let him do it.' Betty got out of the cab and according to her statement:

> I saw he was attacking her and she yelled again, 'Stop him'. They were right beside me and Ricky [Karl] asked me to help him. Ricky got her down on the ground and I held her legs ... Ricky then put his hands around her neck and I thought he was strangling her. She made a gurgling noise and I saw blood coming from her mouth and her head was bleeding. She was struggling and Ricky tightened his grip around her throat. I still held on to her legs and Ricky took hold of her throat for about ten minutes before she became limp. I thought she was dead then.[8]

Betty also admitted helping Karl carry the woman to the stream when he said he was going to throw her in. In her statement she claimed: 'I told Ricky not to throw her in so we left her there... . We then made sure there was nothing lying on the ground and drove away.'[9]

Incredibly, the woman they had attacked – Violet Hodge (18) – survived. She was adamant that she had not been left by the side, but had been thrown into the water.[10]

After their attack on Miss Hodge, they drove back to Betty's bedsit on King Street. He dropped Betty at the door, carried up Violet's suitcase which had been stored in the back of the truck, and then parked the lorry at Ravenscourt Park. Once inside, they

---

7. Crim 1/482 Hulten
8. Crim 1/482 Jones
9. *Ibid*
10. *Western Daily Press* 16 December 1944

eagerly went through the contents of the suitcase, and Betty also had a look through Violet's handbag, which she had left on the seat of the cab of the truck. Karl had already gone through the bag but after finding only photographs and papers, had thrown them out of the truck window as they drove along. It was only after they got into the light at Betty's bedsit that Betty kept the bag. It was only when they got into the light of the bedsit that they noticed there were large patches of blood on Karl's clothes. His only reaction to this was to say to Betty, 'You will have to get my valise tomorrow' so he could get some clean clothes. With that they went to bed.[11]

The couple stayed in bed until 2.50pm on Friday 6 October. When they got up Karl gave Betty a luggage ticket and she picked up his valise (a B4 bag in the name of Werner J. Meier) from Hammersmith Metropolitan Station. Once she returned with the case, Karl changed into a pair of clean green officer's trousers from the valise and put the bloodstained 'pinks' back in their place. Karl said he was going to get rid of them but Betty said she would sponge them out and take them to a cleaners.[12] Karl then went out about 4.30pm; he apparently did not tell Betty where he was going but said he would be back about 6.00pm. He actually went to visit his regular girlfriend Joyce Cook. When he did not show up at 6.00pm, Betty decided to wait for him. Sure enough, at 11.30pm she heard Karl's whistle from the street. She went down to the street and Karl said, 'Come on let's go and get a taxi.' Betty freely admitted:

> I knew the meaning behind his words and that he wanted me to go with him to rob a taxi cab driver.
> We walked along Hammersmith Road and stood in a shop doorway opposite Cadby Hall. After about ten minutes a grey Ford car approached us very slowly like a taxi cab, it was coming from the direction of Hammersmith Broadway. I yelled 'Taxi' and it stopped. Ricky thought it was a Naval car and stopped in the shop doorway while I went over to speak to the driver. I said, 'Are you a taxi?' and he said, 'Private hire, where do you want to go?' I replied, 'Wait a minute' and went back to Ricky. I told him it was a private car and he asked how many men were in it. I told him only the driver so we went across to the car and Ricky asked the driver to take us to the top of King Street ... the driver told Ricky that the fare would be ten shillings and Ricky said, 'That's all right.'[13]

---

11. Crim 1/482 Jones
12. Crim 1/482 Hulten
13. Crim 1/482 Jones

Karl told the driver he wanted to go just beyond the roundabout
at the Hammersmith end of the Great West Road and explained
what happened next in his statement:

> When we got to the roundabout I took my pistol [a standard US
> Army .45 Remington Automatic]. Just as the car was coming to
> a stop I pulled the slide back and cocked the pistol ... . It was
> about 0100 hours when we got into the car and it must have
> been about 0115 hours[14] when I told the driver to stop. When
> the car stopped I was holding my loaded and cocked pistol in
> front of my chest. When the car stopped I looked over toward
> Georgina. As I was looking back toward the front again I pulled
> the trigger, just as I pulled the trigger the driver, who I later
> learned to be George Heath, raised up and reached over the
> back set to open the left rear door. He was reaching back with
> his left arm. When I pulled the trigger I intended to pull the
> trigger and fire the pistol. I intended to fire the pistol through
> the car but I did not expect George Heath to raise up to open
> the door just as I did it.[15]

George Heath, the rugged taxi driver with the cleft chin

---

14. Crim 1/482 Bill Hollis, nightwatchman at the nearby Hudson car depot
    in Chiswick, would testify that he heard a muffled gunshot coming from the
    London end of the bypass at 2.30am on the morning of Saturday 7 October
15. Crim 1/482 Hulten

Heath slumped to the side. Karl got behind the steering wheel and told Betty to search Heath for his wallet. After a couple of minutes Karl drove away and, after they had been travelling for a short while, he told her to take everything out of Heath's pockets.

Betty said she found Heath's wallet containing four pound notes on the left-hand outside pocket of his overcoat. She also found his identity card from which she learned his name and address, as well as a cheque book, driving licence, personal photographs and letters. Betty continued:

> From his trousers I took a pound in silver and a few pennies which I put in my pocket. From other pockets I took a big brown fountain pen, a silver pencil, a long silver cigarette case which had a funny sliding action to open ...[and] an expensive looking cigarette lighter with a snap down action. I put all these in my pocket. Ricky then asked me if Heath had a watch and I found a wrist watch on Heath's left wrist and I gave it to Ricky. I think I took everything from his pockets. All this time Ricky was driving fast along the road and I sat back examining the things I had taken from Heath's pockets.[16]

They then drove to Staines, Middlesex, and about a mile past the police station Karl turned off to the left, onto a dirt road, and after a short distance pulled the car onto the grass of Knowle Green, which Betty thought looked like 'a sort of common'. There were only a few houses nearby, certainly nothing too close to where they had stopped, and the place was cloaked in darkness. If Karl or Betty knew the area, or if it was a lonely spot selected at random, was not clarified in their statements. It was probably the latter as nether mentioned the place by name.

Betty had admitted to helping Karl move what they assumed was the dead body of Violet Hodge to the bank of the River Thames at Runnymede by carrying her legs. However, both were reticent to admit that they actually threw her in. When it came to the disposal of Heath's body, Betty distanced herself further again, stating, 'He got out and dragged Heath's body from the car and rolled it into a ditch.'[17]

At Betty and Karl's trial, PC Thomas Walton, who had examined and recorded the crime scene, was asked specifically if there had been any indication of Heath's body having been

---

16. Crim 1/482 Jones
17. *Ibid*

dragged to the ditch. PC Walton was clear in his reply – there were no drag marks.[18]

Karl was probably more realistic in his statement:

> I got out and walked around the rear of the car. Georgie got out on the right side of the car and walked round to the front of the car. I opened the left front door and put my arms through his [Heath's] armpits. I raised him up and pulled him out of the car. His feet dropped to the ground. Georgie picked up his feet and we carried him to a ditch [that] was about three feet from the car.[19]

Karl then span the car round and back onto the road, bumping over the grass as he did so, and drove back to Hammersmith, looking at the things they had taken from Heath's body along the way and throwing things they did not want, such as photographs from his wallet, out of the window. They parked up at the Old Gaumont, went to have something to eat at the Black and White Cafe on Hammersmith Broadway, and walked back to Betty's bedsit where they spent the night together.

Neither seemed unduly worried about the body being discovered. George Heath was found later that same morning. Auxiliary fireman Robert Balding, a lending-library librarian who was attached to the NFS at the Ship Garage on London Road in Staines, came off duty at 9.00am and was walking home across Knowle Green when he spotted the body of a man lying in a ditch. Mr Bolding had wondered if the man was drunk or needed medical assistance so he bent down, shook him and looked at his face. The man was clearly dead and he immediately fetched the police.

Once the scene had been recorded, Heath's body was removed to Feltham Mortuary where it was formally identified by Winifred Heath as that of her husband George Edward Heath (34) of 5 Hards Cottages, West Street, Ewell, Surrey. They had one son. George Heath was a former member of the Metropolitan Police War Reserve and had worked as a chauffeur for the well-known firm, Messrs Godfrey Davis Ltd in the West End. More recently he had worked as a self-employed private hire car driver. A post-mortem examination was carried out by Harley Street pathologist Dr Robert Teare, who recorded his findings as follows:

---

18. Bechhofer Roberts C. E. (ed.), *The Trial of Jones and Hulten* (London 1945)
19. Crim 1/482 Hulten

I found the entrance wound of a bullet on his back, one inch to the right of the mid-line level with the sixth rib. I found the exit wound on the front of the chest an inch and three quarters from the mid line and the level of the right third rib. It had perforated the spinal canal and damaged the lung. He would have been paralysed within half a minute at the most. He would have lived 15 minutes at the most after the injury.[20]

Heath's wife pointed out he would have been driving his Ford V8 saloon car, and a police search for the vehicle was rapidly underway.[21]

Meanwhile, it was Saturday and Karl and Betty were going to enjoy some of their ill-gotten gains. Karl sold Heath's watch and lighter and used the proceeds to take Betty to the dog races at White City. They won £7 and then went to see Deanna Durbin and Gene Kelly in *Christmas Holiday*. Unfortunately, they weren't allowed to spend the night together as Betty's landlady, Mrs Evans, was going to be in all day Sunday. He would have to get a hotel room – at least that is what Betty assumed. Chances are, he made a beeline to his regular girlfriend Joyce Cook.

On Sunday night Karl was back and he and Betty went out. This time he said, 'We'll go see if we can find a girl', meaning go find a girl to rob. He tried a run over to Reading but drew a blank and decided to try the West End. While driving around Piccadilly, a prostitute wearing a fur coat caught his eye. Turning to Betty he said, 'I'll get the girl and get the coat.' But a policeman was standing nearby and Karl thought better of that plan, at least for the moment, and carried on driving, even giving some soldiers a lift during the night. He and Betty had a meal at a cafe on Wood Lane, Shepherd's Bush at 7.00am on Monday 9 October, then went back and slept at her room until 1.40pm when Karl got up and went out. He drove over to Joyce Cook's place at 159 Fulham Palace Road.

George Heath's murder was now featuring in the local and national press. Photographs of him showed a ruggedly handsome man with a cleft chin. The name stuck and the case was soon dubbed 'The Cleft Chin Murder'. Throughout the press coverage, there was no mention of Heath's missing car so Karl was convinced detectives weren't looking for it. He was wrong – the make of the car, and its registration plate RD 8955, had been widely circulated to policemen on their beats and motor patrols.

20. Crim 1/482 Statement of Dr Robert Teare
21. Crim 1/452

Police officers removing George Heath's Ford V8 saloon from Lurgan Avenue, Hammersmith

Karl parked the Ford V8 on Lurgan Avenue, which runs behind Fulham Palace Road, and it was here, at 8.10pm, that the car was spotted by PC 579 William Waters of F Division. Waters used a nearby police box to notify his station immediately and DI Percy Read and Sergeant Dowell soon joined him, keeping watch to see if the driver returned. Their patience was rewarded at about 9.00pm when Karl emerged and got behind the wheel. Police officers moved in. Sergeant Dowell dragged Karl out of the car and stood him up facing the wall. He was searched and a loaded Remington automatic pistol, with the safety off, was recovered, along with a magazine containing six rounds of ammunition.

Karl Hulten was taken to Hammersmith Police Station where he initially gave his rank and name as Second Lieutenant Richard John Allen, but eventually admitted he was Pte Karl Gustav Hulten. Betty Jones was picked up soon afterwards and would initially provide Karl with the alibi that he had been with her, in her room, all night on the night of the Heath murder.

It had been a gruelling experience for Betty, who popped into a cleaners on Hammersmith Broadway shortly after leaving the police station on 11 October having given her first statement. There she bumped into Henry Kimberley, a WRPC she had known as a customer when she had been a waitress at Paul's Cafe on King Street, Hammersmith. Kimberley had not seen her for a couple of years since she left the cafe and she had changed quite a bit since then. Enquiring how she was, she told him she had just been in the police station regarding this murder, held up a newspaper and pointed to an article about Heath.

Kimberley asked her what she had to worry about and she said, 'I know the man they have got inside, but it would have been impossible for him to do it as he was with me all Friday night.' Kimberley tried to change the subject, saying she looked tired, but Betty replied, 'If you had seen someone do what I have seen done you wouldn't be able to sleep at night.'[22] At this point the constable was convinced that she had valuable information about the murder and contacted DI Tansill, who had taken her statement hours earlier. They went straight to see Betty at her bedsit. She was surprised to see them but soon admitted that she had lied in her statement and said she would now like to tell the whole truth. She agreed to return to the police station where she told them her version of events in remarkable detail.

Confronted with what Betty said in her new statement, Karl gave his version of events the following day. They are both remarkable documents, not just because of the frankness and detail in their accounts but because they also provide a fascinating insight into their psychology.

At no point did Betty do a single thing to help Violet Hodge when she was being attacked. In fact, she confessed that she had helped to restrain her and watched as Karl strangled her. In their statements, neither Betty nor Hulten ever showed sympathy for their victims nor any remorse for their actions. What little shock was expressed came from Betty, and it appeared to be something of an afterthought, expressed in words akin to dialogue she had lifted from gangster films of the time. She did not scream, sob or appear shocked when she described the shooting of taxi driver George Heath. She had no compunction about going through Heath's pockets, and even seemed to express satisfaction as she sat back in her seat looking at the items she had just taken from the pockets of a man who had been shot and lay dying, or dead, directly in front of her. Only at the end of the night, when she was back inside her bedsit with Karl, did Betty claim the following conversation took place:

> I said, 'He's dead isn't he?' and he said 'Yes'. I said, 'That's cold blooded murder then, how could you do it?' and he said, 'People in my profession haven't the time to think what they do.' Indoors we examined all of Heath's things we had taken. Then we went to bed.[23]

---

22. Bechhofer Roberts, *Trial of Jones and Hulten*
23. Crim 1/482 Jones

At the time the case generated much debate in the press about 'delinquent girls'. Betty was described as 'impressionable', and she most certainly was, but the question remains to what degree? It is highly probable that if she had never met Karl, she would never have embarked on this murder spree on her own. However, her statements failed to convince that her time with Karl was spent under duress.

Such callous behaviour committed by couples is rarely recorded so candidly in statements. Usually, one suspect will blame the other in an attempt to exonerate themselves. Betty came in very late to make such allegations. It was late October 1944, while she was on remand at Holloway Prison, that she first wrote a letter to DDI Wilfred Tarr, the officer in charge of the case, requesting a visit. Tarr duly came and conducted an interview during which Betty claimed, for the first time, that she had been terrified into acting as she had because she had been threatened by Karl Hulten.[24] Acting under duress would become the mainstay of her defence at their joint trial, which opened on 16 January 1945. The judge, Mr Justice Charles sought to clarify why she had left it so late to make that claim:

> Judge: 'Now the greater part of your evidence is that step by step you were terrified, dazed, frightened, ordered to do this, ordered to do that. Why didn't you say a word of that to the police?'
>
> Jones: 'Because I didn't think it concerned me, that I would be drawn into it.'
>
> Judge: 'You didn't think it concerned you? Why do you think it concerns you today?'
>
> Jones: 'Because it has all been explained to me now.'[25]

Whether it had been explained to her by a fellow prisoner, or her defence team, did not need to be asked. Betty had lost much of her credibility. The newspaper stories of the striptease dancer and the 'gangster' captivated the attention of the British public as each new witness let loose their revelations.

What is not generally realised is that the trial focused on the murder of George Heath. Legal counsel had agreed to concentrate

---

24. Bechhofer Roberts, *Trial of Jones and Hulten*
25. *Ibid*

on that one charge, and accounts of the earlier incidents were not presented to the court.

Looking at the case files, comparing the statements of Betty and Karl, and considering the chain of events, the dynamic between the pair fits the profile of a killer couple. Joint culpability of this nature is very rare, but it has been seen in more recent cases such as in the 'Moors Murderers' Ian Brady and Myra Hindley, and Fred and Rose West.

On 23 January 1945, the jury of nine men and three women retired to deliberate. One hour and fifteen minutes later they returned a verdict that found both defendants guilty of murder, but recommended mercy be shown in the case of Betty Jones. Neither Betty nor Karl responded when asked if they had anything to say before sentence was passed. Mr Justice Charles then donned the black cap and pronounced the sentence of death on them both. Karl Hulten remained impassive. Betty Jones clutched a small white handkerchief. She looked broken as she sobbed and was on the point of collapse when she was taken down, and had to be assisted from the dock. Both of them immediately appealed against their sentences.

The British public were rarely keen to see a woman sent to the gallows, especially in the more enlightened years of the mid-twentieth century. Many people were also clearly moved by Betty Jones's youth – she was still only 18. The 'gunman's moll' story certainly suggested a young, pretty and impetuous young girl being led astray by a hardened gangster. The matter was also discussed in the House of Commons. Since 1900, the sentence of death had been carried out on twenty-eight people under the age of 21 and not one of them was a woman. Elizabeth Jones was granted a reprieve and her death sentence was commuted to one of imprisonment.

George Orwell would comment in his essay 'Decline of the English Murder', published in February 1946:

> Considering that only ten women have been hanged in Britain this century, and that the practice has gone out largely because of popular feeling against it, it is difficult not to feel that this clamour to hang an eighteen-year-old girl was due partly to the brutalising effects of war.[26]

---

26. Orwell, George, 'Decline of the English Murder' published in *Tribune* 15 February 1946

Because Jones was under 21, she began her sentence in Aylesbury Borstal and was released in 1954 after serving nine years.

Karl Hulten's appeal was turned down. Despite a personal visit from the American Ambassador to the Home Secretary Herbert Morrison to try and persuade him to grant a reprieve, Karl Hulten was hanged just five days after his twenty-third birthday by Albert Pierrepoint at Pentonville on 8 March 1945.

Interest in the case lingered for a long time, and the morbid curiosity of the general public saw Heath's Ford V8, in which he was murdered, put on display, doing the rounds at fairgrounds. In 1989, the film *Chicago Joe and the Showgirl* starring Kiefer Sutherland as Karl Hulten and Emily Lloyd as Betty Jones brought the story to a new generation.

The tragic postscript to the story is that of Violet May Hodge, the young Bristol woman so callously attacked and thrown in the river by Karl and Betty, and who was so fortunate to survive. She was, unsurprisingly, left a changed woman. To add insult to injury she was barred from her local pubs because of her association with the case. Violet went to demand an explanation from one of the licensees at one of the premises on Bridewell Street in Bristol. A row erupted, police were called, she bit a policeman's hand after he asked her to go away quietly and it took three people to restrain her. Brought before Bristol Police Court in December 1944, Violet Hodge was found guilty of disorderly conduct and assaulting the police, was fined three pounds and was bound over to keep the peace for a year.[27]

She would be back in court in January 1946 for assaulting a policewoman under similar circumstances. When she was brought before the magistrates she said: 'You are picking on me all the time just because I was in the Cleft Chin case. I'll show you what I think of you', and with that she hurled one of her shoes at the bench. Fortunately, the shoe missed the court clerk and the magistrates. Miss Hodge was remanded and the medical officer was asked to give a report on her mental stability. She failed to appear for the second court hearing and a warrant was issued for her arrest. She arrived late claiming she had been delayed, was arrested on arrival and informed she would be remanded in custody until the following day. She was taken down from the dock kicking and struggling by three police officers and two policewomen.[28]

---

27. *Western Daily Press* 16 December 1944
28. *Western Daily Press* 24 January 1946

In 1947, Violet Hodge was back in Bristol Magistrates' Court again. She had broken the terms of her probation, which had been imposed after the two previous offences, because she had failed to notify the authorities of her change of address from Bristol to London. She said this was simply because she had been trying to make a fresh start and did not want her new friends to know about her past issues. She was sent to prison for two months. Perhaps with some irony, underneath the report on her imprisonment was published in *The Western News* was this quote from Psalm 32: 'Blessed is he whose transgressions are forgiven, whose sins are covered.' [29] I sincerely hope that one day Violet Hodge got the help and care she so clearly needed.

---

29. *Western Daily Press* 28 April 1947

CHAPTER 9

The Colne Strangler
(Colne, Lancashire 1941 and
Ellough, Suffolk 1944)

The Moving Finger writes; and, having writ, Moves on: nor all thy Piety nor Wit Shall lure it back to cancel half a Line, Nor all thy Tears wash out a Word of it.
Rubáiyát of Omar Khayyám translated by Edward FitzGerald

During the Second World War there was no national police database of unsolved crimes, forensic technology was quite basic when compared to what is available today and DNA testing was decades in the future.[1] The pressures of wartime crime stretched CID and police to the limit. The huge numbers of troops and transient people around the country – be they refugees or those bombed out from their homes – and the limited communications between police forces across the country meant it was highly likely predatorial murderers, and even serial killers, were operating in Britain over the war years and remain undetected to this day. Some may well be revealed over years to come. The frustration is that many items of evidence collected for the cases at the time, which may have proved a vital clue if they could only have been tested for DNA, have been lost, destroyed or contaminated over the eight decades since the murders took place.

Modern researchers of crimes committed during the Second World War also have to face the fact that many of the suspects, and those involved in the cases as witnesses and investigating officers, are now dead. Any links between murders committed with a similar *modus operandi* in different parts of the country, after all these years, tend to be very hard to prove conclusively. But occasionally there are historic cases that press the question, is there a connection or is it just a coincidence? The case of the Colne strangler is one of those cases.

---

1. The first person to be convicted of murder on the basis of DNA evidence was Colin Pitchfork in 1988.

In March 1941, a number of lone women on public roads in the Colne area of Lancashire were stalked and attacked by an unidentified male assailant during the blackouts. The hallmark of the attacker was that he suddenly grabbed them by the throat. Most of the women he assaulted did not immediately report the matter to the police or, if they did, were apparently not taken seriously. Reports were not published in newspapers, women were not put on their guard and the violence used in the attacks escalated. At around 9.15pm on Monday, 24 March 1941, domestic servant Teresa Baldwin (16) was walking back from work to her home at 3 Reedley Road, Burnley. Her journey took her along the leafy and quiet Reedley Drive and it was here a man suddenly came out of the shadows and attacked her. She had to fight for her life to escape her assailant and reported the attack to the police.

It is not clear exactly what the police did after this attack was reported to them; there was no mention of it in the newspapers the following day, or even in the local evening papers on the dark, wet night of Tuesday, 25 March.

Let us pay a brief visit to the village of Trawden, in the Pendle district of Lancashire, just a few miles from Colne. It was a village like many others in the industrial north at that time, where most residents lived in rows of small slate-roofed terraced houses and cheek-by-jowl cottages built from the large cut blocks of local stone. Most folks living in the village had grown up in the village, were employed in the local mills, socialised together and tended to know each other, at least by sight.

The industrial village of Trawden, near Colne. Lancashire, home of Eileen Barrett

They spent their evenings as members of local groups such as the St John Ambulance Brigade, Civil Defence, Home Guard, Scouts or Guides, especially because these groups were needed for wartime duties. They went down the pub to meet up with friends and take part in darts competitions, they tended their allotments, and they relaxed at home with their families listening to the radio. Come the weekend they attended local sports matches and, for a night out, they might catch a bus to Colne to 'go to the pictures' and see what was on at the cinema. Many still went to church or chapel on a Sunday.

One of the young stalwarts of the church community of St Mary the Virgin in Trawden was Eileen Barrett (19). The only daughter of volunteer ambulanceman Allan Barrett, manager of the Ceresco poultry food business in Swan Croft, Colne, and housewife mum Ida, Eileen was the older sister of Colin, a schoolboy at Clitheroe Grammar School. They all lived together in Back Side Farm Cottage with Ida's mum, dear old Granny Caffrey, round the corner at Proctor Croft.

Eileen had worked hard at school and progressed to Colne Grammar School and Alston's College in Burnley. After she left college, she worked as a cashier-secretary at the Royal Insurance Company on Grimshaw Street. She loved sports and outdoor activities; she played for a girl's hockey team, was an officer in the Girl Guide troop attached to St Mary's, and a group fire watcher in the village. Intending to volunteer to do something more for the war effort, under the National Service scheme, she had recently resigned as secretary of the parochial church council. She was the sort of daughter any parents could be proud of. She had boyfriends, but nothing too serious, and her life revolved around the church. Eileen may appear to our modern eyes to have been living rather a staid life but values were different then and, for many, the life she was living was one to aspire to, and worthy of respect in working-class communities in the 1940s. Eileen was a tall and attractive young woman who dressed smartly, but not decadently, and was intelligent and charming. Known for her bright outlook on life, she was well-known and well liked in Trawden.[2]

Eileen did not go out at night very often unless it was to attend the groups or social activities connected with the church or Civil Defence work. However, with wartime shortages becoming more acute by the month, she wanted to learn how to make her own clothes so she had enrolled in evening classes at the Technical

2. *Nelson Leader* 28 March 1941

Eileen Barrett

School in Colne. Looking outside at the grotty weather on that March night she told her mother she didn't feel like going, but she had been working so hard on the party frock she had been making during the course, and it was the last night of term. She was also due to sit an exam the following Saturday, so she decided to go. She picked up her attaché case containing the dress, told her mum she would not be late back and off she went. She left the cottage to catch the bus at 6.40pm that would get her to Colne in time for the 7.00pm start of her class. Once she arrived at Colne, her bus stop was on the corner of Linden Road and Albert Road, only about 30 yards from the entrance of the Technical School.

Eileen's class ended at shortly after 9.00pm and her classmates dispersed into the blackout on that dark, rainy night soon afterwards. Elizabeth Kelsall of Birchenlee Farm, Colne, had been at the class with Eileen. Leaving the classroom shortly after her, she remembered seeing Eileen standing alone at the bus stop. Local man Robert Duerden was walking up Albert Road that night. At approximately 9.20pm, when he was about 10ft past the bus stop, he heard a woman's scream coming from behind him. He stood for a second or two then shouted, 'Are you all right?' but could not see anybody. He went to where the scream had come from and found Eileen standing under the street lamp near the bus stop.

Albert Road, Colne. The bus stop on Linden Road corner where
Eileen Barrett was fatally stabbed is on the left of the bus on the
photograph

George Keith, the newly appointed Colne postmaster, had
been sheltering in a shop doorway as he waited for his bus when
he heard the scream. He also came running over and arrived as
Mr Duerden was asking her what was the matter. Clearly shaken
by what had happened to her she replied, 'I have been hit in the
back by a man whilst I was waiting for a bus. He got hold of my
throat.' Looking around to see if he could spot her assailant,
Mr Keith spotted 'the fleeting figure' of a man running away
down Linden Road and into the dark wet night.

Clearly frightened by the experience and undoubtedly in
shock, Eileen said she had felt something pierce her back but did
not think she had been seriously injured, just hurt by the blow,
so she continued to board her bus along with Mr Duerden and
Mr Keith who were also making for the Yorkshire side of town.
They travelled with her to the Heifer Lane bus depot. During the
journey she told George Keith she did not know the man who
had attacked her. He recalled that Eileen kept moaning while she
was on the bus but he attributed this to the pain of the blow she
had been delivered. When they arrived at the bus depot there was
more light and he could see she was looking very pale. It was only
when he put his arm around her to assist her from the bus that
he noticed her clothes were saturated with blood and it appeared
that she had been stabbed in the back.

An ambulance was summoned to the depot and she was rushed to Hartley Hospital. On arrival, she was still conscious. She took some brandy, thanked the men who had assisted her then lost consciousness and died from an internal haemorrhage just minutes later.

Detective Sergeant Noel Stirzaker stated at the inquest that he had received information at 10.00pm that a girl had been stabbed in the back and had been taken to Hartley Hospital. By the time he arrived at 10.20pm she was already dead. He examined the body and found a wound in her back near her right shoulder blade. Stirzaker then took possession of the girl's clothing, most of which was stained with blood. Upon examination of her coat, costume jacket and woollen jumper, Stirzaker also found cuts that coincided with the position of the wound in the shoulder. At 10.30pm, Eileen's father was notified by a police officer that his daughter had died, and he was taken to Hartley Hospital where he formally identified her body.

DCS Peter Gregson Head of Lancashire Constabulary CID was put in charge of the investigation. Working with DCI John Woodmansey, the pair were soon on the spot where the attack took place. They were later joined by members of the staff of the North Western Forensic Science Laboratory. Police searched for the assailant and the weapon through the night to no avail.

The official announcement of Eileen's murder was made on 25 March. The Chief Constable of Lancashire, Captain Archibald F. Hordern, spoke to reporters at Nelson Police Station about what they had managed to ascertain about Eileen's murder and revealed that a similar incident had occurred about the same time on Sunday, 23 March, just two days earlier, a few miles away at Reedley. Police were concerned that these crimes were committed by the same man. The difference was that this woman had escaped. To ensure she remained safe Hordern did not name the victim (Teresa Ann Baldwin), only describing her as a domestic servant. Hordern explained that she was walking home along Reedley Drive when she had been grabbed by the throat by a man who threatened to kill her. She had fought hard and after a violent struggle had managed to get away. If they managed to catch Eileen's killer there was a chance Teresa Baldwin could identify him.

While careful to play down the suggestion of a serial attacker, in order to avoid panic, press reports stated that it was possible the attack and murder 'could be the work of a maniac'.[3]

---

3. *Nelson Leader* 28 March 1941

A further witness soon came forward. One of the masters at the Technical School had noticed a man standing in the main exit at the time the evening classes ended on the night Eileen was murdered. He noticed him because he had turned away, as if to shield his face, as the teacher walked out the door. His description of the man was released to the press as a man they wished to talk to. He was described as 'Aged about 28, 5 ft. 7 in. to 5 ft. 9 in.; medium build; wearing a Trilby hat and a fawn raincoat.'

Another witness, a female employee of the Co-operative Society, also came forward to tell police that when she was passing the doorway of the Co-op nearest Linden Road, at between 9.15pm and 9.20pm on the night of the murder, a man had said 'goodnight' to her. He was in the shadows so all she could see was that he was wearing a light raincoat. When she passed by again, two or three minutes later, he repeated his remark.[4] Other witnesses had also seen the man running towards Linden Road from Albert Road at the time of the crime. A description of this man was published in the press as 'Aged 35 or 40 years, about 5ft 7 inches tall, broad build, round face, wearing a dark cap and dark overcoat with big collar and white scarf, prominent teeth.'[5]

Despite continued police appeals neither man ever came forward, nor was either man positively identified. Despite a thorough police search, including the dragging of Vivary Bridge Mill dam and a search of the sludge, no murder weapon was found. A post-mortem examination of Eileen, conducted by Blackburn pathologist Dr Bailey, revealed she had been killed by a knife with a doubled-edged blade about 5 ins long and ½ in wide, with a very sharp point.

Over the days and weeks that followed, hundreds of people were interviewed by the police and some women told stories of having been followed by a suspicious man. A few even claimed he had seized hold of them, but the police stated in the press that 'close enquiry into such statements had shown little to substantiate them.'[6]

The local newspapers covering Eileen Barrett's funeral on Saturday, 29 March 1941, spoke of Trawden being 'a village in mourning'. Local people lined the route, standing in silence as the cortege made its way through the streets to the church. Inside were her family, friends and a congregation of people from across the

---

4. *Burnley Express* 30 April 1941
5. *Nelson Leader* 10 April 1941
6. *Burnley Express* 2 April 1941

area. Among those paying their respects were representatives of the various churches, community groups and organisations Eileen had been connected with, and the schools she had attended. Many wept openly. There were more than seventy wreaths, including one from Teresa Baldwin. The long-serving and well-loved vicar, Reverend Canon Hugh Dempsey, conducted the service and the last rites at the graveside as Eileen was buried in the churchyard of St Mary, the church that had played such a big part in her life. Canon Dempsey never spoke a truer word than when he said of Eileen that day, 'A beloved soul had been taken from our midst.'[7]

When the inquest was reconvened, tributes were paid to the 'extensive, exhaustive and intelligent' enquiries conducted by the police, including the tracing and interviewing of more than 200 people who had attended the Co-operative whist drive and dance held in the municipal hall on the night of the murder, especially those who had parked their cars down the side of Linden Road. By the time the inquest was over, 5,000 people had been interviewed and statements had been taken from 574. But it seemed the darkness of the night and the blackout on the night of the murder, combined with the lack of any motive, saw their investigations lead nowhere. The jury returned a verdict of 'Wilful murder by person or persons unknown'. In his summing up, coroner F. Rowland described it as a brutal crime and sincerely hoped the murderer would be brought to justice one day.[8]

Nevertheless, the investigation carried on and newspapers continued to publish renewed appeals for witnesses and information. But as the months passed, leads dried up and eventually the appeals stopped appearing in the papers and police resources had to be directed to new cases.

Over the next half century the murder of Eileen Barrett faded from many memories until it hit the press again in 1996 when an 83-year-old man in a Colne residential home told staff he had been responsible for the murder. The police were informed and DC Ian Gibbs of Colne CID contacted headquarters to consult the case file from half a century before. When Gibbs interviewed the pensioner, he claimed that he had been drunk and wished to retract his confession. There were also inconsistencies between his version of events and the narrative recorded in the case file. A little more research also provided the perfect alibi, the man's wartime army records were accessed from the Ministry of Defence and

---

7. *Nelson Leader* 4 April 1941
8. *Lancashire Evening Post* 24 June 1941

they showed he had actually been posted overseas for the whole of 1941. No further action was taken against the elderly man. But that may not be the end of the story.

Let us now return to the war years and the wintry morning of Thursday, 9 November 1944, when the body of a young WAAF was spotted by Wilfred Payne as he was cycling to work as a stoker along the Ellough Road in Suffolk. She was lying in a ditch on the south side of the road near the junction which borders the concrete road known as Green Lane near the rural village of Ellough. Mr Payne stopped at the main guard house at RAF Beccles and reported what he had seen to the duty corporal, Bethune Darling Riddell. RAF Police Corporal Stockley, who was also present, went straight to where they had been told the body was lying and Corporal Riddell telephoned the East Suffolk Police at Worlingham.

Claude Ernest Fiske, an electrician's mate and special constable from Derby Road, Beccles, was not far behind Wilfred Payne when he was cycling along the Ellough Road at about 8.00am. After spotting the body in the ditch, he stopped, dismounted from his bicycle and went to check for signs of life. The WAAF's uniform appeared to have been disarranged, her buttocks had been exposed and were bloody. Mr Fiske held one of the girls legs to see if there was any sign of life. It was cold and stiff. As he was doing this, RAF Police Corporal Stockley arrived and said he wanted to move the body. Mr Fiske told him to leave the body where it was.

Leaving Corporal Stockley to keep guard over the body, Claude Fiske went to the guard room, spoke to the corporal on duty and asked him to telephone East Suffolk Police at Beccles. PS Hardwicke was rapidly on the scene, closely followed by Inspector William Bryant from Beccles Police Station. It was horribly apparent that the young WAAF had met her death by foul play. Inspector Bryant called Dr Clermont Grantham-Hill to attend and remained at the scene until the doctor, DI George Read and other officers from East Suffolk Constabulary CID arrived and began to document and photograph the scene leaving everything in situ as found. Inspector Read recorded his immediate observations of the body:

> In the ditch I saw the body of a female dressed in the uniform greatcoat of a member of the WAAF. She was obviously dead. The head was bare and the body lay prone – head towards the west – arms stretched down alongside the body. The head was turned slightly to the right and the face rested on some brick rubble which formed a small dam across the ditch. The body and the legs were also straight, the feet being extended and resting

on the ground and about ten to twelve inches apart, the toes
pointing inwards. To the east of the feet, lying in the ditch about
thirty six inches away from the feet, I saw a woollen scarf bag
and 12 inches further east I saw a WAAF cap ... the greatcoat
was disarranged ... both buttocks were exposed and naked ...
the right side of the collar on the body was torn away from the
shirt and lying on the face. The right side of the shirt was open
and the button hole torn. The tie appeared particularly tight
around the neck, the knot being a little right of the midline.[9]

The body was rapidly identified as WAAF Aircraftwoman (ACW)
1st Class Winifred May Evans (27), who was attached to the Air
Sea Rescue Squadron at RAF Beccles. For the police officers
who saw her body it was tragically clear that Winifred had been
subjected to an extremely violent, sexually motivated attack and
murder. Once he had been informed of the serious nature of the
crime, Lieutenant Colonel A. F. Senior, Chief Constable of East
Suffolk Constabulary, wasted no time bringing in Scotland Yard
officers to take charge of the investigation.

The Yard assigned one of its most experienced officers to the
case, the now DS Ted Greeno, who headed for Suffolk immediately,
taking Detective Sergeant Frederick Hodge with him. Home
Office pathologist Dr Keith Simpson had also been called in and
Greeno collected Simpson from his flat on Weymouth Street as the
first snow flurries began to fall. They ended up driving through
the teeth of a blizzard to the rural village of Ellough near Beccles.
By the time they arrived at the murder scene, at around 10.00pm,
the body had been covered with tarpaulin and the whole area was
blanketed with snow.

Keith Simpson recalled how he first saw the body:

> The girl was lying prone, face down, her body and legs straight
> and her arms almost straight by her sides. She had been wearing
> full uniform, including her greatcoat, which together with her
> tunic, shirt and vest, had been drawn up over the back of her
> shoulders, her slacks and knickers, together with suspenders
> and a sanitary pad, had been torn down.[10]

Once Simpson completed his examination at the scene, the body
of ACW Evans was removed to Beccles Hospital mortuary where

---

9. MEPO 3/2282 Statement of DI George Arthur Read
10. Simpson, Keith, *Forty Years of Murder* (London 1978)

he performed the autopsy with his old friend Eric Biddle, the pathologist at East Suffolk and Ipswich Hospital.

After discussing the post-mortem findings with Greeno, they formed a picture of how and when Winifred had been attacked and killed. They narrowed the time of her death to between 12.10am and 12.25am on 9 November 1944. There was no sign of a preliminary struggle, no defensive injuries and no trace of skin under her fingernails from scratching her attacker. Both detective and pathologist agreed Winifred must have been grabbed suddenly and taken by surprise. She tumbled into the ditch, landing on her right-hand side and was then rolled onto her front and her face was pushed so hard into the ditch that her lip split. Her assailant had then jumped on her back so hard he burst her liver and bruised her lungs. He then tore off her clothes and raped her. Simpson noted clear asphyxial haemorrhages on her scalp, face, neck and lungs. Press reports stated that Winifred had been strangled to death with her own neck tie, which had been tied off with a sailor's knot. Her autopsy revealed she had died because her killer had applied such compression on her chest and lungs by violent kneeling upon her and holding her face down forcing it into the mud of the ditch, he had asphyxiated her.

Police tracked down the friends and comrades of ACW Winifred Evans at the Ellough airfield site of RAF Beccles, less than a mile from where her body was found. Those who knew her well called her Winnie, and described her as a nice girl, attractive, softly spoken with fair hair and lovely eyes. She had been serving as a wireless operator in the signals section. She had only been there since October, after being posted from Gosport. For the most part she was quiet and reserved but she was also a very good dancer. Her WAAF pal Florence Cook was asked about Winnie by a reporter and she said, 'She clung on to the sense of right and wrong, things that were done and were not done by which she had been brought up, and if anyone tried to "get fresh" with her she used to slap them.'

Before she had been called up in January 1943, Winnie had been working as a bought ledger clerk at the Victoria Instrument Company in Acton, London, living with her married older sister, Ivy Roberts, and her husband John at 'Rockhurst', Acton Lane, Harlesden. Mrs Roberts was interviewed by a reporter from the *Sunday Pictorial* and said:

> Winnie had not wanted to go into the forces but it was a case of the Services or a factory, and she chose the air force and chose,

as always in her life, to start from scratch with the other girls who would be new as well.[11]

But what many did not realise was that the war years had not been kind to Winnie's family. In 1939 she had been living in Willesden with her parents, William, a housepainter, her housewife mum Eliza, and her twin brothers Lawrence and Leonard. Her mother had died in 1940. Her twin brothers had both joined up as 'sappers' (combat engineers) in the Royal Engineers but Leonard had been killed on active service in the desert in January 1942. Their father died just a few months later in the July. Winnie's family said he died from a broken heart.

On the night of 8 November 1944, Winnie and ten of her pals had been to a dance organised by the American Red Cross USAAF base at Horsham St Faith near Norwich. The night itself had been dark and squally, with a few periods of starlight. Visibility had been down to 10 yards and the journey there and back from the dance through the blackout had been slow. By all accounts, the event itself had been enjoyable. Winnie had spent it in the company of her good friend, WAAF Corporal Margaret Johns, with whom she lived with ten other ACWs in Hut 22 on the WAAF camp of the base. Neither had drunk to excess. They had got back to Beccles at midnight; Winnie changed into her battledress trousers and was on her way to report for night duty at her station headquarters signal office where ACW Marjorie Mellows had agreed to stay on duty so that Winnie could go to the dance. Corporal Margaret Johns was going to the ablutions hut and walked to the main site entrance with Winnie. Margaret asked if she wanted her to see her to the door but Winnie said, 'Oh, it's too late for you to come round with me. I'll hurry along on my own.'[12]

Corporal Johns then went to the ablutions hut, which was located about 80 yards away. She had gone through the outside door and then through the second door, about a yard or so inside, into the main washroom where she heard someone moving about inside. She switched on the light. To her surprise, instead of a WAAF there was a uniformed leading aircraftman (LAC) standing against the wall near the open inner door. Corporal Johns recalled:

He looked at me but said nothing. I then said to him. 'What are you doing here?' He replied. 'Isn't this Number One site?' I said,

11. *Sunday Pictorial* 12 November 1944
12. MEPO 3/2282 Statement of Corporal Margaret Elizabeth Johns

Members of the Women's Auxiliary Air Force and Women's Land Army at a dance on a USAAF base in Suffolk, 1943

'No. It's the WAAF's site on the WAAF site' He then said. 'Well, how do I get to No 1 site then?' I told him to get out and find his own way back. He replied. 'I can't, I am drunk and I can't see. Will you show me the way?' I told him again to go and as he moved from the wall, he staggered. I felt convinced he was drunk and I pushed him along in front of me to the main road.[13]

Corporal Johns had sent him on his way along the main Ellough Road. In the meantime Winnie had found the dark too disorientating and had returned to Hut 22 and was able to borrow a cycle lamp from her friend, Liverpudlian Leading Aircraft woman (LACW) Audrey Shipley. She then hurried off on her way to duty. When Winnie did not arrive at the signals office there was

13. *Ibid*

no undue alarm – they assumed she had got back from the dance and had gone to bed and would sort it out in the morning. When ACW2 Mellows and ACW2 Frances Chitty were released from duty in the signals office later that night, they cycled back to the hut they shared with Winnie and saw she was not in bed. Neither thought they had passed her on the road they had cycled along, so they assumed she had travelled there by another route and they had missed each other. ACW Mellows did, however, say later:

> I saw a light shining about 30 yards along the road in the direction of the spot where the deceased was found. The light was similar to that of a torch and was about 3ft from the ground as if it was being held by someone. I did not pay much attention to it. I only got a fleeting glance of it. I think I said to Chitty, 'I am glad we didn't go round the short way.' [14]

Winnie Evans would have left the camp after going back for the lamp shortly after the LAC had been sent on his way from the ablutions hut by Corporal Johns and the pair would have been on the Ellough Road at the same time. He probably spoke to her suggesting they walked together. He was, after all, in uniform and perhaps he lulled her into a false sense of security as they walked together through the darkness, then suddenly launched his attack at the junction with Green Lane.

DS Greeno wanted to see if Corporal Johns could identify the LAC she had encountered in the ablutions hut. Fate was on his side, and on the afternoon of 10 November there happened to be a pay parade for 280 Squadron where every aircraftman in the local base would be lined up. It was the biggest, and easiest to arrange, line up Greeno had ever had. The payments were made in alphabetical order. It is likely one of the men on parade spotted Corporal Johns, and a plainclothes policemen, and suspected what was going on as he made himself conspicuous by not answering when his name was called for pay and stepping out from the 'H' men. He stood at the back of the room and was paid with the 'R' men instead. Corporal Johns was sure she recognised him as the man she had encountered in the ablutions hut on the night of the murder.

The man in question was LAC Arthur Heys (37) and Greeno had him brought in for questioning at Beccles Police Station immediately after the end of the pay parade. If initial impressions were anything to go by, Heys did not appear a likely murderer, he

---

14. MEPO 3/2282 Statement of ACW Marjorie Joan Mellows

One of the country roadways near Eye in Suffolk

was a family man with sons aged 13 and 11 and a daughter aged 10. His RAF comrades would, however, later comment that when Heys had a few drinks he would easily lose his temper and even become violent. LAC Goddard was among a number of those who had seen this for himself and recalled an incident at RAF Strubby in Lincolnshire when Heys had struck a corporal and would have caused the man some serious injury had he not been stopped. [15]

When asked if he had been in the WAAF washroom, he answered calmly that he wished to counter any claim that he had been inside and said he had been in the doorway of the ablutions hut instead. So, he admitted he had been there. Heys also claimed that he had walked straight back to his camp, keeping to the main road all the way, and had got back to his barrack hut no later than 12.30am.

It is worth noting that Heys was actually billeted on Site 3 – not the Site 1 he was asking directions to – so he had told Corporal Johns a lie that night. He could not excuse the muddle by saying he was drunk, as when he had reported his bicycle stolen around an hour earlier at Beccles Police Station, he had no problem stating his address as Hut 38, Site 3, RAF Camp, Ellough. [16]

15. MEPO 3/2282 Note by Ted Greeno
16. MEPO 3/2282 Statement of Police WRPC Matthew Robert Mason

When Heys' comrades in the barrack hut were asked about his movements on the night of the murder, they were sure he had not arrived back between 1.00 and 1.30am. Apparently LACs Heys, George and Sheratt had cycled to Beccles for a night out, met colleagues from their hut and squadron associates at the Black Boy and the Suffolk pubs and then went to a dance at the Caxton Pavilion Dance Hall near Beccles Railway Station. Heys, who was seen to have drunk nine pints of beer during the course of the evening, was described as being 'merry and having enough to drink'.[17] They said he stayed to the end but disappeared soon after the end of the dance. His pals were all back in the barrack hut they shared by 11.00pm.

Heys could not find the bicycle he had borrowed for the night and wanted to report it stolen. He first encountered WRPC Bertie Moore on town patrol at 10.45pm when he was on duty at the Public Hall Corner on Station Road. Heys told him about the missing bike and Constable Moore directed him to the police station. WRPC Moore saw Heys again when he was on Blyburgate, the road leading out of Beccles towards the RAF camp. Heys was walking up the middle of the road, the rain was pouring down and he asked Moore for directions to the camp. Moore told him the way and recalled later that when he first met Heys he appeared to be the worse for drink but on the latter occasion, when he saw him about 11.20pm, 'his condition had definitely improved, although his breath smelled very strongly of drink.'[18] He walked off, soberly, in the direction Moore had given him. Travelling at a standard walking pace of 3 ½ miles an hour, Heys would have reached the WAAF site in approximately twenty-six minutes.

WRPC Matthew Mason was on duty at Beccles Police Station when Heys was brought in to see Greeno. Mason had taken down details from Heys when he came to report the stolen bicycle. The bike, by the way, was found where Heys had left it, he just could not find it in the blackout. Mason said he hadn't noticed anything untoward on Heys' hands, such as cuts or scratches, when he was taking down the details of the missing bicycle. When he saw Heys' hands again after the pay parade, he noticed they showed fresh scratches. These had not been caused by a human hand, but by the sharp thorn bushes in the ditch where Winifred had been murdered. There was also a fresh tear in his greatcoat, which looked like it might have been caused by

---

17. MEPO 3/2282 Statement of WRPC Bertie Leonard Moore
18. *Ibid*

barbed wire. There was barbed wire near the ditch where the murder took place. Greeno asked Heys to roll up his trousers and he noted there were bruises on his knees and shins. Heys claimed they were old and had been caused by him knocking his legs while at work and playing football.

Greeno instructed another detective to fetch Heys' kit and shoes from his barrack block so they could be examined forensically. Under the instep of one was mud and brick dust, just like the mud from the ditch. On the morning after Heys had come in so late, LAC Redmonds, who slept opposite Heys in the barrack hut, noticed how unusually muddy his shoes were. Other men from his hut also recalled how he had skipped breakfast, preferring to stay and sponge his uniform clean with a wet rag and a towel. Heys then carefully burnt the rag he had used to remove the 'dirt' in the hut stove, which he had lit (this in itself was unusual because station orders forbade the lighting of stoves in huts before 4.00pm) so that he could dry his clothes. Heys' jacket and trousers would still test positive for blood stains but they had been cleaned and proved too weak to enable a blood group to be detected. When asked if he could explain the presence of the blood stains, Heys claimed they had occurred when he had helped a fellow LAC after he came off a bicycle and cut himself, back in October.

Long strands of fair female hair were also found on his trousers, tunic and even on his clothes brush. Professor Simpson examined the hair in detail and compared it with Winnie's. It was a match for colour and length. The hairs even showed they had been freshly waved with curling irons and Winnie was known to have borrowed some tongs to wave her hair before she went to the dance on the night she was killed.

Heys had been on leave shortly before the murder and had gone to visit his family, so perhaps he could argue the hairs on his uniforms had been picked up from his wife. DS Greeno dispatched Inspector George Read of Beccles CID to see Heys' wife and children to interview them and collect hair samples. None of them matched the ones found on Heys. Unfortunately, in 1944, forensic science and technology was just not advanced enough to prove conclusively that any of these clues actually linked Heys to the murder site or to Winnie Evans.

There was also a curious mix of red, brown and yellow brick rubble in the ditch where Winnie had been murdered. Investigating officers checked around the area and around the camps to see if there were similar patches elsewhere, but nothing quite like it could be found. However, this distinctive combination of brick rubble was found on the soles of the shoes worn by Winnie, and on the shoes worn by Heys. Heys' very muddy boots also suggested that rather than walking back to his barrack hut by road like the others, he had crossed the agricultural fields instead.

Heys had certainly given those he shared a hut with pause for thought. When the news of the murder reached the men's camp on 9 November, and the place buzzed with conversation, but he had not joined in. When he was released after his first interview with the police and had returned to his base, he went for a cycle ride with LAC Hunter. Hunter spoke about the police activity in the area as the fields, ditches and dykes were searched. As they cycled past Green Lane, Heys pointed out where the body of the murdered WAAF had been found. This was long before the exact location was made common knowledge.

The combination of witness statements that proved he had lied about the time he had returned to his hut, and the fact he had been caught acting suspiciously in the WAAF camp close to where Winnie had just left, Greeno felt he had enough to arrest Heys for murder and leave it to a jury to decide the matter in court.

Greeno arrested Heys at 10.00am on 5 December 1944 and took him to Beccles Police Station where he informed Heys that he was not satisfied with his story, and that he would be detained in connection with the murder. Greeno recalled that Heys gazed at the floor for at least five minutes and looked as though a shiver had gone through him. Then he said, 'I've been thinking. I can't see what evidence you have to connect me. Can't you tell me.' Greeno said he could not tell him at that stage and he let Heys stew. He was then formally cautioned by Inspector Read, and after another long pause he said, 'I didn't do it.'[19]

Heys appeared before a special magistrates' court at Beccles on 6 December, where he was remanded until 15 December, on which date he was further remanded until 3 January 1945, and held at Norwich Prison pending trial. As the date of the preliminary hearing approached a letter, bearing a Norwich postmark, claiming to come from the real murderer, was received by Heys' commanding officer. Addressed to Officer Commanding Air Sea Rescue Squadron, Beccles, Suffolk, the letter written in blue pencil crayon, in block capital letters, began with a request that the officer passed the letter 'to the solicitors of the airman so wrongly accused of the murder of Winnie Evans.' It went on to claim the unnamed author had arranged to meet Winnie that night, that he had walked

---

19. Greeno, Edward, *War on the Underworld* (John Long 1960)

with her along the lane in the dark and she had told him about the 'drunk airman' in front of them. The letter then rambles on claiming, 'I must have gone mad' and 'I was most indecent.'[20]

Could this letter really have come from another killer and absolve Heys of the crime? No. Investigations uncovered that Heys had managed to smuggle the letter out from Norwich Prison. Apparently, he had been allowed to circulate, work and exercise with other inmates, and he could have passed it to one of the prisoners who was regularly taken by transport provided by the War Agricultural Committee to work on local farms. One of the civilian drivers of the lorries admitted he posted letters given to him by the prisoners.

The letter contained several points that only Winnie's killer would have known. He mentions that she was 'unclean' (menstruating), and that she had been carrying a cycle lamp which he had taken and would never be found. Indeed, it was missing and has never been found. Crucially, he mentions the 'drunk airman' and, as the prosecution would point out in court, only two people were aware of his existence on the WAAF site, Corporal Margaret Johns and Heys himself.

Arthur Heys was tried before Mr Justice Macnaughten at Suffolk Assizes at Bury St Edmunds in a hearing that lasted 22–24 January 1945. The letter was read out in court and was pivotal to the outcome of the case. Despite being written in block capitals, in an attempt to disguise the writer's own handwriting, it was examined by Scotland Yard's fingerprint and handwriting expert Supt Fred Cherrill who compared it with samples of Heys' handwriting. Cherrill identified a number of common characteristics; indeed he would point out in court that characteristics in block letters are even more significant than ordinary handwriting. In the case of Heys, it was the way he formed his capital letter Ps in both letters. Cherrill had no doubt that both letters had been written by Heys.[21] Far from taking himself out of the equation by concocting that letter, Heys may as well have put the hangman's noose around his own neck.

In his summing up, Mr Justice Macnaughten described the murder as 'more savage and horrible than any in my experience of crime'.

The jury took just forty minutes to come to a unanimous verdict of guilty. When asked why sentence of death should not be passed

20. Greeno, *Underworld*
21. *Ibid*

on him Heys replied, 'God knows I am innocent of this foul crime. I know God will look after me. I am not afraid.'[22] Just before he turned round to be taken down, he looked up at the gallery where his wife had sat throughout the trial. She was in floods of tears. Alfred Heys was executed at Norwich Prison by Thomas William Pierrepoint, assisted by Stephen Wade, on Tuesday, 13 March 1945.

ACW 1st Class Winifred May Evans was buried near her remaining family at Willesden New Cemetery and is commemorated with a Commonwealth War Graves Commission headstone. Her killer paid the ultimate penalty for his crime. The attack on Teresa Baldwin and stabbing of Eileen Barrett remain unsolved.

With many county and borough police forces operating in their own bubbles, and with no central police registry of unsolved crimes, many crimes during wartime were put on the back burner if leads ran dry. There was none of the technology we take for granted today: the Police National Computer was still decades away. Even in the 1970s, the amount of card indexes, files and paperwork generated by the Yorkshire Ripper inquiry was so heavy, the upper floor of Millgarth Police Station in Leeds where the incident room was based had to be reinforced after concerns the floor was no longer able to cope with the weight of it all.

The escalation of violence and evolution of method with each attack exhibits a pattern that can be easily recognised from modern profiles of predatory sex offenders and serial killers. The *modus operandi* of the Colne Strangler and Heys was similar too. Each young woman was alone during a blackout and was subjected to a sudden, surprise attack. The attacks also took place on public roads, which had numerous places for the perpetrator to hide as he waited for a suitable victim, and multiple routes by which he could make his escape. Both early attacks began with a grab to the throat. Teresa Baldwin had to fight hard to fend off her attacker. Eileen Barrett was taken by complete surprise and killed by a deep penetrating stab from a knife. The attack on Winifred Evans was so sudden she did not have a chance to fight back either, and her killer satisfied his sexual desires by raping her.

Descriptions of Heys during his appearances in court state that he was a large-framed man. The HMP Norwich Record of Executions Book recorded his height as 5ft 5 ins and notes his build as 'sturdy'. Corporal Margaret Johns who encountered him in the women's ablutions at RAF Beccles described him as '5ft

---

22. *Diss Express* 26 January 1945

7 inches tall, well built, full face, clean shaven, dark eyes'.[23] The man witnesses spotted running towards Linden Road from Albert Road in Colne after Eileen Barrett was stabbed was described as 'Aged 35 or 40 years, about 5ft 7 inches tall, broad build, round face'. Heys was 33.

Heys had been born in Colne, grew up in the area and knew it well; in fact, he could have known every dark doorway, alley and blacked-out street. He was living with his wife and three children on Harold Street, just five minutes' walk away from the bus stop on the corner of Linden Road and Albert Road where Eileen Barrett had suffered the stab wound that would kill her. He had been employed as a silk cloth weaver at a number of mills in the Colne area up to 1939, but during the early war years had set himself up as a shoe repairer in Colne.[24] As a cobbler, he would have used a variety of sharp knives for cutting, shaping and trimming leather. He would have also owned a sharpening stone that would have not only kept his working knives in tip-top condition, but also any other blades he may have acquired. Heys worked long hours repairing shoes out of a shed in his garden and would have been able to come in and out of the garden gate without disturbing his family inside the house or arousing any suspicion. The shed would have provided an ideal place for him to clean up and change clothes.

Heys' father, Edward, had committed suicide by hanging at the family home on Spring Garden Road at Colne when Arthur was aged 5 in 1913, and his mother, Mary Isabella, had died from heart failure in June 1941. There was no history of mental illness in the family. Heys had a criminal record dating back to March 1923, when he had been convicted at Colne Police Court for stealing tools. In May 1935 he had received eighteen months hard labour at Preston Sessions for shopbreaking and larceny, and asked that sixteen other offences be taken into consideration. Three years later, in October 1938, he was convicted again at Preston for warehouse breaking and larceny. Heys enlisted in the Royal Air Force on 12 August 1941, after which the attacks stopped in Colne. However, attacks on women in the dark on RAF stations where Heys was based occurred around the country. Two instances were quoted in the case file.

The first was on 23 June 1943, at RAF Leuchars, Fife. ACW Margaret Jamie Scott was asleep in her barrack room when she was seized by the throat by the hands of a man in an LAC uniform

---

23. MEPO 3/2282 Statement of Margaret Elizabeth Jones
24. MEPO 3/2282 Greeno

who compressed her windpipe. Fortunately she was able to get a scream out and her assailant fled. The file notes:

> Enquiry regarding this assault shows that Heys was interviewed and at the material time was absent from his billet and put forward the excuse that he was in the lavatory lying on the floor where he vomited through excessive drinking. He denied the assault and could not be identified.[25]

On 20 December 1943, at 7.15am, ACW Alice Emily Hayes WAAF, who was stationed at RAF Thornaby in North Yorkshire, was walking from WAAF quarters to the dining hall when she was attacked from behind by a man who forced her back over a bench in a shed but then suddenly fled. Heys was at RAF Thornaby at the time of the attack but was not connected with this assault.

DS Greeno left just one note on the file regarding the murder of Eileen Barrett:

> Incidentally it must be noted that in March 1941, a female was murdered in Colne, Lancashire, by being stabbed in the back by a sharp instrument whilst in the street. This murder still remains unsolved. Heys was at the time living in Colne as far as I can ascertain he did not come under notice in connection with this enquiry, because apparently he was never thought of, therefore no evidence was obtained to connect or eliminate him. Heys' presence in Colne at that time has now been brought to the notice of police in that district by me and further enquiries are in hand.[26]

Sadly, there is no publicly accessible record of what the outcome of these enquiries were, or whether they ever were actually carried out.

Hopefully police will reopen the case file one day, if only to investigate Heys and rule him out as a suspect. Or perhaps these similarities will prove to be more than just coincidences and the family of Eileen Barrett will finally know the identity of her killer, and maybe take some comfort in the knowledge that he had been brought to justice.

---

25. MEPO 3/2282 Greeno
26. *Ibid*

CHAPTER 10

The Witchcraft Murder
(Upper Quinton, Warwickshire 1945)

There are more things in heaven and earth, Horatio, than are dreamt
of in your philosophy.

Hamlet, William Shakespeare

Witch hysteria manifests with the greatest intensity when society is under pressure, such as at a time of war. Historically, in rural communities when hysterical behaviour, such as accusations of witchcraft, has manifested, it was usually directed at the most marginal people. Poor widows, without children or family to support them, have been particularly vulnerable. Often reduced to living on the fringes of communities, in hovels, many of them earned a meagre living selling remedies they created from the herbs and plants they found growing wild in the hedgerows around them. Some would earn a bit more by telling fortunes and making love potions. If the cures, potions and predictions worked, the poor widow would soon be attributed magical powers. By that same token, if someone bore a grudge against her, or was looking for a scapegoat, that same woman could also become the target of accusations of malevolent 'bewitchment', such as causing the stillbirth of a baby, the death of a cow that provided income for a family, or the poor yield or failure of a locally grown food crop.

This phenomena is well evinced by the number of accusations of witchcraft and trials during the period of the English Civil War (1642–1651), when Matthew Hopkins was proclaimed 'Witchfinder General' and he and others earned a bloody living by being called in by local magistrates to conduct interrogations and search the bodies of those accused of being witches for marks of the Devil.

David Pinner drew on many of those themes for his novel *Ritual* (1967), which he sets in a rural Cornish village that kept itself detached from mainstream society. *Ritual* inspired the film *The Wicker Man* (1973), set on the remote Scottish island of Summerisle. Both book and film explore the beliefs and rituals that might be long held and accepted as normal and necessary in a remote country village, isolated community or island, but in their most extreme manifestation would horrify the more enlightened norms, values and laws of the modern world. *Ritual* and *The Wicker Man* are, of course, fictional. Our final case is one of a real murder which begs the question, could a long and lingering belief in witchcraft in rural Warwickshire really lead to a ritual murder?

The story begins at dusk, as householders were drawing their curtains and blinds and people were rushing home from work to get inside before the evening blackout on 14 February 1945. The war was going well in Europe but despite applications from local politicians to regional commissioners claiming that the likelihood of air raids had been greatly reduced and the continued enforcement of blackout night after night was bad for morale, our streets in city, town and countryside remained in darkness each night.[1]

Edith Isabel 'Edie' Walton (33) lived in the rural village of Lower Quinton, Warwickshire. This idyllic place lies at the foot of the ancient Meon Hill, with the neighbouring villages of Upper Quinton and Admington; in 1945 there was a resident population of less than 500 people living in these villages, but just 2 miles away there were 1,046 prisoners of war (POWs) in Long Marston POW camp. The area was, and still is, distinguished by a number of sixteenth and seventeenth-century thatched, timber-framed houses and cottages, images of which could quite happily adorn the lid of any chocolate box. Edie resided with her uncle, farm labourer Charles 'Charlie' Walton (74), in the centre cottage of a block of three numbered 14, 15 and 16 Lower Quinton, which stood then as now on the corner of Friday Street, just across the road from the medieval St Swithin's Church.

Charlie Walton had married his cousin Bella Walton in 1914. Bella's brother, George Walton, had married Elizabeth Shaw in 1909. They had been blessed with little Edie in 1911 but Elizabeth died suddenly in 1914 so newlyweds Charlie and Bella adopted little Edie. The three of them lived an ordinary, quiet country life together but sadly Aunt Bella died in December 1927, leaving just Charlie and Edie. Edie cooked for her uncle and looked after the domestic arrangements in the cottage, acting very much as his housekeeper. She also worked as a printer's assembler at the Royal Society of Arts, which had relocated from London to Lower Quinton to escape the air raids on the city.

---

1. *Aberdeen Press and Journal* 14 February 1945

Charles Walton

Charles Walton lived in the centre cottage, number 15, in what was then a block of three timber framed cottages numbered 14, 15 and 16, Lower Quinton

Charlie suffered with rheumatism and sciatica and both conditions had become progressively worse over recent years, to the degree that his back had become bent and he often had to walk with the aid of a rough stick he cut from a hedge. Otherwise he was in pretty good health and still worked casually on local farms, doing small manual jobs such as hedge laying and ditching, but he had his rules. Charlie would not work on Saturdays or Sundays, nor if it was wet, if there was too much wind or if there was fog, snow or ice on the road. He seldom worked a full week.[2] He kept himself to himself but Edie described the man she knew and had lived with for most of her life in a statement to the police:

> He was an extremely good tempered man. I have never known him to lose his temper or use bad language. I have never heard him speak badly of anyone or to have a quarrel with anyone.... . He was friendly with everyone but no one ever visited him at the house. He didn't go out in the evenings and very seldom went into a public house. He was always happy and contented with his life.[3]

The only close friend Charlie had was another local man named George Higgins (72), who lived at Fairview. The pair regularly worked together hedging and often went out for walks on Sunday evenings in the summer.[4]

Charlie had been employed by Alfred John Potter (41) on Firs Farm for about twelve months. On the morning of 14 February, as Charlie and Edie ate breakfast – Charlie usually had two slices of toast and a cup of coffee – he told Edie he would be back up on Firs Farm doing some hedge cutting that day. Charlie was a creature of habit, a steady and reliable old country man. He would usually leave for work at 8.30am and return about 4.00pm. He would only take a piece of cake with him, wrapped up in a blue sugar bag, to eat at midday and would have his proper meal when he got home. When he set out, Charlie had not been carrying any tools as he tended to leave his hedge-cutting implements where he had been working. Edie also knew he occasionally carried a purse with a few shillings in it, but on the morning of 14 February he had left that at home. She left a meal out ready for when her uncle got in and she set off for work at 8.30am.

Charlie would *always* be at the cottage when Edie got in from work at about 6.00pm. When Edie returned home that night there was no light in the house, the meal she had left for her uncle had not been touched and there was no sign of Charlie. It was so uncharacteristic of her uncle not to be home that Edie was concerned. She went round to their neighbour of twenty-three years, farm worker Mr Harry Beasley (46) who lived in

---

2. MEPO 3/2290 Statement of Edith Isabel Walton 23 February 1945
3. *Ibid*
4. MEPO 3/2290 Statement of George Higgins 24 February 1945

the adjoining cottage of 16 Lower Quinton with his wife and family. Edie told him her uncle was not home and asked him to accompany her to see if they could find him.

Edie and Harry – who had always got on with Charlie and agreed that it was out of character for him to not be home in the evenings – made their way to the fields of The Firs and spent about half an hour looking for Charlie with no success. They even asked the woman who was staying in a caravan on the adjoining field if she had seen him that evening, but she had last seen him when he passed her by that morning on his way to the field where he was working.

Becoming increasingly concerned, Edie and Harry went to see Farmer Potter at his house at about 7.00pm to see if he could tell them where Charlie had been working. In the statement she gave to the police on 16 February 1945 Edie Walton recalled:

> I said, 'There must be something wrong' to which Mr Potter replied, 'My God, there must be.' He then came with us and took us across some fields. Mr Potter said, 'I have to do the milking on a Wednesday. I came to the field to cut some hay at twelve o'clock and saw your uncle was at his work.' We then went on up the fields and Mr Potter said, 'This is the hedge he was on.' Mr Beasley was walking a little in front and all of a sudden he told me to stop where I was. He came straight back to me and said, 'My God, he's gone.' I became hysterical and they would not let me go near the body.'[5]

According to Harry Beasley:

> When we reached the hedge of the field at Hillground Mr Potter said, 'This is where he was working.' At this time Mr Potter and I were walking in front and Edith was behind. I think Mr Potter and I saw the body of Mr Walton together. It was lying in the corner of the field. I noticed at once that the face was covered with blood and that a trouncing hook was sticking in the throat. I turned at once and prevented Edith coming any further.[6]

Mr Potter had guided Edie and Harry to a field known as Hillground, on the north flank of Meon Hill about a mile from the main Stratford on Avon to Campden Road. Charlie's blood-spattered body was lying close to the hedge on the far side of the

---

5. MEPO 3/2290 Walton
6. MEPO 3/2290 Statement of Harry Beasley 18 February 1945

field on the boundary where Mr Potter's farm joined the land of neighbouring farmer Allan Raymond 'Ray' Valender.

Edie was screaming and sobbing. Harry Beasley tried to comfort her as best he could. He had also noticed a man walking towards Upper Quinton along the other side of the hedge in Ray Valender's field. By the time they reached Charlie's body the man in the other field was about 50 yards away. Mr Beasley recalled:

> I said to Mr Potter, 'For God's sake call that man whoever it is.' Mr Potter called to him and the man came back and Mr Potter spoke to him over the hedge and said, 'Look over there' and pointed to the body. Mr Potter added, 'Go down to Valender's, phone to the police and bring them here as quick as you can.'[7]

Harry soon realised the man he had spotted, and whom Potter had just dispatched to telephone for the police, was Harry Peachey of Upper Quinton. Mr Beasley then set off to walk the inconsolable Edie home. As he was about to leave, either Beasley said he would fetch a stretcher or Potter suggested a stretcher should be fetched to help get the body down. Harry Beasley met his wife and a Mrs Nicholls on the way and handed Edie over to them. He then called for Mr Nicholls, who lived on Friday Street, and his own brother Fred. They fetched the stretcher from the ambulance that was kept at Firs Farm and took it to where Charlie's body lay.

Harry Peachey had actually been up to a nearby field to check on the progress of some beans he had planted and was walking home when he had been hailed by Farmer Potter and asked to phone the police. All he could see over the hedge was Edie Walton being held by Harry Beasley. She was sobbing terribly so when he got to Ray Valender's house and asked him to call the police, he told him it was a matter concerning Edie.

The call from Ray Valender was received at 6.50pm by PC Jim Lomasney at Long Marston Police Station. Valender relayed what he had been told, and said, 'There is a girl at the foot of Meon Hill and there is something seriously wrong with her.'[8] PC Lomasney arrived at Valender's at 7.15pm and accompanied Harry Peachey and Valender to find the spot. As they got close to the place where Peachey had been hailed, Valender shouted, 'Where are you Alf?' Mr Potter called back, 'Here I am' from

---

7 MEPO 3/2290 Beasley

8. MEPO 3/2290 Statement of PC 173 Michael James Lomasney, Warwickshire County Constabulary 1 March 1945

the corner of his field. PC Lomasney then climbed over the
boundary fence, followed by Valender and Peachey. Mr Potter
was standing about 25 ft from the corner of the field near an
RAF cable pole, dusk was falling fast and visibility was becoming
poor. PC Lomasney asked, 'Where is she?' Potter replied, 'Look
over there, in the corner.'

As they approached and saw a male body, PC Lomasney
exclaimed, in typical country-copper style, 'It's not a girl then.'[9]
Visibility was so poor the constable wondered if it might be
the body of an airman, but he flashed his lamp and realised it
was a civilian. PC Lomasney asked, 'Who is it Alf?' Mr Potter
replied, 'It's old Charlie Walton.'[10]

He conducted a brief examination of the body and in his
statement PC Lomasney said, 'I noticed that the trousers were
unfastened at the top and that the flies were unbuttoned. The
jacket and waistcoat were also unfastened. A belt lay loosely
across his thighs. I noticed that the braces were broken at the back
and undone at the front.'[11]

PC Lomasney went through Mr Walton's pockets. He found
the blue sugar bag the cake had been wrapped in, with a few
crumbs inside, in his left-hand jacket pocket. There was also a
piece of silver watch chain in the bottom right-hand waistcoat
pocket, but there was no sign of a watch. PC Lomasney described
the wounds that had been inflicted on Charlie in his statement:

> I looked closely at the wounds and found that the blade of
> a hedging hook and the tine of a two tine fork were inserted
> into the man's neck and throat. I felt the handle of the fork
> near its extreme end and found that it was firmly fixed in the
> hedge.[12]

It was clear there had been foul play so PC Lomasney asked
someone to go and telephone Stratford Police to inform them
that a man had been murdered and to ask someone in authority
to come at once. Ray Valender commented in his statement:

> Potter seemed very hesitant about doing this and said, 'If I can get
> through' as if he expected it to be difficult to get the phone call
> put through. I straight away volunteered to go and use my phone

---

9. MEPO 3/2290 Statement of Harry Peachey 18 February 1945
10. MEPO 3/2290 Lomasney
11. *Ibid*
12. *Ibid*

and this I did. I thought Mr Potter was very shaky and scared at this time. This struck me as peculiar because he is a strong man and not one I would have expected to have been so upset.[13]

As PC Lomasney and Mr Potter stood waiting, the constable asked Potter when he had last seen Charlie alive. He replied, 'About ten minutes or a quarter past twelve when I came to feed the cattle and sheep down there. He pointed towards his house. I noticed some calves in the field where the body lay.'

PC Lomasney also took the opportunity to return to the body and use his torch to take another look around the area. He said:

I saw a walking stick on the ground about three and a half yards from the body. I was lying near the fence between Potter's Field and Valender's bean field. I picked it up and found blood and hairs adhering to the handle end. I showed it to Potter and said, 'Look at the blood and hair.' He said, 'It is, as well.'

It also gave PC Lomasney a chance to observe Mr Potter's behaviour. His comments are interesting and give more than a hint that Potter was already drawing suspicion:

Potter seemed very upset. He was shivering and complained of being cold. Peachey was standing more or less in the background all this time. Looking back I think that Potter appeared more worried than one would have expected him to be. I have known him for over five years and he is not a demonstrative sort of fellow. He is used to seeing animals slaughtered and is accustomed to the sight of blood. He said, 'It's a devil, this happening on my land. What will the public say? You know what they are round Quinton.'[14]

He also noted that when Harry Beasley arrived with his brother, and Mr Nicholls with the stretcher, Mr Potter said, 'I'm famished, I'll be getting home.' That certainly struck PC Lomasney as odd, especially as he was leaving before the arrival of Stratford Police, and especially as the murdered man was one of his employees and had been killed on his own farm land.

Just before Potter departed, Inspector Chester and Detective Sergeant George Bailey arrived, followed a few minutes later by police surgeon Dr Archibald McWhinney and PC Benton from

13. MEPO 3/2290 Statement of Allan Raymond Valender 8 March 1945
14. MEPO 3/2290 Lomasney

Stratford. Dr McWhinney conducted the first detailed examination of the wounds that had been inflicted upon Charles Walton:

> The body was lying on its left side with the knees and hips in a bent position and was about 1 yard from the hedge facing the body and 2 yards from the hedgerunning at right angles to this hedge. There was a gash on the right side of the neck and the cut ends of the main vessel and the lacerated trachea (windpipe) could be seen. The blade of the bill hook was in situ in the wound. The tip of the blade being at least buried 4 inches in the tissue at the root of the neck. The head was turned to the left and the handle of the bill hook laid across the face in a position nearly parallel to the long axis of the body.
>
> In addition to the wound already described, the face was impaled by a pitch fork, one prong which had entered on either side of the face. On the right side the point of entrance was just below and in front of the angle of the jaw and on the left side appeared to be at a somewhat lower level. The handle of the fork had been pressed backwards and the end of the handle was wedged under the cross member of the hedge behind the head, thus anchoring the head to the ground. The handle of the bill hook, which was lying free, was approximately parallel with the handle of the fork.[15]

The pathologist, Professor James Webster, director of the West Midland Forensic Science Laboratory, arrived at 11.30pm and carried out his examination of the body and the scene of crime. His initial observations all chimed with Dr McWhinney, and Professor Webster added:

> There was a great deal of blood in the region of the head and it was obvious that he had severe injuries seeing that a hedging hook and both prongs of a hay fork were thrust deep into the tissues of his neck and upper thoracic cavity. His head gear had fallen off and was just below his head. His left hedging glove was between the bent left elbow and his left side.
>
> The right hedging glove was on the ground to the left of the body on a level with the groins ... I removed the hook and the fork and it required considerable effort to pull both of these out. The hook was superimposed upon the fork and the prongs of the fork had been plunged into the body a full three quarters of their length. The handle of the fork, moreover, was

---

15. MEPO 3/2290 Statement of Dr Archibald Renwick McWhinney 18 February 1945

forced under a cross-piece in the hedge and the body had to be slightly pulled down in order to release this.[16]

Everything pointed to Charlie having been hit about the head with his stick, then pinned to the ground by the hay fork being plunged through his neck, while the slashes to his throat were delivered using the slashing hook. Both medical men agreed that the injuries that had been inflicted on Charlie had could not have been self-inflicted.

Police photographer PC Arthur Nicholls of Warwick had arrived on the scene around the same time as Professor Webster and took photographs by the light of battery torches of Charlie's body in situ on the field. Charles Walton's body was removed at about 1.30am on 15 February. Placed onto the stretcher, he was lifted over the fence then put on a hand cart and trundled across the fields to a waiting ambulance at Upper Quinton and taken to the General Hospital Mortuary, Stratford-on-Avon. More photographs were taken by PC Nicholls before and after the body was washed.[17] An autopsy was then carried out by Professor Webster in the presence of Dr McWhinney.

Professor Webster reported his findings at the inquest convened by George Frederick Lodder, coroner for South Warwickshire at Stratford Town Hall on Tuesday 20 February:

Mr Walton had received serious injuries inflicted by his stick, the hedging hook and the hayfork that he had been using had been plunged into his body for three quarters of the length of the prongs.

Several ribs on his left side were broken. There were bruises as well as cuts on the man's head and an injury to the back of the left hand such as might be received when defending himself against a cutting instrument.

The main wound was in the neck and was obviously made by more than one blow with the slashing hook; in fact three separate and distinct blows had been delivered by a cutting instrument.

All the main vessels of the neck were severed. Other wounds in the neck were caused by the prongs of the hayfork. One prong of the hayfork had punctured a lung.[18]

---

16. MEPO 3/2290 Webster, Professor James, Report on Autopsy 16 February 1945
17. MEPO 3/2290 Statement of PC 148 Stanley Arthur Nicholls, Warwickshire County Constabulary
18. MEPO 3/2290 Webster

The body of Charles Walton photographed where he was found near the hedge on the field known as Hillground, on the north flank of Meon Hill, 14 February 1945

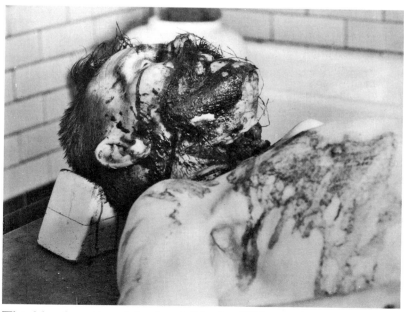

The blood-spattered body of Charles Walton, General Hospital Mortuary, Straford-on-Avon,14 February 1945. Note no cross was carved into his chest

Professor Webster placed the time of Charles Walton's death as between 1.00pm and 2.00pm on 14 February.

The murder investigation was initially led by Supt H. Simmons of Warwickshire Police. The problem that confronted the investigating officers was that there was no immediately apparent motive. Charlie was not carrying any money, nor was he known as the sort of man to carry large amounts of cash or valuables.

There was also the question of why had Mr Walton been found with his trousers undone. There was a local rumour that he had stashed quite a bit of money away; perhaps his trousers had been disturbed because his killer thought he had been wearing his savings in a money belt?[19]

Another possible scenario was that the rheumatoid old man would have been at his most vulnerable as he prepared to defecate in the field. His left hand could have been cut as he attempted to fend off his attacker as he clawed his undergarments and trousers back up with his right hand. His stick, and working tools would have been left to the side as he prepared to relieve himself, and could have easily been picked up and used against him. The hail of blows to his head would have quickly stunned him and his rheumatism and half-hitched trousers meant he fell back allowing his killer to pin him to the ground and slash his throat.

It was also rather odd that Charlie was found wearing just a watch chain but the cheap white metal half hunter watch bearing the name if its stockist, Edgar Jones, Stratford on Avon, that he always had in his pocket on the end of the chain, was missing. Detective Sergeant Webb would comment later to his biographer that he considered it inconceivable anyone would have killed Charlie simply to obtain that watch.[20] A search was carried out over the fields where Charles had been carried, in case his watch had fallen out of his clothes or a pocket as he was being taken to the ambulance, but it did not turn up. In view of the injuries that had been inflicted on him, there were concerns that the attack had been carried out by a maniac who was still at large. Police began a thorough search of the countryside for clues, the missing watch and the culprit, over a wide radius of Walton's thatched cottage.

A number of local people jumped to the conclusion that the murderer was likely to have been one of the many Italian POWs working in agriculture in the area. Police visited the Italian POW camp at Long Marston and all prisoners known to have been

---

19. MEPO 3/2290 Webster
20. Fairlie, *Reluctant Cop*

working outside of the camp on the day of the murder were searched and interviewed with the aid of camp interpreters. Nothing untoward was revealed. The investigations kept drawing blanks and late on the night of 15 February, the chief constable of Warwickshire County Constabulary put in the request for assistance from Scotland Yard.

Chief Inspector Bob Fabian and Detective Sergeant Albert Webb were dispatched, post haste, and arrived on the morning of 17 February, bringing DS Saunders of Special Branch, who spoke fluent Italian, as interpreter. He would spend two weeks on the POW camp investigation. Further enquiries were made at the local British Army military garrison at Long Marston. In total, hundreds of soldiers and Italian POWs were interviewed and all statements were followed up and checked. There was not a single authentic case where any of the POWs had been discourteous to the villagers, or any incident of rage or violence.[21]

The caravan on Firs Farm, which Edie and Harry had called at while searching for Charlie, was occupied by Flight Lieutenant Thomas Woodward, who was stationed at RAF Honeybourne, and his wife Maud. Their caravan had a good view of the field where Charlie had been working. Both were interviewed and confirmed that they had only seen Charlie walking to work in the morning and had not noticed anybody else on the day of the murder. On that day, Mrs Woodward had been busy attending to their baby and Flight Lieutenant Woodward was at his aerodrome. Occupants of nearby cottages were also questioned. Soldiers who had been on Meon Hill, and those who had been working in nearby fields, were traced and interviewed. Enquiries were also carried out door to door across Upper and Lower Quinton but all to no avail. Those who knew and worked with Charlie spoke of him as an inoffensive man, content with his lot in life, who kept himself to himself and minded his own business. He would speak to others to pass the time of day and then get on with whatever he was doing. No grudges or disgreements were mentioned to the police.[22]

Police records were checked for any persons with a criminal history in the area. The only person who drew any real suspicion was Mr Walton's employer Alfred Potter, the man believed to be the last person to have seen Charlie alive, and a man who could not get his story straight. On the night the murder was discovered, witnesses and police officers recalled that Mr Potter had clearly

21. MEPO 3/2290
22. MEPO 3/2290

Alfred Potter

been in some discomfort at the murder scene but officers had put that down to stress.

Over subsequent interviews, however, Potter established an account of his movements during the day that simply did not add up when checked with statements from other witnesses. He was keen to try and show that he had not been nearer to the murder site than about 100 yards, and only then in passing, but by his own admission to PC Lomasney on the night of the murder, as they stood near Charlie's dead body, he had been in that field feeding cattle earlier that day. Firs Farm cowman Charles 'Happy' Batchelor (37) mentioned in his statement:

> The straw laid on the ground in the field next to that in which the body of Mr Walton was found, is straw for feeding the cattle. As far as I can remember the last time straw was laid in this field was Monday 12 February 1945 and I took it up there myself. I know that on the day when Mr Walton was found there were 9 store cattle in the field next to the one in which Mr Walton had been working or in the actual one where he was working.[23]

---

23. MEPO 3/2290 Statement of Charles Henry Batchelor 23 February 1945

In the notes taken by DI Bertie Toombs, when he interviewed Potter at 11.00pm on the night of 14 February, the farmer said he had been for a quick drink at the College Arms with Joseph 'Joe' Stanley, the farmer of White Cross Farm, at 11.55am and had left at 12.00 noon. Mr Stanley would recall that they arrived at the pub at 11.45am, and left at noon. In those fifteen minutes, Mr Stanley said he drank one pint of Guinness and Potter downed two.[24] Toombs noted that when giving his statement, Potter 'specially noticed the time' of when he and Stanley left the pub. People only tend to note the time if they have good reason to make a note of the time, such as keeping an appointment or when attempting to establish an alibi. Potter then stated he 'went straight across to a small field adjoining Hillground' and that he could 'see Walton hedging 500 to 600 yards away'.[25]

In his statement on 17 February 1945, Potter provided more specific details:

> ...at about ten past twelve I went across to Cocks Leys a field on my farm to see some sheep and feed some calves. When I got there it was about twenty past twelve and I saw Walton working at the hedge in the next field. He was about 500 yards away and was working in his shirt sleeves ... I would have gone over to have seen him but I had a heifer in a ditch nearby which I had to attend to. I went straight back home and got there about twenty to one. I then went to see to the heifer.[26]

At the end of his statement, Potter revisited what he had stated earlier, perhaps in response to a question from Detective Webb, who was conducting the interview, asking if he was positive it was Charles Walton he saw in the field:

> Although I cannot be positive I am almost certain it was Walton who I saw working at the hedge at twenty past twelve on 14 February 1945. Whoever it was appeared to be trimming the hedge. From the point where I saw Walton at twenty past twelve to where he had finished working was about ten yards. It would have taken him almost half an hour to have trimmed that amount of hedge.

---

24. MEPO 3/2290 Statement of Joseph Stanley 22 February 1945
25. MEPO 3/2290 Notes taken by DI Bertie Toombs 14 February 1945
26. MEPO 3/2290 Potter

In his report, Chief Inspector Fabian said:

> It will be remembered that Potter, in his earlier statements, said that from the point where he saw Walton working to the point where he later found the body would constitute about half an hour's work. If the man who Potter saw was not Walton it would be interesting to know who did the half an hour's work on the hedge.[27]

In his statement of 23 February, Potter claimed that having had his statement of 17 February read to him there were 'one or two mistakes and I want to put these right.' In the revised version concerning his movements over lunchtime of 14 February, he wished to state that once he had been to the field named Cocks Leys to feed some of his calves and sheep, he had gone home sat down and read a paper for about five minutes, then went to the cowshed and helped Batchelor the cowman machine pulp mangolds for about five minutes. Potter was also careful to indicate his timing could be corroborated by another witness:

> I fed the machine for about five minutes and Batchelor asked me the time and I said, 'If we go and fetch some flour we can see the clock.' I meant the church clock. We then went to the meal house and I looked at the church clock. It was just one o'clock.

Batchelor then went to have his lunch and Potter went to his farm house to have his. He said he remained in the house for 'one hour and ten minutes'. He was very precise about the time. He then went and met Batchelor in the yard and they discussed the best way to move the dead heifer.[28]

Subsequent police enquiries into the statements made by Potter revealed that the heifer he mentioned had been found dead in Doomsday Brook on 13 February 1945. Firs Farm worker Charles Batchelor would recall:

> I was told by a farm labourer on Tuesday 13 February 1945 at about 12.45pm, that a young heifer was dead in a ditch near the road halfway between Lower Quinton and Adminton. I went along and found the heifer was dead having drowned itself. I could not tell Mr Potter then because he was in Stratford

---

27. MEPO 3/2290 Report by Chief Inspector Robert Fabian 5 April 1945
28. MEPO 3/2290 Potter

on Avon. I know the dead heifer was taken out of the ditch by Mr Potter and a Mr Mace, driver of a tractor belonging to Mr Tom Russell of Lower Quinton, about 3.30pm on the following day [14 February] and it was removed by Mr Perkins the knackerman, about half an hour later.[29]

The plot thickened when it emerged that whereas the farm was not in financial difficulty, former employees William Dyde and George Purnell told detectives that Alf Potter 'had difficulty in the past in paying his employees' wages.'[30] Firs Farm was actually owned by Potter's father, and money for payment of the workers had to been drawn through him. Alfred Potter had been drawing weeks of payments for Walton when Charlie had not worked at all and had kept the money for himself. In his statement of 23 February, Potter admitted that he drew money for times when Charlie did not work, and sometimes Charlie had asked him for wages due to him but he did not have the money to pay him because he had spent it. He did say on those occasions, he paid him later in the week.[31] No wonder that the only statement in which there appeared to be any word of Charles Walton expressing dissent was made by Alfred Potter when he described his employee as an 'innofensive type of man but one who would speak his mind if necessary.'[32]

The timings from about 12.40pm were confirmed by Mr Batchelor in his statement.[33] However, a crucial period of about thirty minutes between just after 12.10pm, when Potter said he left to look at the tractor under repair, and 12.40pm, remained uncorroborated. By his own admission, in his previous statements made to the police, Potter had been a few hundred yards away of Charles Walton, and in his line of vision, around the time the murderous attack took place.

The resumed inquest on Tuesday, 20 March was recorded in detail in both the case file and in the *Tewkesbury Register*. This included when, at the coroner's request, Alfred Potter presented yet another version of events concerning his movements on the day of the murder:

---

29. MEPO 3/2290 Batchelor
30. MEPO 3/2290 Fabian
31. MEPO 3/2290 Batchelor
32. MEPO 3/2290 Notes taken by DI Toombs when interviewing Alfred John Potter 11.00pm 14 February 1945
33. MEPO 3/2290 Batchelor

CORONER: 'Did you see him [Charles Walton] early that morning?'

POTTER: 'No sir, not before he began work. I saw someone at about 12.30 but I would not say it was him.'

Potter said he went to the College Arms at about 11.55 a.m with a Mr. [Joe] Stanley. He stayed till about 12 and then went with Mr. Stanley to his (Mr. Stanley's) farmyard where for about 10 minutes he watched Mr. Stanley's tractor being repaired.

Witness then went home and put down the tools he himself had been using. Next he went off up the fields to see the sheep and calves. He gave the cattle a bale of straw and it was while feeding them he saw Walton in the distance. That was about 500 yards away. 'I am not sure it was him' he added 'but I saw someone in shirt sleeves.'

Questioned about this witness said he told the police at the time that he was not sure whether it was Walton.

CORONER: 'At the time you thought it was him?'

POTTER: 'That's right sir.'

CORONER: 'Was he using any tool?'

POTTER: 'Well, I can't say I never saw him move ... I just thought at the time it was him and went on.'

CORONER: 'What time was that?'

POTTER: 'About 12.30.'

CORONER: 'What did you do after that?'

POTTER: 'Went back home.'

CORONER: 'Was anyone at home when you arrived?'

POTTER: 'Mrs. Potter.'

CORONER: 'Did you remain in the house?'

POTTER: 'About five minutes. I then went to the cowshed to help Batchelor, the cowman, to pulp the mangolds.'

Witness said that at one o'clock he went in to dinner and that he left at about 2.10. A heifer had got in the ditch and as his own tractor was too heavy he telephoned to Mr. Russell. He was told that Mr. Russell was at Clopton so he got out the car and went to Clopton. The heifer was got out of the ditch and later witness did the milking.[34]

---

34. *Tewkesbury Register* 24 March 1945; also see MEPO 3/2290

The coroner then asked if Potter had got on well with Mr Walton to which he replied, 'I did sir. I never had a row with any man. I never went to him once in a fortnight. He went on with his work. I trusted him.'

Chief Inspector Fabian informed the coroner that when Potter was interviewed on 17 February he stated that after feeding the cattle he went straight to get the heifer out of the ditch, and now he was telling a different story. The chief inspector wondered which version was right. The coroner then addressed Potter, who had clearly been flustered by Fabian's interjection, directly. The *Tewkesbury Register* reported the following exchange:

CORONER: 'I don't want to unduly press you: which is correct?'

POTTER: 'What I have said now?'

CORONER: 'Were you very disturbed?'

POTTER: 'I was very cut up.'

CORONER: 'Do you know of anybody deceased was unfriendly with, or anybody with a grudge?'

POTTER: 'No-one whatsoever.'

CORONER: 'Did you see anyone?'

POTTER: 'The only people we see are soldiers.'

CORONER: ''Is there anything in your field that might attract anyone?'

POTTER: 'Not that I know of. On the hill just above there are a few rabbits.'[35]

All the inquest could conclude, on the evidence presented, was that Charles Walton had been murdered 'by person or persons unknown'.

It is worthy of note that between his first interview with DI Toombs on the night of the murder, and the inquest in March, the time Potter claimed he had seen Charles Walton at work on the hedge changed from shortly after leaving the pub at noon to about 12.30pm. Potter would also claim he had filled yet more of the time between leaving the College Arms and arriving with his cowman with a previously unmentioned visit to Mr Stanley's farmyard, where Potter claimed he watched Stanley's tractor being repaired for about ten minutes.

---

35. *Tewkesbury Register* 24 March 1945 also see MEPO 3/2290

In a curious addendum that must have come to his mind after he signed off his statement, Mr Stanley stated that at about 12.57am in the morning on Sunday 18 February, he heard four knocks on his front door. People did occasionally knock on his door as a prank when they were returning worse for drink from dances at Ilmington, so he took no notice and did not even look out of the window. However, he recalled, 'After a few minutes I heard someone walking on the bricks towards Mr Potter's house and later I heard Mr Potter's dog bark.'[36]

Was it a prowler or Potter wanting a quiet word with his neighbour in the wee small hours so he could furnish him with an alibi if the police came to take a statement from him?

Potter would also claim to be less sure it was Walton he had seen working on the hedge at lunchtime in each of the successive five statements that he made to police. In his first comments to DI Toombs on the night of the murder, he said he saw Walton actively engaged in work on the hedge. In his account at the inquest, he said he saw a man – whom he could not positively identify as Walton – in shirt sleeves standing still. In a statement made by Charlie's old friend George Higgins who had worked with him hedging for years, he said, 'I cannot think for a moment that he would ever work in his shirt sleeves in the winter.'[37] On the day of his murder Mr Walton had actually been wearing a short-sleeved shirt and a cardigan with long sleeves, and these were shown to Potter.[38] If Potter really had seen the man he described standing near the hedge it could not have been Charles Walton.

Police collected the clothes worn by Alfred Potter on the day of the murder and sent them for examination at the West Midland Forensic Science Laboratory. Before the police took them away, Potter said that they might find blood on his breeches, which he attributed to the recent birth of a calf. Blood was indeed found on his breeches, but they had been so well washed it was impossible to determine if the blood was human or not.

When Alfred's wife Lilian gave her statement to the police some three weeks after the murder took place she corroborated her husband's story. She was quite exact about the time he had been in the house around lunchtime. However, while she could recall the timings around that crucial period precisely, she was hazy about times for the rest of the day and had no recollection of what they

---

36. MEPO 3/2290 Stanley
37. MEPO 3/2290 Statement of George Higgins 24 February 1945
38. MEPO 3/2290 Potter

had eaten for lunch. When asked about Mr Potter's clothes from the day, specifically his breeches, she claimed her husband never cleaned them.[39]

In his first statement to the police, Potter had not mentioned anything about touching the implements used to kill Charles Walton. By the time he made his statement on 23 February, fingerprints had become quite a matter of concern for Potter and were clearly playing on his mind. He said that both he and PC Lomasney had touched the slashing hook embedded in Mr Walton's neck when they had checked to see if he was dead or not. Potter then went on to add how he had expressed concerns about touching the murder weapon and he put quite some effort into claiming he had mentioned this earlier to the police and that his fingerprints might appear on the hook.[40] Curiously, when the tools used to murder Charles Walton were checked for fingerprints no prints were found at all.

The most puzzling element of Alfred Potter as prime suspect in the killing of Charles Walton was the lack of apparent motive. Some former employees spoke of him having a bad temper, especially when he had been drinking, but what could have forced him to inflict such a frenzied attack on an old man? Ultimately, the evidence against Potter was circumstantial and what forensic clues could have been obtained at that time, such as the bloodstains on his clothes, proved inconclusive.

Another curious element to the story was what had happened to Charlie's money. Close friends and family always believed he had 'put a bit of money by' as he had been left £297 after the death of his wife and had placed £200 of it in a deposit account he had with Midland Bank at Stratford on Avon. He had been in regular employment for all of his life and on the days he worked for Mr Potter he was paid 1s 8d an hour. Known to be a man of frugal habits, he had very few friends, was not a drinker nor a gambler, was not known to have had financial dealings with anyone and had few outgoings.

The cottage where Charlie and Edie lived belonged to Magdalen Farm. Charlie paid a rent of 1s 6d a week which he paid to Joe Stanley, who in turn would pay Frederick Frost – the tenant of Magdalen Farm – the entire annual rent once a year by cheque. Mr Frost paid rates and taxes on the cottage too, which was usually

---

39. MEPO 3/2290 Statement of Lilian Elizabeth Potter 7 March 1945
40. MEPO 3/2290 Potter

more than the rent.[41] When Charlie's bank account was checked after his death it came as quite a surprise to find it only contained £2 11s 9d. There were regular withdrawals but no large lumps sums taken out, so what he spent his money on, or if it was being withdrawn fraudulently by somebody else, was never resolved.

The police investigation was thorough and troops from the Royal Engineers used mine detectors along the route from the murder site to the ambulance, to search for Charlie's missing watch. All sorts of rusty old implements were discovered, but no watch. An appeal for information, accompanied by a photograph of a similar pocket watch, was made through newspapers and circulated in the special notices of the *Police Gazette* on 24 March 1945, but again to no avail.[42] It would take fifteen years for some answers when a watch, believed to be the one lost by Charlie, was handed in to the police in 1960 by a workman who had discovered it in the back garden of Charlie's former home. The area in which it had been unearthed had been occupied by a shed at the time of the murder. The questions posed by the discovery were, had Charlie dropped the watch through a gap in the floor of the shed and had meant to retrieve it? Or had it been put there by someone else, perhaps his murderer?[43]

Local gossip can be a dangerous and misleading element during any police investigation but the manner in which Charlie had been killed, particularly the fact he had been pinned to the ground by the prongs of the hay fork and then had his throat cut, had the appearance of a ritualistic killing. This resonated among local people who were often far more aware of the darker and folkloric history of the area than they would openly admit. Some did dare mention it, and from early on in their enquiries it had been suggested to the police that the killing of Charlie Walton may have been connected to local beliefs in superstition and witchcraft.

Such stories can be overegged and muddied with spurious additions. In the years since Charlie's murder, in 1945, some accounts have become embellished with details, such as a cross being slashed across his chest, but there is no mention of this in the original medical or police reports and nor does it appear on the photographs of his body lying, with its shirt off, on the mortuary slab.

---

41. MEPO 3/2290 Statement of Frederick Frost 7 March 1945
42. *Ibid*
43. *Birmingham Post* 26 August 1960

That said, Charles Walton had been born into, had grown up in and had been entirely educated in, a rural agricultural area and had worked all his life on the land. This was a time before the National Health Service when doctors and veterinarians were expensive or even beyond the means of many country folk, so it would be surprising if Charlie had *not* been versed in local superstitions and herbal remedies. There were stories of Charlie talking to birds and having power over the animals but that really should come as no surprise either. Anyone who knows and loves the countryside will have heard country folk talk to birds and animals. Many of those who work with horses and livestock are blessed with the 'horseman's word' or regarded as 'horse whisperers' that can also work on other animals. It may appear magical, but as any countryman would tell you, it is more about being respectful, understanding and being in tune with the animals.

What is intriguing is that hard-nosed Chief Inspector Fabian was drawn to mention the witchcraft and folkloric connections of the case in his autobiography *Fabian of the Yard* (1950). A local folk tale told of the ghostly black dog of Meon Hill that was said to be a harbinger of death, and when Fabian was walking on Meon Hill at dusk one evening, during the investigation, a large black dog ran past him. Shortly behind the dog came a farm boy in his big muddy boots. Fabian asked the boy if he was looking for his dog. The boy went pale and asked, 'dog Mister?' When Fabian explained it was a black dog the boy did not say another word, he just kept on walking.[44]

Stories of hell hounds and night hounds in the villages below Meon Hill are recounted in Reverend J. Harvey Bloom's book *Folklore, Old Customs and Superstitions in Shakespeare Land* (1930). The book also features a story often attributed to Meon Hill but, in fact, is of a plough lad at Alveston, a village about 60 miles away from Lower Quinton. Although often dated to 1885, no date is ascribed to it in Bloom's book. The story tells of how the plough lad encountered a spectral dog on his way home from work on nine successive evenings, but on the ninth night a headless lady in a silk dress rustled by. The next day the boy was informed that his sister had died. The boy's name was Charles Walton.[45]

The Charles Walton who was murdered in 1945 was born in 1870. He would have been 15 in 1885, and about the right age to

44. Fabian, Robert, *Fabian of the Yard* (London 1950)
45. Bloom, Rev J. Harvey *Folklore, Old Customs and Superstitions in Shakespeare Land* (London 1930)

have been the plough lad. The 1881 and 1891 census, however, both record Charles as living with his family in Quinton. He had three sisters but none of them died in 1885. Only one of them, Mary Ann, died at a younger age than the others but that was in 1901 when she was 35. Charlie did, however, come from a large local family and it could be possible that the boy in the book, if not Charlie himself, was one of his relatives.

A 1949 article in the *Weekly Despatch* revealed that DS Alec Spooner, head of Warwickshire CID, had uncovered a 'witch killing' with remarkable parallels to the murder of Charles Walton. It had taken place in the nearby village of Long Compton seventy years earlier.[46]

According to contemporary newspaper reports Ann Tennant (80) had left her cottage to buy some bread from the village shop between 7.00 and 8.00 pm on Wednesday, 15 September 1875. As she returned, she passed a group of harvest field workers who were on their way home after a long day's toil in the fields, carrying their hay forks over their shoulders. One of the labourers, James Haywood (45), suddenly and without saying a word attacked Mrs Tennant with his hay fork, thrusting the prongs into her leg three times before knocking her down with the tines of the fork. He was about to hit her again but farmer James Taylor grabbed the fork and prevented him from delivering any more blows. Mrs Tennant died from the wounds a short while later. John Henry Ivens (16), who had been working with Haywood during the day, said he had threatened some of the women of the village, and added, 'He said they were all witches that had been haunting him all day and he would kill them all.'

The only motive for the attack was described in the press as follows:

> [Haywood] for some time past has been under the impression that he was under the effect of witchcraft and that Mrs Tennant and several other women in Long Compton were witches and he was determined to rid the village of them.[47]

During the course of investigations into Mrs Tennant's murder, witnesses stated that Haywood's parents, and at least one third of the residents of Long Compton, believed in wizards and witches. When the case was brought before the Warwick Winter Assizes in December 1875 it was described as one of curiosity

---

46. *Weekly Despatch* 15 May 1949
47. *Leamington Spa Courier* 25 September 1875

'from the fact it shows that there is a general belief in witchcraft at Long Compton and in other villages of South Warwickshire, among a certain class of the agricultural population.'[48]

Dr Henry Parsey, medical superintendent of the County of Warwick Pauper Lunatic Asylum at Hatton, near Warwick, had examined Haywood and in presenting his evidence stated: 'In South Warwickshire the belief in witches is common, even among people who may be considered sane.'[49]

While in prison awaiting trial, Haywood said he believed his village was 'haunted' by fifteen or sixteen witches, almost all of them old women. He was convinced that he had been bewitched and justified his actions to the prison governor by repeatedly quoting *Leviticus XX 27, Acts VIII 11, Micah V 12* and other passages of Scripture referring to witchcraft and the fate that should befall witches which he had underlined in his Bible. In court at the Warwickshire Assizes, Haywood explained his actions as having 'only killed a witch to take her power off him.'[50]

Haywood was sentenced to be detained at Broadmoor Criminal Lunatic Asylum 'until Her Majesty's pleasure be known'. Having passed sentence the judge, Mr Baron Bramwell, commented to the jury that he felt something should be done to quell the ignorance and superstition in the area, which he considered 'most criminal and most lamentable'.[51]

Among the strange stories attached to Charlie Walton, which have appeared in print since his murder but are not recorded in the police investigation file, is how he had tied a toy plough to the back leg of a 'walking toad' (a natterjack) and sent it across a local farmer's land. In English folklore, toads have always been regarded as mystical creatures, closely associated with witches and witchcraft. Walking toads were believed to do the bidding of witches, such as carrying a curse to your door, or in the case of the toad and the toy plough, would a bring a blight upon your land and its crops. It was also claimed that the locals of the Quintons had recalled that the last harvest had not been as good as it should have been.

Such stories do need to be treated with some caution but there are incidents, which happened during the case, that could be seen as portents by superstitious country people. Only the day before Charlie's murder, Farmer Potter had discovered the carcass of

48. *Reynold's Newspaper* 19 December 1875
49. *Nuneaton Advertiser* 18 December 1875
50. *Ibid*
51. *Ibid*

St Swithin's Church, Lower Quinton, just across the road from Charles Walton's cottage and the churchyard where he was buried

one of his cows in the Doomsday Stream. Chief Inspector Fabian would bemoan the fact that when he tried to interview local people about such matters he was met with 'lowered eyes, reluctance to speak, except to talk of bad crops – heifer that died in a ditch. But what that had to do with Charles Walton nobody would say.'[52]

All in all, more than 4,000 statements were taken but Fabian was left feeling that locals were not as forthcoming as they could have been. He wrote of 'the most innocent witnesses' not being able to meet the eyes of detectives, and doors being slammed in the faces of the Scotland Yard officers. It has been suggested, in some reports and documentaries over recent years, that the local people of Quinton were more open in their responses to questioning than Fabian suggested, but even the pragmatic Detective Sergeant Albert Webb, who also worked tirelessly on the case, would comment that by the time he and Fabian arrived and began their enquiries 'the locals had got very reticent.'[53]

It appeared that the villagers wanted to put the murder behind them, regardless of whether the murderer had been brought to justice or not. As one local said after Fabian explained that he was making enquiries about Charles Walton, 'He's been dead and buried a month now – what are you worrying about?'[54]

---

52. Fabian, *Fabian*
53. Fairlie, *Reluctant Cop*
54. Fabian, *Fabian*

Scotland Yard had to call it a day, but Warwickshire CID did not close the case and the press would return to it again and again. In 1949, a reporter from the *Weekly Despatch* spoke to the parish priest, Reverend Harold Mason, the minister who had officiated at the funeral for Charles Walton four years earlier. The Reverend said, 'I am convinced no one here thinks that way [about superstition and witchcraft] now. Nevertheless, it was the strangest case I ever heard of.'

The reporter also spoke to Arthur Dobson, the elderly village schoolmaster who said, 'Fifty years ago these beliefs were common enough. But I have heard nothing of the sort for a long time. But who can tell what goes on in the minds of some country men?'[55]

However, the argument was reignited in 1950 when Dr Margaret Murray, the archaeologist, anthropologist, historian and folklorist, came to Lower Quinton to investigate the allegations of ritualistic murder. The date and method of murder struck her as significant, as she explained to a reporter:

> In the pre-Christian era, from which many rituals still live, February was a sacrificial month. On this day a human being had to be killed in the belief that his blood would replace the fertility of the soil ... I believe there is a traditional belief in fairies and witches in this village but the villagers fear to talk about it.[56]

After conducting her study she said:

> I am almost satisfied this is a witchcraft murder. There is much to be explained. I think I shall prove that the murder at Lower Quinton was a ritual sacrifice ... I spent a week in the village, which is a very out of the way place, and typical of those where superstitions and beliefs in witchcraft still exist.[57]

DS Alec Spooner had told reporters in 1948, 'I have sworn to solve this murder, and I am not going to give up'[58] and visited the village, and the murder site, on the anniversary of the murder for over a decade. Each year the visit would be reported in the local, and even national, newspapers. Spooner was convinced the killing

---

55. *Weekly Despatch* 15 May 1949
56. *Daily Mirror* 4 September 1950
57. *Ibid*
58. *Birmingham Daily Gazette* 15 February 1954

had been a ritual murder and the perpetrator was a local person who was still living in the village. He hoped his visits would one day spook the assailant into revealing themselves or encourage a witness with key information to come forward. Alec Spooner retired from the police in 1964 and passed away in 1970, aged 66. The case had haunted him since 1945, but he never gave up and believed one day Charles Walton's murderer would finally be identified.

Quinton residents at the time of the murder, and over the years since, have been keen to point out that local people do not believe in witchcraft and had not done so for years. Newspaper and television reporters revisiting the story have found residents increasingly dismissive of any suggestion that witchcraft played a part in the murder. Some locals refuse to talk to reporters at all. Charlie's niece Edie appeared in the BBC documentary *Power of the Witch* in 1971, in which – when interviewed by Michael Bakewell – she dismissed any notion that witchcraft had played a part in her uncle's death, and went on to say that she did not know anything about witchcraft and had never met a witch. However, in the absence of any other motive, DS Spooner was right to pursue the witchcraft angle of the investigation.

Regardless of whether there was a widely held belief in witches among the people of South Warwickshire in 1945, or if there was a culture of silence, or flat denial of such beliefs to outsiders, it would only take one unbalanced individual to become convinced that they were justified in killing someone they believed to be a witch who was causing harm to them and their community. Just like James Haywood had been convinced his actions were justified when he killed elderly Ann Tennant because he believed she was the witch that had put a curse on him at Long Compton in 1875. The only difference is that the killer of Charles Walton committed the murder then walked away, apparently unseen.

No matter what those who consider themselves educated and above such matters may say, fervent and casual belief in folklore and witchcraft still existed in rural counties across Britain in 1945. It is worth noting that the murder of Charles Walton took place less than a year after Scottish medium Helen Duncan was prosecuted under the Witchcraft Act of 1735 and stood trial at the Old Bailey for fraudulent claims. It was also just four years earlier in 1940 that a case was brought before Dereham Magistrates' Court in Norfolk where army pensioner Gordon Sutton had struck his neighbour Melvena Spinks, after she had 'practised witchcraft against him' for the past five years and made his life a misery. Both were bound over to keep the peace for six months.[59]

The manner in which Charles Walton was killed still begs the question, if he was not killed in a manner that had any symbolism, why did the killer go to the trouble of pinning him to the ground with the fork and slashing his throat? Especially after the old man had been beaten to the ground with his stick and could have easily been dealt a fatal blow with the slashing hook, and could have carried on being dealt blows by his attacker until their frenzy was spent.

Whether it truly was a witchcraft murder or not, the finger of suspicion surely points to Alfred Potter. Chief Inspector Fabian was certainly not convinced of his innocence. He recorded his personal observations of Potter in his report of 5 April 1945:

> When interviewed, Potter has always appeared morose and sullen and even when closely interrogated has never lost his temper or become other than respectful. He is unkempt and would appear, on the surface, to be dull witted but I am convinced he is far from that. He is a man of considerable strength and in my opinion, is an extremely cunning individual.[60]

Fabian followed up with a further report on 30 April 1945 in which he noted Charles Batchelor, the cow man and employee at Firs Farm for three years who had corroborated the times and movements of Potter had left his employment shortly after being questioned about the events. Fabian said:

> Whilst I am satisfied that Batchelor's chief reason for leaving Mr Potter is as he states [he was refused an increase in wages by Potter's father] I also think it probable that he had been prompted to leave by suspicions he may have formed regarding his former employers's connection with the death of Charles Walton. Kenneth Eric John Workman, another employee of Mr Potter has also left his employ since the murder ... by his demeanour I am satisfied that he, too, suspects Potter of having some connection with the murder... . Throughout this enquiry Potter has repeatedly failed to disclose to police his movements round about 14 February 1945, until a direct question has been put to him.[61]

59. *Hull Daily Mail* 6 January 1941
60. MEPO 3/2290 Fabian
61. *Ibid*

In later life, when in conversation with crime writer Richard Whittington-Egan, Fabian told him that he was certain of Potter's guilt and that he had killed Charles Walton because he owed the old man a considerable sum of money. Fabian simply didn't have the evidence to prove it in a court of law. He added that he had been unable to name Potter as the killer in his books because of the libel laws.[62]

Alfred John Potter continued to live at Firs Farm, Lower Quinton and died in Stratford on Avon Hospital on 25 March 1961. When probate was granted, despite his wife and children still being alive, his main financial beneficiary of some £600 11s (about £11,500 in today's money) was the Reverend Rhys Ellis Pryce of Stroud.

If Alfred Potter had killed Charles Walton over money perhaps he deliberately added the twist of an apparent ritual murder of a witch? Whether he truly believed Charlie was a witch or not, Potter would have known that by inflicting such injuries, he would stand a chance of deflecting attention away from him as a suspect, seal the lips of superstitious locals, make those who did not believe dismissive of the matter and frustrate the efforts of the police. To this day, the 'Witchcraft Murder' remains the oldest unsolved murder in the Warwickshire Constabulary records.

Writing twenty-five years after the murder, in his book *The Anatomy of Crime* (1970), Robert Fabian was explicit in his views on the matter:

> I advise anybody who is tempted at any time to venture into Black Magic, witchcraft, Shamanism – call it what you will – to remember Charles Walton and to think of his death, which was clearly the ghastly climax of a pagan rite. There is no stronger argument for keeping as far away as possible from the villains with their swords, incense and mumbo-jumbo. It is prudence on which your future peace of mind and even your life could depend.

---

62. *Ritual Killings: Murder Casebook* vol 5 part 71 (London 1991)

Select Bibliography

Bechhofer Roberts, C. E. (ed.), *The Trial of Harry Dobkin* (London 1944)

Bechhofer Roberts, C. E. (ed.), *The Trial of Jones and Hulten* (London 1945)

Bloom, J. Harvey, *Folk Lore, Old Customs and Superstitions in in Shakespeare Land* (London 1930)

Briggs, Susan, *Keep Smiling Through: The Home Front 1939–45* (London 1975)

Buckton, Henry, *Friendly Invasion: Memories of Operation Bolero* (Stroud 2006)

Calder, Angus, *The People's War* (London 1992)

Camps, Francis E., *Medical and Scientific Investigations in the Christie Case* (London 1954)

Camps, Francis E., *Camps on Crime* (London 1973)

Camps, Professor F. E with Barber, Richard, *The Investigation of Murder* (London 1966)

Chapman, Paul, *Madame Tussaud's Chamber of Horrors* (London 1984)

Cherrill, Ex-Chief Superintendent Fred, *Cherrill of the Yard* (London 1954)

Dunboyne, Lord (ed.), *Trial of John George Haigh* (London 1949)

Fabian, Ex-Detective Superintendent Robert, *The Anatomy of Crime* (London 1970)

Fabian, Ex-Superintendent Robert, *Fabian of the Yard* (London 1950)

Fabian, Ex-Superintendent Robert, *London After Dark* (London 1955)

Fairlie, Gerard, *The Reluctant Cop: The Story and Cases of Detective Superintendent Albert Webb* (London 1958)

Gillman, Peter and Gillman, Leni, *'Collar the Lot' How Britain Interned and Expelled its Wartime Refugees* (London 1980)

Gosling, Ex-Detective Superintendent John and Warner, Douglas, *The Shame of a City* (London 1960)

Greeno, Ex-Detective Chief Superintendent Edward, *War on the Underworld* (London 1960)

Hayward, James, *Myths & Legends of the Second World War* (Stroud 2006)

Honeycombe, Gordon, *The Murders of the Black Museum* (London 1982)

Lane, Brian, *The Murder Guide* (London 1991)

Lefebure, Molly, *Evidence for the Crown* (London 1954)

Lefebure, Molly, *Murder with a Difference* (London 1958)

Levine, Joshua, *The Secret History of the Blitz* (London 2015)

Jones, Steve, *When the Lights Went Down* (Nottingham 1995)

Oates, Jonathan, *John George Haigh The Acid-Bath Murderer* (Barnsley 2014)

Oates, Jonathan, *John Christie of Rillington Place* (Barnsley 2017)

Pierrepoint, Albert, *Executioner: Pierrepoint* (London 1974)

Shew, E. Spencer, *A Companion to Murder* (London 1960)

Shew, E. Spencer, *A Second Companion to Murder* (London 1961)

Simpson, Professor Keith, *Forty Years of Murder* (London 1978)

Storey, Neil R., *A Grim Almanac of Essex* (Stroud 2005)

Storey, Neil R., *Hanged at Norwich* (Stroud 2011)

Storey, Neil R. and Kay, Fiona, *The Home Front in World War Two* (Stroud 2017)

Stratmann, Linda, *Essex Murders* (Stroud 2012)

Totterdell, Superintendent G. H., *Country Copper* (London 1956)

Tennyson-Jesse, F., *The Trials of Evans and Christie* (London 1957)

Journals

Camps, Francis Edward 'The Colchester Taxi Cab Murder', *Medico-Legal Journal*, vol. 17, no. 1, 1949

Simpson, Keith, 'Rex v. Dobkin: The Baptist Church Cellar Murder', *Medico-Legal & Criminological Review* 132, 1943

Simpson, Keith, 'The Luton Sack Murder', *The Police Journal* October–December 1945

All files quoted in the text and footnotes are from The National Archives

Newspapers quoted are in the footnotes

Acknowledgements

The author would like to express his thanks to the following for their kind help with the research for this book. The National Archives, The British Newspaper Archive, The National Justice Museum, Nottingham, Newcastle City Library Local Studies, Tyne & Wear Archives, Bradford Police Museum, Essex Police Museum, Wandsworth Prison Museum, Suffolk Police Archive, HM Prison Norwich, Lieutenant Colonel Martin Valles USAAF (Retd), Stewart P. Evans, Fred Feather, Linda Stratmann, Dr Geoffrey Clayton, James Hayward, Stewart McLaughlin, Dave Schrader, Greg Lawson, Richard C. Cobb, Rob Clack, Delianne Forget, Eve and Steve Bacon, Dave Brown, Lauren Davies, Brian Young, and the many past and present members of the medical and legal professions and retired police officers who have discussed historic cases and candidly shared their expert opinions with me over the years. I am particularly grateful to Dr Jonathan Oates for reading my draft chapters on Christie and Haigh, his sage comments and thoughts were much appreciated. I would also like to express my appreciation to the wonderful team at Pen and Sword Books, it is a pleasure to work with them. Last but by no means least I would like to thank my partner Fiona, my family and friends for all their love and support as I wade through the archives and travel around the country researching historic crimes.